CITY ON THE LINE

How Baltimore Transformed Its Budget to
Beat the Great Recession and Deliver Outcomes

Andrew Kleine

Foreword by Peter Hutchinson

ROWMAN & LITTLEFIELD
Lanham • Boulder • New York • London

Executive Editor: Traci Crowell
Assistant Editor: Mary Malley
Senior Marketing Manager: Karin Cholak
Interior Designer: Rosanne Schloss

Credits and acknowledgments for material borrowed from other sources, and reproduced with permission, appear on the appropriate page within the text.

Published by Rowman & Littlefield
An imprint of The Rowman & Littlefield Publishing Group, Inc.
4501 Forbes Boulevard, Suite 200, Lanham, Maryland 20706
www.rowman.com

Unit A, Whitacre Mews, 26-34 Stannary Street, London SE11 4AB, United Kingdom

British Library Cataloguing in Publication Information Available

Library of Congress Cataloging-in-Publication Data Available
ISBN 978-1-5381-2187-0 (cloth: alk. paper)
ISBN 978-1-5381-2188-7 (pbk.: alk. paper)
ISBN 978-1-5381-2189-4 (electronic)

∞™ The paper used in this publication meets the minimum requirements of American National Standard for Information Sciences—Permanence of Paper for Printed Library Materials, ANSI/NISO Z39.48-1992.

Printed in the United States of America

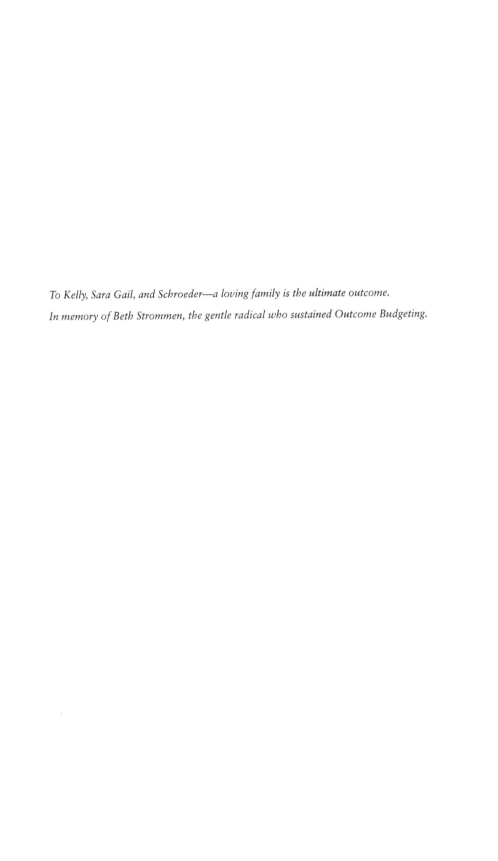

To Kelly, Sara Gail, and Schroeder—a loving family is the ultimate outcome.

In memory of Beth Strommen, the gentle radical who sustained Outcome Budgeting.

Human progress is furthered, not by conformity, but by aberration.
—H. L. Mencken, the "Sage of Baltimore"

Contents

■ ■ ■

Foreword

■ ■ ■

WHAT YOU ARE about to read is a very unusual book. It is a lively combination of stories well told, lessons learned, and vital advice—about budgeting: outcome budgeting, to be specific. It does a masterful job of connecting Outcome Budgets to strategic planning, performance management, the STAT process, and all of the other tools needed to effectively manage a government and successfully deliver results.

When it comes to directing and controlling what gets done and how in government, nothing is more powerful than the making and the management of the budget. When it comes to communicating what matters, nothing is more compelling than the processes and priorities of the budget. When it comes to focusing the attention and driving the behavior of employees, nothing is more effective than the rules and results of the budget. Nothing. No speech, no election campaign promise, no executive order, no press conference, no good intention can overcome the pervasive power of the budget.

I learned these lessons the hardest way possible—by humiliating myself in front of our state's union shop stewards. I was the commissioner of finance for Minnesota. We had a budget shortfall. The governor expected me to come up with a solution. I did. He asked me to share it with our union leaders. I did. I failed.

I was pretty naïve and went to the meeting convinced that with my charts and graphs and a call to do what was right for our citizens,

I could win them over. I didn't get through the first chart before they started chuckling. By the time I finished they were laughing out loud. So I asked, "What the heck's so funny?" "Well," one of them said, "it's pretty clear that you don't know what the heck you are talking about." (I wondered how he knew.) "How do you know that?" I asked. "Look," he said, "here's how it works. Every year in May we paint every building in our department inside and out. We can't save money because we are wasting our time spending it." "Well that's crazy!" I said. "Of course," came his reply, "and worse, this happens during the opening of the fishing season when we all want to be at the lake." "But why are you doing this?" came my next question. "See, you really don't get it, do you? May is the month before June, and June is the end of the fiscal year. If we have any money left in our budget at the end of the year the angels of death from your department will scoop it up and take it back to the treasury. And as they fly away they will tell us, 'if you didn't need this money this year you won't need it next year,' and they cut our budget. You can give all the speeches you want about savings, but the system is telling us louder and more powerfully than you can, 'spend the money, spend the money!' And we do, even if it's crazy."

That day I learned that the budget system—the processes by which we make and manage our finances—was running the government, not us. I learned that every organization produces exactly the results that its systems are designed to produce (even crazy results). If we want different results, we need a different design.

How we budget, where we start, what questions we ask, how we answer them, and what we reward are all a matter of design. They are choices. The choices in the budget design at work in Minnesota at that time, and still in most governments today, were made decades ago. They were part of a revolutionary redesign that was implemented to take control over the chaos and corruption in government over a hundred years ago. Today we call that design bureaucracy—and we don't mean it as a compliment. But it did exactly what it was designed to do: it brought order and control to the process of raising and spending public resources.

It is also the only design that most of us have ever known. In fact, we think it is the *only* design. We are wrong.

In August of 2002, Governor Gary Locke of Washington found himself in a deep budget hole. Locke knew how to budget. He had been an executive of Washington's largest county and chaired the Appropriations Committee when he served in the state senate. As a result, he knew that the budget design that got his state into this mess would not get him out. He knew he needed a new design.

The design we developed and implemented for the first time in 2002 we called Budgeting for Outcomes or Outcome Budgeting. It worked. The story of how it happened and how it works we recounted in our book *The Price of Government*.

Andrew Kleine, a true government innovator, has picked up the story from there. In a decade of using Outcome Budgeting in Baltimore, he continuously improved the design and used it to drive better outcomes for his city. This book, appropriately titled *City on the Line: How Baltimore Transformed Its Budget to Beat the Great Recession and Deliver Outcomes*, tells that story. It can serve as a guide for every government in how to use the power of the budget to deliver results that matter to those it serves. Doing so, now more than ever, is essential to assuring the legitimacy of our vital public institutions.

Peter Hutchinson
Minneapolis, Minnesota
May 12, 2018

Peter Hutchinson has served as a deputy mayor in Minneapolis, Superintendent of the Minneapolis Public Schools, and commissioner of finance (CFO) for the State of Minnesota. He cofounded the Public Strategies Group, was president of the Bush Foundation (Saint Paul, Minnesota), and led public service strategy for Accenture. He coauthored *The Price of Government* with David Osborne.

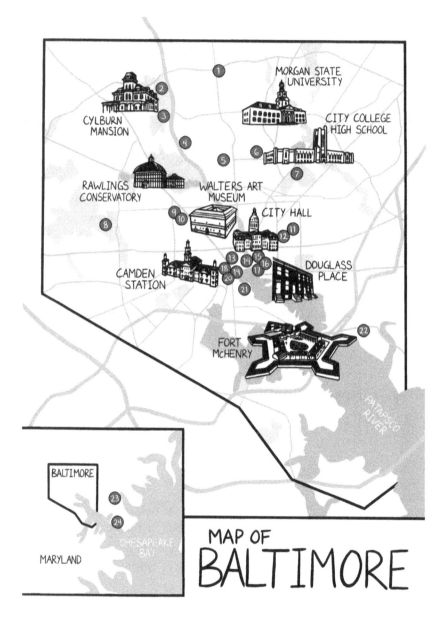

MORGAN STATE
UNIVERSITY

CITY COLLEGE
HIGH SCHOOL

CYLBURN
MANSION

RAWLINGS
CONSERVATORY

WALTERS ART
MUSEUM

CITY HALL

CAMDEN
STATION

DOUGLASS
PLACE

FORT
McHENRY

PATAPSCO
RIVER

BALTIMORE

MARYLAND

CHESAPEAKE
BAY

MAP OF
BALTIMORE

MAP KEY

1. Grace United Methodist Church
2. Cylburn Arboretum
3. Camp Small
4. Baltimore Polytechnic High School
5. Johns Hopkins University
6. Waverly Neighborhood
7. Clifton Park
8. Gwynns Falls/Leakin Park
9. Sandtown-Winchester
10. Gilmor Homes
11. Northeast Market
12. Johns Hopkins Hospital
13. Battle Monument
14. War Memorial
15. Phoenix Shot Tower
16. Power Plant Live
17. National Aquarium
18. Convention Center
19. McKeldin Square
20. Inner Harbor
21. Federal Hill
22. Amazon Distribution Center
23. Back River Wastewater Treatment Plant
24. Sparrows Point

Introduction

■ ■ ■

THINKING OUTSIDE THE BLACK BOX

Politicians like to make big promises, and the people want to believe them. I learned this in sixth grade, when a student council candidate named Darren McCants told a gym full of classmates that if they voted for him, they would get longer recesses and chocolate milk in the cafeteria. The crowd went wild, and Darren won in a landslide. Like many politicians who are better at campaigning than governing, Darren didn't deliver. This book is about how public servants can keep their promises by turning the most change-resistant bureaucracy in government—the budget process—from a force for unnecessary paperwork into a force for good.

My story begins in early 2008. The Great Recession had just begun (though we didn't know it yet), and I was sitting in the executive conference room of Baltimore's historic City Hall, waiting to interview with Mayor Sheila Dixon for the budget director job. All around me, hanging on the walls, were drawings of Baltimore's luminaries. The ones I recognized included Billie Holiday, Thurgood Marshall, Babe Ruth, and, of course, Edgar Allan Poe.

My knowledge of Baltimore didn't extend much beyond the Inner Harbor, the city's waterfront showpiece of tall ships, shops, restaurants, and the National Aquarium. I was not oblivious to Baltimore's challenges, though. Several years earlier, as a board member of a nonprofit affordable housing lender, I had toured the Sandtown neighborhood on the west side (which in 2015 would be the epicenter of civil unrest following the death of Freddie Gray, a young black man in police custody). Chesapeake Habitat for Humanity was seeking financing to renovate vacant row houses, and I went to check out the project. What I saw and heard made a deep impression.

We drove through block after block of abandoned, boarded-up buildings and vacant lots, remnants of the city's depopulation. From a peak of nearly one million in 1950, Baltimore's population has fallen by more than a third. In the 1990s, Baltimore lost residents faster than any other large city, shrinking by 11.5 percent (for comparison, Detroit lost 7.5 percent of its residents during that decade). More devastating than the blight was hearing from the principal of a public elementary school, who told us that most of her students came to school hungry every day and many were abused and neglected by drug-addicted parents. The extreme social and emotional problems in the classroom made teaching and learning nearly impossible.

In part because of that visit to Sandtown, I was willing to take a large pay cut from my federal job at the Corporation for National and Community Service (the agency that runs the AmeriCorps volunteer program). However naïve the notion might have been, I thought I could help to solve Baltimore's problems. I had worked "inside the beltway" for nearly fifteen years and was itching to get closer to the front lines of public service, where I could have a more direct impact on people's daily lives.

I was also fed up with federal budgeting. I knew from having been deep inside the process, as a program examiner at the White House Office of Management and Budget, that I was powerless to bring order to the multitrillion-dollar mess in Washington. Baltimore's budget seemed like something I could get my arms around.

Mayor Dixon radiated energy. At fifty-four, she kept herself fit by riding her bike almost every day. She sat down for our interview, but I could tell she was the kind of person who would rather be up and moving. A former Head Start teacher, she put me at ease with her smile and started in.

"The budget is like a $3 billion black box to me," she said. "The decisions brought to me are at the margins, which means that, as far as I know, 99 percent of the budget is basically on autopilot."

It is a common mayor's lament. When they are elected, mayors feel like they can change the world. Before long, they realize that changing the draperies in their office is complicated. City budgets are layered with the costs of decades of decisions, wise and foolish, and endless details that have to be pried out of wary bureaucrats. You can understand why a mayor would throw up her hands.

I was ready for this moment. On the first day of my federal career, as a budget analyst in the US Department of Transportation, I was sent to a "train the trainer" session on the new Government Performance and Results Act, or GPRA. GPRA requires federal agencies to set goals, measure results, and report on progress. As a twenty-four-year-old fresh out of public policy school, I soon found myself standing in front of rooms full of managers twice my age, teaching them how to develop performance measures for the programs they ran. If my fear didn't kill me, I thought my students might. They had seen management fads come and go, and had little patience for another one.

In spite of the indifference, cynicism, and even verbal abuse I encountered in my trainings, I was inspired by GPRA and have devoted my career to using performance measurement to improve the results government delivers to citizens. More specifically, I have sought to connect performance measurement to budget decisions so that government gets the most possible value for each tax dollar spent.

I became a voracious reader of books that almost nobody else reads—books about how to improve government management. One such book, *The Price of Government: Getting the Results We Need in an Age of Permanent Fiscal Crisis* by David Osborne and Peter Hutchinson, became my bible. It explains how Washington State's governor, Gary Locke, tried something called Budgeting for Outcomes (BFO) to allocate dollars in a way that better reflected citizens' priorities and rewarded programs that got proven results.

If I were a superhero, I would be called Good Government Guy. When a mayor needed help, I could remove my jacket and tie and rip open my button-down to reveal a T-shirt with GGG embla-zoned across the chest. I wasn't born on the planet Krypton, but my upbringing in Lansing, Michigan, imbued me with a civic spirit and a public finance bent. My mother ran a child abuse prevention non-profit and served on the school board. My father was a government economist and ultimately became state treasurer. They showed me that with leadership from competent, compassionate people, government can do great things.

I didn't use the superhero routine with Mayor Dixon, but I told her that BFO would be a good fit for Baltimore, where getting the most out of every dollar is critical, because there are never enough of them. BFO would give her insight about how the city's money was spent and specific recommendations for redirecting funds to her priorities. She was no wonk, but she could see that BFO would give her more control of the city budget. Thus started the adventure that this book is all about.

Baltimore, Maryland, may seem an unlikely source of lessons on government innovation. It is affectionately called "Charm City," but its history of social disorder has given rise to mocking slogans like "Harm City" and "Bodymore, Murderland." A former mayor declared Baltimore "the City That Reads," which was quickly lampooned as "the City That Bleeds."

At a conference in Sydney, Australia, a few years ago, I found out that people halfway around the world know Baltimore, but only because of the HBO series *The Wire*, a crime drama that vividly depicts the city's drug trade, police bureaucracy, politics, schools, and other troubled institutions. As an aside, there is a city budget director character in *The Wire*, and I found myself laughing ruefully as he tried in vain to talk the mayor out of using the rainy-day fund to pay for police salary increases.

What viewers of *The Wire* probably don't know is that Baltimore is forging a new reputation for smart government. It pioneered the much-copied CitiStat to track agency performance and became a leader in BFO—which we came to call Outcome Budgeting. Thanks to these practices, together with long-term financial planning and many tough decisions by Mayor Dixon and her successor, Mayor Stephanie Rawlings-Blake, no city has a better story of managing through the Great Recession. On the other side of that fiscal crisis, Baltimore had a larger fund balance, lower property taxes, reduced retiree benefit liabilities, a shrinking structural budget deficit, and a $1 billion school modernization plan—not to mention a higher bond rating.

This book is about Baltimore, certainly, but it is more so about how to use budgeting to drive innovation and get great things done in cities, counties, states, and any other organization struggling to turn resources into real results. You will learn about

- making outcomes the starting point for budgeting;
- funding outcomes instead of organizational units;
- using data and evidence to make budget decisions;
- fostering competition and collaboration to get the best from your services;
- rewarding services that get results and repurposing dollars from those that don't;
- engaging citizens in the budget process;
- shifting the budget debate from squeaky wheels to value for money; and
- creating a culture of innovation.

Finally, you will learn about completing the performance circle by connecting strategic planning, budgeting, and accountability for outcomes. I call this OutcomeStat, and it represents a new idea for how to manage government.

My decade in Baltimore was arguably the most tumultuous in the city's long history, save for wartime. It was marked by political scandal, economic crisis, and civil unrest. The murder rate fell to the lowest point in generations, then exploded to record highs. New waterfront development and neighborhood investment brought hope of renewal, but the half-century trend of population loss paused only briefly.

Like the city, Outcome Budgeting remains a work in progress, and always will be. I didn't write this book to declare "Mission Accomplished." I wrote it in the hope that others could find lessons in the ups and downs and ins and outs of what Baltimore's been through so far. Just as we learned from Outcome Budgeting pioneers like Dallas; Fort Collins, Colorado; and Redmond, Washington, we were sought out for advice by Los Angeles, Atlanta, Seattle, Philadelphia, and other cities looking to spend smarter. I want to share what we told them with a broader audience.

I am also motivated by my belief that at a time when our politics seems more divided than ever, Outcome Budgeting can be a unifier. Even partisans can agree on the outcomes we want for communities, things like safer neighborhoods, healthier babies, more jobs, and shorter commutes. Conservatives will love how Outcome Budgeting uses data and evidence to prioritize government spending, drives more efficient service delivery, and shines a spotlight on waste. Liberals will love how Outcome Budgeting brings people together around long-term solutions to our toughest problems, makes room for investments that turn people's lives around, and rewards innovation. In our world of fake news and alternative facts, Outcome Budgeting is a return to reason.

I know I have thousands of compatriots around the country who want to revolutionize the way government works and over-throw the outdated thinking that holds us back from achieving great outcomes, or even just making the organization we work in a little more effective. I will introduce you to some of them in these pages. I will also tell you about many of the books that have shaped my thinking and inspired me to keep swinging my pickax to break down the resistance to change. If this book can do the same for a few others, I will consider it a success.

1

Outcome Budgeting 101

■ ■ ■

Cartoon 1.1 Dilbert Cartoon *Source:* DILBERT © 2008 Scott Adams. Used By permission of ANDREWS MCMEEL SYNDICATION. All rights reserved.

DILBERT CARTOONS ARE funny because they hit so close to home. I started my job as Baltimore's budget director in April 2008, and within two weeks I was in front of the city council to defend a budget I had nothing to do with creating. It was trial by fire, but I survived and we got the budget passed on time. What happened next was comical.

After the budget was adopted, I was told by the finance director that one of my jobs was to explain how the budget supports the Mayor's Objectives. "Okay," I said, too embarrassed to admit that I had never heard of the Mayor's Objectives. I asked around the budget office and got blank stares. After a few days hunting through City Hall, I finally found them on the desk of the mayor's communications director. I asked him if I could make a copy. "You can have that one," he said, between bites of a sandwich.

7

The objectives were well intended (if wordy) and covered all the bases: public safety, health, education, cleanliness, jobs, neighborhoods, and government efficiency. There was just one problem. These objectives were little more than campaign slogans. They were not used to develop the budget, and there were neither plans to achieve them nor measures to track our progress.

I did my best to match up the Mayor's Objectives to what was funded in the budget, all the while thinking how backward this was. It was a classic case of putting the cart before the horse, and a perfect illustration of why the budget process needed to change.

There is perhaps no force in the universe greater than the inertia of a city budget, which is why the Mayor's Objectives were an afterthought instead of the inspiration for Baltimore's spending plan. From the moment I swiped those objectives off the communications director's desk, my mission was to seek the real prize, public management's Holy Grail: a budget that maximizes results per tax dollar spent, otherwise known as Value.

I mentioned in the introduction that the Outcome Budgeting idea I pitched to Mayor Dixon came from a book called *The Price of Government*. Published in 2004, it generated some buzz in the wonky world of good government types like me. Fifteen years later, the book is all but forgotten. I know this because whenever I speak at conferences about my work in Baltimore, I ask if anyone has read it. I am lucky if I get one hand in the air—and these are people who are trying to figure out how to get better results for citizens. I have taken to giving away a copy to the person who asks me the best question at the end of the talk.

This chapter will introduce you to what Outcome Budgeting is all about and how it represents a revolutionary shift from the traditional budgeting process that is still used in some form by 99 percent of state and local governments. The rest of the book will be a report from the front lines of the budget revolution, after ten years of insurgency against the status quo. I will tell stories of wins and losses, give you tools to try it yourself, and show you how the hard lessons led us to an exciting new idea for managing government called OutcomeStat.

The central idea of Outcome Budgeting is that budgeting should be about purchasing results. By results I mean measurable improvements to whatever it is you are trying to make better. In Baltimore, the Mayor's Objectives—which we later renamed Priority Outcomes—were the results we wanted to achieve.

Another way to think about purchasing results is getting value for your money. "Value" is something that everyone understands. It is that balance of price and quality that we look for when we are buying a car, a dishwasher, or even a pound of ground beef. It just isn't normally applied to government spending. When we introduced Outcome Budgeting to agency heads and program managers, we told them that value is results per dollar spent. This equation is government's bottom line. We wanted them to write budget proposals that boosted the bottom line in one of three ways, shown in box 1.1

The wise guys always ask me, "What about more results for more money?" My comeback line is, "That's too easy," but the fact is, for most state and local governments, there is no "more money."

The Price of Government was written in the wake of the dot-com crash and the recession that followed, which blew huge holes in state and local budgets. The authors were motivated by two observations.

The first was that most mayors and governors were doing all they could to avoid reckoning with hard choices. They balanced their budgets by raiding reserves and other funds, delaying capital investments, and making across-the-board cuts that punished high-value services and protected ones that couldn't demonstrate results. When those expediencies weren't enough, they used accounting gimmicks or inflated revenue projections. Not only did they thin the

Box 1.1	Value

More results for the same money

OR

The same results for less money

OR, BEST OF ALL

More results for less money

soup of government services, they also put their cities and states on a less sustainable fiscal path.

The second observation was that fiscal stress was here to stay. Sure, the economy would recover, but the combination of an aging population, ever-growing health-care costs, and resistance to tax increases (among other factors) would produce perpetually unbalanced budgets.

As it turned out, the dot-com recession was soon followed by the housing bubble. In Baltimore, which relies heavily on property tax revenue to fund city services, this bubble was a bonanza. Swelling property values gave the city five straight years of revenue surpluses, which mostly went to good use in building up the rainy day fund, fixing infrastructure, cutting taxes, and expanding after-school programs. It also gave city leaders a vacation from dealing with the structural budget deficit and other fiscal challenges that had plagued Baltimore for decades.

Of course, we all know how this story ends. The Great Recession is nothing to joke about, but I often tease my predecessor, Ray Wacks, that he left me holding the bag. Ray, the jovial dean of Maryland budget directors, had been with Howard County, the state's wealthiest, for some twenty-five years before venturing to Baltimore to see how the other half lives. After three years of figuring out what to do with excess cash, Ray went back to Howard County. He says it was because the new county executive gave him an offer he couldn't refuse, but I suspect it had something to do with the fact that property transfer tax revenue was dropping and the city had imposed a hiring freeze. The storm was coming.

I'd like to think it's only a coincidence that the Great Recession and I arrived in Baltimore at about the same time. When I talk at conferences about managing the crisis, I sometimes open with a slide showing a man standing under his own personal storm cloud. That's how I felt at times.

During the slow and uneven recovery from the Great Recession, it was common to hear economists telling us that these conditions were a "new normal" and that we wouldn't soon see a return of

Photo 1.1 How I Felt Sometimes *Source: iStock/quisp65*

robust growth. Some eight years after the recession officially ended, Baltimore was still struggling with annual budget shortfalls, and we were worried that the next recession was overdue. Whether our fiscal crisis is permanent or cyclical, the need for a budget process that improves results is abiding. That probably seems like common sense, but in reality it is a radical concept.

OLD WAY, NEW WAY

I find that the best way to explain the radicalism of Outcome Budgeting (the "New Way") is by comparing it to traditional budgeting (the "Old Way") (see table 1.1).

Starting Point

Old Way budgeting starts with the amount budgeted or spent in the previous fiscal year. This amount is called the "base." The base—plus

Table 1.1 Old Way/New Way

Old Way	New Way
Starting Point: Last year's spending	*Starting Point:* Next year's goals
Funding Targets: By agency	*Funding Targets:* By priority outcome
Agency Submission: How allocation will be spent	*Agency Submission:* Proposal to achieve results
Debate: What to cut	*Debate:* What to keep

adjustments for inflation and other unavoidable costs of maintaining current service levels—is considered an entitlement by agency heads. Protecting the base becomes a badge of honor for these leaders, which is why inertia is the defining feature of most public budgets and why many public officials treat the budget process like a game instead of a serious effort to derive value from taxpayer dollars. I will discuss budget games later in the book, but suffice it to say that government line-item budgets are written in a code that would confound Alan Turing, the British mathematician whose breaking of German ciphers in World War II was celebrated in the Oscar-winning film *The Imitation Game*.

If projected revenues fall short of what's needed to fund current services, the Old Way solution is some sort of across-the-board reduction, or "haircut" in the budget vernacular. That is the only "fair" way, after all. It is also the path of least resistance for mayors and governors, who find it is easier to tell agency heads and advocacy groups that everyone is sharing the pain equally than to have to explain to them that their favorite service was cut (or eliminated) so that a higher-priority service with better results could be fully funded or enhanced. The fact is that an honest conversation about how the budget represents priorities and performance is a fantasy in most places, because the budget process is not about those things.

Elected officials know very little about what is going on inside the base budget and what constituents are getting for their money. They may know from the phone calls and emails that come to their office if this or that service is falling short. They may even have some statistics about how services are performing, like the number of missed trash pickups or the time it takes to fill a pothole. What they're missing is any clue about whether citizens are getting their money's worth or whether current budget allocations are optimized to get them the big, long-term results they want for their city or state. Mayor Dixon was no Archimedes, but her instincts told her that incremental budgeting took the longest lever she had to move the bureaucracy—control of how money is spent—out of her hands.

New Way budgeting starts with the measurable results we want—less crime, higher student test scores, smoother streets, cleaner air, you name it. There is no such thing as a base, and the process that follows is an open competition for the best ideas, strategies, and investments that will "move the needle" on those results. It is the traditional budget process turned on its head.

Baltimore's list of Priority Outcomes and Indicators evolved over the years. The first version was developed from Mayor Dixon's six objectives. At a retreat with the mayor and her team, we came up with seventeen sub-objectives and eighty Key Indicators. The sub-objectives and indicators for just one of the objectives are shown in figure 1.1—all twenty of them!

We had a measure for practically everything city government did, which is fine for management but not all that useful for budgeting, especially Outcome Budgeting. We were supposed to be setting priorities so we could focus our resources on what mattered and actually make some progress. Having eighty key measures is like making eighty New Year's resolutions. Most of us have difficulty keeping one; city governments are no different. In retrospect, we should have spent a lot more time thinking about what really mattered, but one of the biggest challenges of running a city is finding time to think.

In the six months that followed our retreat, a political drama unfolded that forced us to rethink everything. In December 2009, Mayor Dixon was convicted of stealing gift cards intended for poor children. On February 5, 2010, the day before the final-decisions meeting for Baltimore's inaugural outcome budget, she resigned as part of a plea deal and city council President Stephanie Rawlings-Blake was sworn in to replace her.

The sudden mayoral transition was Outcome Budgeting's first existential threat. I can only imagine what was going through Mayor

Figure 1.1 Mayor Dixon's Objectives and Measures

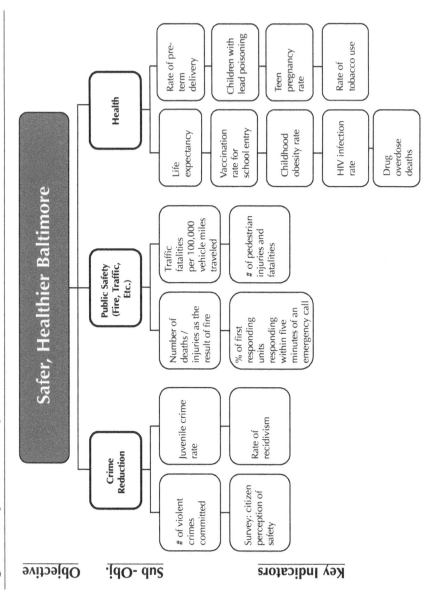

Objective	Safer, Healthier Baltimore
Sub-Obj.	Crime Reduction · Public Safety (Fire, Traffic, Etc.) · Health

Key Indicators:

Crime Reduction
- # of violent crimes committed
- Juvenile crime rate
- Survey: citizen perception of safety
- Rate of recidivism

Public Safety (Fire, Traffic, Etc.)
- Number of deaths / injuries as the result of fire
- Traffic fatalities per 100,000 vehicle miles traveled
- % of first responding units responding within five minutes of an emergency call
- # of pedestrian injuries and fatalities

Health
- Life expectancy
- Rate of pre-term delivery
- Vaccination rate for school entry
- Children with lead poisoning
- Childhood obesity rate
- Teen pregnancy rate
- HIV infection rate
- Rate of tobacco use
- Drug overdose deaths

Source: Baltimore Bureau of the Budget and Management Research

Rawlings-Blake's mind as she sat through that budget meeting on her first full day in office. Remember, the Great Recession had just passed and left the economy in shambles. We were wrestling with a $120 million budget shortfall and had actuaries warning us that without major reforms, we would be looking at a $65 million spike in the cost of our largest pension plan.

Stephanie Rawlings-Blake was destined to be the mayor of Baltimore, just not this soon. Her father, Howard "Pete" Rawlings, had been the powerful chair of the Maryland House Appropriations Committee for more than ten years, until he died of cancer in 2003. She was elected to the city council at the age of twenty-five and was a few months shy of forty when she took the oath for the top job. She was an ally of Mayor Dixon, but where Dixon was gregarious and street-smart, Rawlings-Blake, an Oberlin grad, was reserved and book-smart. Thankfully, I had worked hard at selling her on Outcome Budgeting when she was council president, and she embraced it as mayor.

At her swearing-in and in her campaign the following year, Mayor Rawlings-Blake talked of making Baltimore "Better, Safer and Stronger" and growing the city's population by ten thousand families in ten years. Her themes are reflected in her Priority Outcomes. Mayor Dixon's objective to "Strengthen Baltimore's economy by increasing the tax base, jobs and minority business opportunities" became simply "A Growing Economy" under Mayor Rawlings-Blake. This may seem like superficial sloganeering, but the spirit of boiling the outcomes down to their essence extended to getting more focused about priorities. That spirit shows in the twenty-one Key Indicators (plus two initiatives) she used—perhaps still too many, but far more manageable than the hodgepodge we started with (see table 1.2).

One step we took to zero in on priorities was conducting the city's first ever community survey. We got back our first survey results in the fall of 2009, and though there weren't any huge surprises, we now had data on how our residents thought about the importance of various city services, their levels of satisfaction, attitudes about quality-of-life issues such as safety and cleanliness, and behaviors such as transportation choices and visiting parks. We repeated the

Table 1.2 Mayor Rawlings-Blake's Priority Outcomes and Key Indicators

Priority Outcome	Key Indicator
Better Schools	A Safe and Healthy Start
	Kindergarten Readiness
	Academic Achievement
	College and Career Readiness
Safer Streets	Shootings
	Property Crime
	Citizen Perception of Safety
Stronger Neighborhoods	Blight Elimination
	Neighborhood Investment
	Sustainable Transportation
	Recreation Visits
A Growing Economy	City Resident Employment
	Jobs in Baltimore
	Visitors in Baltimore
Innovative Government	Lean Government
	Innovation Fund
A Cleaner City	Recycling Rate
	Citizen Perception of Cleanliness
	Cleanliness of Waterways
	Energy Usage
A Healthier City	Heroin-Related Deaths
	Citizen Mental Health
	Childhood Asthma

survey every year, and not only did it inform what we measured, it was our data source for several Key Indicators and service performance measures. You'll learn more about how we used the survey in later chapters

Funding Targets
Outcome Budgeting's most disruptive innovation is the way it allocates funding to start the budget planning process. In Old Way

budgeting, each agency is given a funding target. The target is typically the base level (last year's spending with adjustments for inflation, etc.), with a percentage reduction if money is tight. In this model, agency funding is predictable and so are the services and results that will be purchased with that funding. If you think you are getting the best possible results for the dollars you are spending, then I suppose this model makes sense.

The New Way is to allocate funding to outcomes instead of agencies. The truth about most governments is that, over time, the way base funding is organized has become disconnected from the results that political leaders want to achieve, the needs of the community, the performance of services being funded, and the conversion of dollars into units of service performance, such as trash pickups, street light uptime, or high school graduates.

My mental image of traditional agency budgets is silos, each representing insular thinking and a barrier to working together to meet common goals. I was reminded of this image every day when I looked eastward from City Hall and saw Baltimore's historic Phoenix Shot Tower (photo 1.2), which was once the tallest structure in the United States. A shot tower works by pouring molten lead from a platform at the top down through a funnel and into cold water at the bottom, producing shot pellets for rifles and cannons. The Phoenix Shot Tower is an apt metaphor for traditional budgeting: it has stood for more than a century since being rendered obsolete by better methods for making ammunition.

To connect (or reconnect) resources and outcomes, we have to break down the heavily fortified silos of agency budgets and replace them with large pools of funding dedicated to the outcomes we seek. Chapter 2 will go deep into how this works and why it makes agency heads nervous.

Agency Submission

When funding targets are allocated to agencies, the pressure is off agency heads to justify the existence of services, or even their funding levels. Service performance is often an afterthought in Old Way budget discussions, because performance management and budget

Photo 1.2 Phoenix Shot Tower *Source: Flickr user: Mark Peters*
https://www.flickr.com/people/sneakerdog/.

are separate departments. An across-the-board cut may cause some prioritizing and efficiency inside agencies, though it is just as likely to be "absorbed" by spreading dollars thinner and degrading performance, or using gimmicks to forestall the tough choices.

In Baltimore, agency budget submissions in the days before Outcome Budgeting consisted of line-item entries into the central budget system and cursory PowerPoint presentations in front of the mayor and senior staff. Wasteful spending on low-priority and low-performing services flew under the radar while agency heads used their face time to brag about past accomplishments and warn of all the bad things that would happen if the agency had to take the across-the-board cut. Is it any wonder that Mayor Dixon called this "black box" budgeting?

New Way budgeting is a whole different ballgame. Agencies (and private and nonprofit organizations, if you want to boldly go where no one has gone before) are invited to submit proposals for each service they want funded. The proposal explains how the service will contribute to achieving one or more of the mayor's Priority Outcomes and includes performance data and evidence to back up the plan. It's more work than Old Way budgeting, for sure, but it's the best way I know to count every dollar and make every dollar count. Chapter 2 will explain services and the important role they play in Outcome Budgeting. Chapter 3 will explain what makes for a great budget proposal.

Budget Debate

Starting with the base budget as a given inevitably leads us to focus on incremental changes to the base, which represent a mere fraction of the budget as a whole.

In the absence of meaningful and reliable information about how well services perform and what, if any, difference they make in people's lives, funding levels become the measuring stick for how much good government is doing. They also become a source of pride for agency heads. Debates rage and advocates mobilize around even small budget reductions, more because of what they symbolize than the measurable impact they have on results (which is rarely well understood).

Budget debates remind me of the ancient story of the blind men and the elephant. Each man feels a different part of the large creature, and they spend a lot of time arguing about whether it is a rope, a tree, or a wall. They can't see the big picture. In the same way, legislators, advocates, and agency heads have a hard time seeing how a reduction in one part of an enormous budget allows for the preservation or enhancement of funding—and, more importantly, results—in another part of the budget.

New Way budgeting can help shift the budget debate from "What to Cut" to "What to Keep." As you will learn in chapter 4, the heart of Outcome Budgeting is rating and ranking service proposals based on how closely they align with Priority Outcomes and how well they perform in achieving measurable results. The highest-ranked services are funded first, and the lowest ranked services fall below the line at which available funding has run out.

This approach to budgeting allows the public to see how each service fits into the city's strategy for improving outcomes. It also makes the funding trade-offs crystal clear and provides data and evidence to explain every budget decision.

Ultimately, the budget is a political document. No matter how rational you make the budget process, the end product will never be purely rational. City leaders will disagree about priorities, underperforming services will be funded because they are popular, and vocal interest groups will sometimes get their way regardless of what the data and evidence say. My measure of success is to keep upping what I call the "Outcome Quotient"—the percentage of the budget that makes sense and moves the needle toward better outcomes.

THE OUTCOME BUDGETING CYCLE

You've probably noticed that this book is part memoir, part manifesto, and part manual. This chapter is an overview of both the theory and practice—the Why and How—of Outcome Budgeting, intended to whet your appetite for the rest of the book. The Old Way/New Way comparison is the Why. For the How, I want to walk you through the Outcome Budgeting Cycle, from start to finish. To help make your

Figure 1.2 Outcome Budgeting Cycle

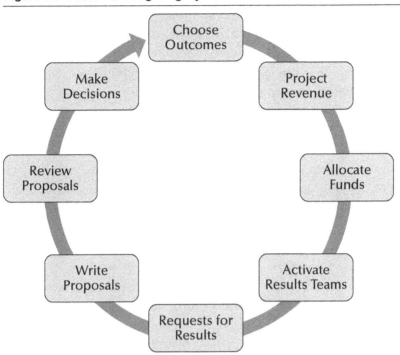

reading of this book efficient, I will point out where you can find further discussion of each phase of the cycle (see figure 1.2).

Phase 1: Choose Your Outcomes

As I have explained in this chapter, the starting point for Outcome Budgeting is deciding what outcomes you want to achieve for your city (or other kind of organization) and how you will measure your progress toward those outcomes. The budget process and the budget itself will be organized around these outcomes. They should reflect the aspirations of your residents (or customers) and leadership. As I've noted, in Baltimore, we used a survey to help us understand what mattered most to city residents.

Phase 2: Figure Out How Much Money You Have to Spend

The Price of Government devotes twenty-two pages of small print to the matter of determining how much taxpayers are willing to pay for government services, in terms of cents per dollar of personal income. The bottom line is that people constantly demand more and better services from government but don't want to pay for them with higher taxes. This mismatch between citizens' expectations of government and their willingness to pay for it bedevils elected officials everywhere. Budgets have to be balanced, even if citizens aren't.

Baltimore is a city where the need for government services is high, but the tax base is low. As a result, its tax rates are by far the highest in the state—54 percent above the statewide average by one index. Conservative commentators blame the high tax rates for all of the city's ills and have convinced many people, including some liberal mayoral candidates, that cutting the property tax rate in half will spur an almost-immediate economic renaissance. The reality is far more complicated, but there is no denying that high taxes make the city less competitive for new residents and businesses.

Being caught between cries for more police presence, after-school programs, street repaving, and so forth on one side and appeals for tax relief on the other seems like a no-win situation. It doesn't have to be, if you can make better use of the resources you have, which is what Outcome Budgeting is for.

Our approach to the price-of-government question was simple. We wanted to deliver progressively better services at a progressively lower cost to taxpayers. Each year, we projected our available resources with the assumption of incremental property tax reductions—consistent with our ten-year financial plan—and no use of fund balance or reserves to make ends meet.

The concept of planning a budget within a preset spending limit is familiar to anyone who has managed anything, from a household on up, but it is not how everyone thinks about budgeting. One Baltimore city council member insisted that Outcome Budgeting should be about figuring out how much it would cost to achieve each outcome, then setting tax rates to provide the necessary funding. I could see where he was coming from, but I had to tell him, "Councilman, that's called Fantasy Budgeting."

Phase 3: Make Your Funding Allocations

Once you know how much money you have available, the next step is to allocate those dollars by outcome. This allocation method was introduced in the Old Way/New Way section above and will be a major focus of chapter 2.

Phase 4: Activate Your Results Teams

Results Teams are teams of employees and citizens—one for each outcome—that issue guidance to agencies about what they are looking for in service proposals, review and rank the service proposals, and recommend to the mayor an "investment portfolio" that delivers the best possible results for the dollars allocated. Chapter 4 is all about Results Teams.

Phase 5: Issue Your Requests for Results

David Osborne and Peter Hutchinson likened Outcome Budgeting to purchasing results. In this case, Results Teams are the buyers, and agencies (and possibly other organizations) are the sellers. In the world of purchasing, the Request for Proposals (RFP) specifies what the buyer is looking to obtain via a contract. Several of the cities and states that have implemented Outcome Budgeting adopted purchasing parlance in describing the strategy documents that guide service proposals—hence, the Request for Results (RFR).

Ideally, RFRs are derived from a citywide strategic planning process that has identified and prioritized strategies for achieving the outcomes. In Baltimore, we started Outcome Budgeting without such a strategic plan. The city just didn't have one. As a result, Outcome Budgeting became the stand-in for a strategic plan, and remained so. Results Teams were tasked with writing RFRs, which ultimately reflected their subject-matter expertise and research, not a comprehensive and inclusive planning exercise.

Aristotle is credited with the idiom, "Nature abhors a vacuum," meaning that empty spaces don't stay empty for long (my desk being Exhibit A). Outcome Budgeting wasn't alone in trying to fill Baltimore's strategic vacuum. Individual agencies wrote their own strategic plans, which were not always connected to the outcomes being used in the budget process. Task forces were convened around pressing issues, producing more plans. Foundations, trying to be helpful, gave the city money to make yet more plans, around such things as sustainability and economic growth. Eventually, we had at least four different sets of "outcomes" and zero consensus on which star we were supposed to be following.

Surveying the panoply of goals, measures, and strategies that built up over the first five years of the Rawlings-Blake administration made me realize two things. One, Outcome Budgeting is a poor substitute for strategic planning. Its purpose is to align resources with a strategic plan. Two, the city needed a unified strategic planning program. This is the origin story of OutcomeStat, which is the subject of chapters 8 and 9.

Incidentally, I think Aristotle would have been down with Outcome Budgeting. He saw happiness as life's ultimate outcome and extolled the virtues of common purpose over the narrow interests that tend to dominate our politics. He also famously said, "Our problem is not that we aim too high and miss, but that we aim too low and hit."

Photo 1.3 Aristotle *Source:* Ludovisi Collection

Phase 6: Write Your Service Proposals

Service proposals explain how "sellers" (agencies or others) will convert dollars into results. Outcome Budgeting is only as good as the service proposals it inspires.

Two of the chief complaints I hear about Outcome Budgeting are that it is too much work and comes down to a writing contest. Chapter 3 is all about why service proposals are important and how to write great ones (even if you're not Shakespeare).

Phase 7: Review Your Service Proposals and Make Recommendations

Results Teams review and rank service proposals, seeking to understand how well they fit with the outcomes and how effectively they perform. This review process is described in chapter 4.

Phase 8: Make Your Budget Decisions

I have told you why shifting the budget debate from What to Cut to What to Keep is hard. Similarly, when times are good and revenue projections are up, evidence-based strategies to improve outcomes can easily take a back seat to less effective uses of new money, such as expanding popular but low-performing services or funding "feel good" initiatives with no track record or even logic model to suggest they will work. Chapter 5 shows how Outcome Budgeting can help the best ideas prevail.

On paper, it is hard to argue with Outcome Budgeting. Who would object to making more informed, strategic decisions about spending tax dollars? In real life, change is hard, and when you start pushing in a new direction, you get pushed back. Chapter 2 is about crossing the Rubicon to Outcome Budgeting, and what we encountered on the other side.

FIVE TAKEAWAYS

1. **Government's bottom line is Value,** which I like to think of as Results per Dollar Spent. Value is hard to measure with precision in the public sector, but your goal should be to have data that tells you if you are getting more results for the same dollars, the same results for fewer dollars, or more results for fewer dollars.

2. Baltimore started Outcome Budgeting with eighty indicators, way too many for a budget process meant to steer dollars to priorities. We eventually homed in on twenty-one Key Indicators, three or four for each of our Priority Outcomes. We didn't have the resources to do everything well. If you have the same problem, **spend time having hard conversations, inside and outside the organization, about what's most important.**

3. In Baltimore, Mayor Dixon realized that she only had a handle on a fraction of the city's vast budget; most of it was a "black box" to her. Traditional budgeting rolls the "base" budget forward year after year, with only marginal changes. **Outcome Budgeting demands accountability for every dollar.** This doesn't mean starting each year's budget from scratch, but it does mean justifying that each service is aligned with your priorities and performing well.

4. **In a good budget process, the debates are about what should be funded and how to fund those things.** The tradeoffs required to fund those things should be made as clear as possible. Make the fight about What to Keep, not What to Cut. If we can agree on the Keeps, the Cuts become easier.

5. Budgets are political documents. Don't fool yourself into thinking that Outcome Budgeting will take the politics out of budgeting; it won't. **Your goal should be to maximize what I call the "Outcome Quotient":** the proportion of the dollars in your budget that demonstrably support your priorities and do so effectively.

FIVE QUESTIONS

1. For your city (or state or organization), what would be five Priority Outcomes?
2. Choose one outcome. What three measures would you use to track your progress?
3. Based on what you've read so far, what do you think are the three best selling points for Outcome Budgeting?
4. What are the three biggest questions or concerns you have about Outcome Budgeting?
5. Do you think Outcome Budgeting would be more useful during a recession when overall spending has to be reduced, or in good times when surplus revenue is available?

FIVE RESOURCES

1. Hutchinson, Peter, and Osborne, David. (2004). *The Price of Government: Getting the Results We Need in an Age of Permanent Fiscal Crisis*. New York: Basic Books. This is the book that introduced Outcome Budgeting to the world. The Introduction and Part One tell the story of Governor Gary Locke's effort to implement Outcome Budgeting in Washington State.
2. Atteberry, Darin, and Cates Barnett, Camille. "Your Budget: From Axe to Aim," *Public Management*, May 2007. This article is a great primer on Outcome Budgeting. It describes the steps Fort Collins, Colorado, took to get started with Outcome Budgeting, the benefits it experienced, and lessons learned.
3. Elmer, Eva, and Morrill, Christopher. "Budgeting for Outcomes in Savannah," *Government Finance Review*, April 2010. This is another article about a city's Outcome Budgeting implementation. It focuses on things to consider before getting started and the role of teams in making Outcome Budgeting successful.
4. Kamensky, John M., "Baltimore's Outcome Budgeting Approach," *IBM Center for the Business of Government*, October 16, 2013. A handy summary of the steps in Baltimore's Outcome Budgeting process, written by an outsider.
5. Bykowicz, Julie. "Dixon Resigns," *Baltimore Sun*, January 7, 2010. This article details Mayor Dixon's downfall, which is discussed briefly in this chapter.

2

Outcomes vs. the Org Chart

■ ■ ■

WHEN IT COMES to budgeting, agencies don't matter. There, I said it. We are so used to city budget books with a chapter for each agency, and city councils calling up agencies one at a time for budget hearings, it is hard to imagine any other way. I'm here to say that planning budgets around agencies is the wrong way. Agencies are indispensable, of course. They are the organizational units that deliver services to the public. But when it comes to deciding how tax dollars should be allocated, we should only care about the outcomes we want to achieve and the services and other investments that, collectively, move us toward those outcomes.

After Mayor Dixon gave the green light to Outcome Budgeting, the first phone call I made was to Mary Suhm, then the city manager in Dallas. Dallas was the first large city to try Outcome Budgeting, and I wanted to learn from Mary's experience. We talked for at least an hour and a half, and near the end of the call, she said something I'll never forget. When I asked her how much Dallas spends on its police department, she told me she had no idea. "I can tell you what we spend on public safety," she explained, "but not the police department."

Mary's lesson was that while the folks inside City Hall may be preoccupied with the size of agency budgets, citizens don't care. Citizens want to feel safe, live in a clean city, get to work and shopping with ease, and see their children do better than they did. *How* city government delivers on these outcomes is not nearly as important as *how well* it does so. Case in point: if we make the mistake of confusing the amount we spend on the police department with how safe citizens should feel, or how much the crime rate will change, we miss the full range of possible strategies for improving public safety. This is what happens when cities use across-the-board cuts to balance their budgets and exempt police from the cuts. They do it because public safety is the top priority, without thinking hard about how best to make their city safer.

Baltimore spends the largest portion of its General Fund budget on the police department and has more police officers per capita than all but a few cities. Historically, it is hard to correlate spending on the police department with the crime rate. The forces that cause crime are larger than any police department can control. Every year during budget hearings, children's advocates and a bloc of progressive city council members argue for shifting funding from law enforcement to longer-term solutions for preventing crime, such as mentoring, job training, recreation, and even street lighting.

In fact, Baltimore has reduced the size of its police force and increased spending on preventative measures in recent years. This budget shift is no accident. It started with the way funding is allocated in the Outcome Budgeting process.

MONOPOLY MONEY

Babak Armajani was my spiritual leader for Outcome Budgeting. Known as "Armi" to his friends and colleagues, he cofounded Public Strategies Group (PSG), the small St. Paul, Minnesota, consulting firm that I hired to help me get Outcome Budgeting off the ground in Baltimore. Armi was passionate about making government work better, and he shared his passion with thousands of public servants through his teaching, writing, and coaching. Not long before his untimely death in 2013, he wrote, "I believe that for democracy to realize its full potential, government needs to delight citizens with its services. For the past 30 years, I've been trying to figure out how to make WOW! service happen in government."

Armi wanted Mayor Dixon and her senior team to look at the city's budget with fresh eyes. He asked them, "If you were starting over, how would you spend the city's money?" At one of the mayor's staff meetings, he placed seven paper bags on the conference table, each labeled with the name of a Priority Outcome. He then gave each team member $100 of Monopoly money and asked them to drop it into the paper bags according to how they think the city should allocate its tax dollars.

As you can see from the pie charts shown in figure 2.1, the way the senior team divvied up the Monopoly money bore no resemblance to how the city was actually allocating the budget. The Monopoly budget reflects the leaders' instinct that a balanced investment strategy across all the outcomes would get the best results. In the real budget, nearly half the money was going to a single outcome: public safety.

When Armi revealed these pie charts to the team, the reaction was a mix of embarrassment and frustration. Some felt like the Monopoly game was just a cute consulting trick that made them look ignorant

Figure 2.1 Monopoly Money Game

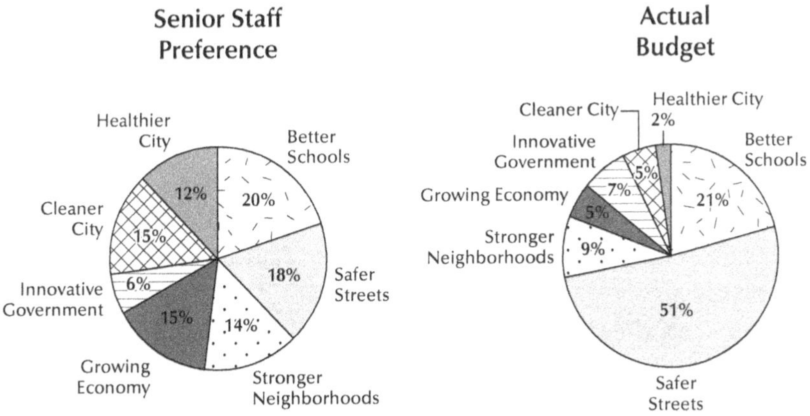

Senior Staff Preference

- Healthier City: 12%
- Better Schools: 20%
- Safer Streets: 18%
- Stronger Neighborhoods: 14%
- Growing Economy: 15%
- Innovative Government: 6%
- Cleaner City: 15%

Actual Budget

- Cleaner City
- Healthier City: 2%
- Innovative Government: 5%
- Better Schools: 21%
- Growing Economy: 7%
- Stronger Neighborhoods: 9%
- Safer Streets: 51%

Source: Baltimore Bureau of the Budget and Management Research

about the budget. Those who got the point of the exercise were at a loss for how spending could ever be brought in line with the outcomes they wanted.

Armi's obituary in the Minneapolis *Star-Tribune* noted that his family couldn't remember him losing at Monopoly once in forty years. He won this time, too, by giving the mayor a clear picture of how she should evolve her budget in the years to come. "Evolve" is the operative word, because it takes time to reorient a multibillion-dollar organization without causing all kinds of problems, from union unrest to service disruptions. We started with a small step. In a year when we had to cut $120 million from the Current Level of Service budget, we allocated the largest percentage share of the reduction to the Safer Streets outcome.

One last thing about Armi: In late 2012, he sent me an email saying that Baltimore had instituted what he believed to be "the nation's most sophisticated and advanced version of budgeting for outcomes in a city government." I cherish these words, and a copy of his message has a permanent place on the corner of my desk.

SERVICES

Agencies may not matter in the budgeting process, but the services they deliver matter a lot. The types of services government provides, how well the services perform, and whether they make people better off are essentials of community well-being.

After citizens and their elected leaders have decided on the outcomes they care most about and the amounts they are willing to spend on each one, the next step in Outcome Budgeting is for participants—be they government agencies, nonprofits or businesses—to make service proposals.

Services, then, are the building blocks of the budget. But what exactly is a service? How you answer this question will determine how well you are able to connect resources to results, make your budget accessible to the average citizen, and hold people in your organization accountable for performance and financial management.

Box 2.1 illustrates how we defined a service in Baltimore:

Box 2.1 | Service

An activity or set of activities performed by city government that

- has identifiable costs for budgeting purposes;
- has a clear public purpose and measurable results;
- has clear lines of accountability for its performance and financial management; and
- is discrete, that is, it is not overly dependent on other services to achieve its results and does not combine activities with substantially differing results, funding streams, lines of accountability, and so forth.

Services are the means to achieving desired outcomes for city residents.

When we got started with Outcome Budgeting in Baltimore, the term "service" was not used in budgeting or accounting. Summary budget publications were organized by fund and agency, presumably so that only seasoned budget analysts could make any sense of them. Those with the temerity to venture into financial details below the agency level would discover something called "programs."

Studying the city's programs felt like traveling back in time. Most programs were artifacts of org charts from the 60s and 70s. They no longer reflected how the city served its residents; perhaps they never had. Many had become bloated with activities that were only loosely related to one another, and none had performance measures. Unlike Marty McFly, I had not gone back to the future. The program structure was badly outdated and needed a reboot.

The first agency I worked with to redefine programs into services was the Department of Recreation and Parks. I gave the agency head the definition of a service shown in box 2.1 on this page and told her, "After you've broken down what you do into services, ask yourself two questions about each of them: One, would this service make sense to a citizen? Two, can I tell the story of how this service is performing with five measures or fewer?"

The graphic in figure 2.2 shows a before-and-after transformation that fitness mogul Joe Weider would have been proud of. From four amorphous programs, Recreation and Parks defined eleven services that make sense to the agency's customers and are understandable even for taxpayers who don't use the city's parks, pools, and recreation centers.

Over the course of a year, we worked with every agency—from the police department to the Bureau of Municipal Zoning Appeals—to restructure their budgets around citizen-centric services. In the process, we pushed performance measurement to all corners of city government. The stage was now set for a new kind of budget. Activities and functions that were hidden within sprawling programs would now see the light of day, for better or worse. The mayor, the city council, and the public (heck, let's not forget the budget director) would actually be able to evaluate how the city was spending money and what we were getting in return.

GO FISH

Besides transparency, accountability, and all that good stuff, the new services had another benefit that I didn't fully expect. Like a giant game of Go Fish, when every agency's cards were on the table,

Figure 2.2 Defining Recreation and Park Services

Old Programs	New Services
Regular Recreation Services	Community Recreation Centers
	Aquatics
Special Recreation Services	Therapeutic Recreation
	Senior Recreation
General Park Services	Youth and Adult Sports
Administration	Special Recreation Facilities
	Urban Forestry
	Park Maintenance
	Horticulture
	Park Programs and Events
	Administration

matching and stealing ensued. We called it collaborating and competing and encouraged agencies to work together (or with outside partners, like nonprofits) and, if they had the guts, make a play for a service run by another agency.

One of Baltimore's gutsiest bureaucrats is the aptly named Michael Braverman, then a deputy housing commissioner who had the thankless job of enforcing codes and issuing building permits. His bid to take over burglar alarm collections from the police department was an early win for Outcome Budgeting.

A native of Queens, Michael is compact and intense—a fighter who has needed every bit of his New York City swagger to take on incompetence and patronage over his thirty years in city government.

Michael's parents worked together as a dentist and a hygienist. They would have loved for their only son to join the family business, but he had a different calling. When the City University of New York started a new law school dedicated to public interest law, Michael was one of the first to sign up. He wanted to be a community organizer and decided to start his career in Baltimore, the off-beat, welcoming city he fell in love with as an undergrad at Johns Hopkins. "I figured the pay for community organizers was about the same in Baltimore and in New York, but Baltimore was a much cheaper place to live," he told me. "My friends thought I was crazy."

Working as a prosecutor in the Baltimore City State's Attorney's office, Michael filed the first lawsuit under an ordinance that he helped write to go after landlords for drug nuisance properties. He didn't stop there, initiating the Community Anti-Drug Assistance Project and cofounding the Baltimore Community Law Center, a nonprofit that assists residents in fighting crime, blight, and other social and economic problems.

When Martin O'Malley was elected as mayor of Baltimore in 1999, he recruited Michael to head the housing department's litigation unit. Michael relished the opportunity. He knew that one bad property can ruin an entire block and wanted to use the law to save neighborhoods. First, though, he had to turn around an office that didn't know how many cases it had, who they were assigned to, how long it took to file charges, and how cases turned out. He found boxes filled with unfiled cases, some more than two years old. His predecessor had spent $35,000 on software to organize the cases, but it hadn't worked.

He also found that the staff did not share his interest in using metrics, standards, and technology. The resistance was not quiet. One staff attorney repeatedly told him to leave her alone, using expletive-laden language to get her point across. When he fired her, he was labeled a racist by a powerful state lawmaker, who called for his head. Michael survived, and it wasn't long before he had cleared the backlog and was proactively filing charges against slumlords.

Michael's results got him promoted, and his operation is a national model, with one-stop shopping for building permits, quick response to service requests, and data-driven code inspection—so data-driven that he can tell you how much private investment has resulted from his enforcement actions. Michael credits his staff: "Ronald Reagan called government a refuge for the incompetent," he says. "For years, it was hard to convince good people to work for me, because government was no longer a noble calling. Thankfully, the millennial generation showed up with a renewed ideal of public service."

Outcome Budgeting appealed to the data junkie in Michael. He liked that it demanded answers from services. What are you doing? What is your evidence of success? How can you improve? Why should we invest in you? "I wanted to tell our story, and I saw an opportunity to be rewarded for good ideas."

One of those ideas was that the property registration software he was writing could be used to collect burglar alarm registration fees. The police department was paying a collection agency 35 percent of the fees it brought in, but revenue was low and citations for non-payment were rare. Michael proposed to bring the collection work in-house and aggressively pursue unpaid bills. It worked. Revenue doubled in two years.

Michael's burglar alarm registration proposal paved the way for other service takeovers. The Department of Public Works took over rat control from the Health Department. In our annual citizen survey, rat control stood out for having the largest gap between its importance

Figure 2.3 Service Importance/Satisfaction Matrix

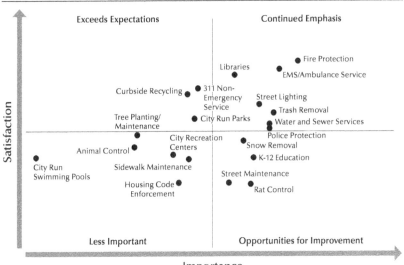

Source: Baltimore Bureau of the Budget and Management Research

rating (high) and satisfaction score (low). In the importance–satisfaction matrix (see figure 2.3), it fell squarely in the quadrant labeled "Opportunities for Improvement." Public Works proposed that its street and alley cleaning crews could be a force multiplier for identifying and baiting rat burrows. As of 2016, these crews were inspecting every alley in the city for burrows on a twenty-one-day cycle, which happens to be the gestation period for a rat.

From rats to rugrats, Baltimore's Head Start director, Shannon Burroughs-Campbell, proposed to assume operation of two childcare centers run by the Department of Housing and Community Development (HCD). Under HCD, the centers were losing enrollment and, even though the service was called Early Childhood Education, there was no evidence of academic progress. Shannon's great idea was to convert the childcare centers to Head Start centers and give summer learning opportunities to 1,100 more children—with no additional funding. She did it in part by finding efficiencies, including consolidating into one center and replacing cooks with caterers at half the cost.

THE ORG CHART PUSHES BACK

Bringing Outcome Budgeting into Focus

Even eight years later, it is still a little hard for me to read the focus group report from the first year of Outcome Budgeting. From where I sat, I could see that the new process had helped the mayor prioritize spending and balance a historically tough budget without making across-the-board cuts or raiding reserves. I could also see that the process had generated a long list of new and innovative ideas for improving city services. Michael Braverman's burglar alarm proposal was just one of many.

Agency heads saw things differently. As the Fiscal 2011 budget cycle was wrapping up, we invited twenty of them to sit down with a facilitator to talk about what they had just been through.

On the whole, the agency heads believed in the principles behind Outcome Budgeting: planning strategically, rewarding innovation, measuring performance, and focusing on value. As one put it, "Outcome Budgeting presented a good opportunity to get a broader view of decisions we make and why . . . to get the total picture instead of silos." They also liked how Outcome Budgeting promoted teamwork within and among agencies. "More people were involved in the budget process than ever before," one said. "The right hand now knows what the left is doing." Another explained, "I really got to understand my agency operations and got into communication with other agencies to try to cooperate."

Concept—check. Implementation—not so much. Some of the criticism we heard was no surprise. Even with training and coaching, writing service proposals for the first time under tight deadlines was "terrifying" and "high stress." The large budget shortfall meant that cuts were inevitable. A common lament went like this: "People were told there would be an opportunity to fund innovative projects, but the cuts were so deep that wasn't true."

My biggest mistake that first year—the biggest source of frustration and confusion for agency heads—had to do with funding targets. Since we were new at Outcome Budgeting, we had two rounds of service proposals so that agencies could get Results Teams' feedback before submitting their final proposals. In the first round, we went by the book and put no limits on the funding levels agencies proposed. The whole idea was to get away from dollar targets, which might suppress creativity. We wanted to let 1,000 flowers bloom, not 725.

The result was a set of proposals that totaled $200 million more than the revenue we had available. I panicked. I couldn't ask the Results Teams to cut that much from the proposals. In retrospect, that's exactly what I should have done. Instead, I issued agencies what I called "Planning Levels" (not targets, you got that?) that they would have to meet with their second-round proposals. I hated to do it, and I hated it even more after I read the focus group commentary. Here's a sampling:

> "Targets undermined the entire process."
> "I was surprised that we were given targets for proposals. It gave the impression that at the end of the day, it ended up being the same old budget process with a lot more work."
> "My staff were deflated after we got targets."

The truth is that the targets did not undermine the entire Outcome Budgeting process, but the fact that they undermined confidence in the process is all that matters. I erred by imposing targets in the middle of the process, and I compounded the error by not doing a good enough job of explaining my decision to agency heads and Results Teams.

After much soul searching, I have concluded that targets (or planning levels, or funding parameters, or whatever euphemism you prefer) can have a legitimate role in Outcome Budgeting. Outcome Budgeting is about getting the best possible results from *available resources*; it is not a blue-sky exercise. Scarcity forces us to be creative and resourceful. It drives innovation. In Baltimore, we found a happy medium by giving agencies planning "parameters" along with the opportunity to propose funding enhancements. We used the term "parameter" because the dollar amount was not a final allocation. Results Teams were free to recommend whatever funding level they saw fit for each service, based on its priority and performance.

Targets were followed closely by transparency on agency heads' gripe list. They wanted more information about how their proposals were ranked by Results Teams and how those rankings translated into budget decisions. They felt they were missing the bigger picture of what changes actually resulted from Outcome Budgeting. Many suspected that "core" city services would be fully funded, regardless of the quality of their proposals. In the spirit of transparency, I will share with you a few of their choicer comments:

> "If there had been some integrity to the process, it would have been palatable. I got to a point where I knew it was BS and ended up feeling like we just had to get something in."
> "It was clear that they were going to do what they wanted to do and what we were submitting didn't really matter."
> "After all the talk about performance, there are still sacred cows."

I could go on, but this is not fun for me. The point is that the budget office asked agency heads, fiscal officers, and Results Team members for their feedback, listened to them, and made changes. The biggest changes were about communication and transparency. Results Teams started face-to-face conferences with agency heads and gave them detailed feedback on how their services were rated and ranked. In table 2.1 you can see a summary of what we heard from the focus groups the first year and what we did about it. We repeated this kind of review and revision every year, because we wanted Outcome Budgeting to keep getting better.

Tell Me How You Really Feel

When I talked to my counterparts from other cities about Outcome Budgeting, they always asked me if I had to overcome resistance from agencies. My stock answer is that all agency heads will tell you that budgets should be based on performance and results. Some actually believe it. Others, deep down, wish they could go back to the old way of budgeting. An agency head in the first focus group was blunt about it: "Give me a budget target and let me determine how to spend the money. If I go over budget, fire me." This reaction was not unexpected. In her memo to agency heads kicking off Outcome Budgeting—which is shown in figure 2.4—Mayor Dixon tried to prepare them for change, using vivid language. "Fiscal officers will struggle to present budget requests differently," she wrote. "Program

Table 2.1 Focus Group Feedback

Feedback	Fixes
• Planning levels undermined the process; same old budget process in disguise • Funding cuts were so severe there wasn't anything left for innovation	• No planning levels will be given. Agencies will submit current level of service and a proposed level of service. • Establish an **Innovation Fund** for one-time investments with demonstrated payback in terms of budget savings, revenue, or results.
• Process is too time-consuming for both agencies and Results Teams • Timelines too tight; don't allow for cross-agency collaboration	• Streamline the budget process; less voluminous, more focused proposals. Modify the web tool to ask for more specific, space-limited information. One round of proposals instead of two. • Assign one or more **efficiency teams** to examine cross-cutting operational or management issues, such as mowing of city property.
• Process lacked transparency. Agencies and Results Teams weren't able to connect proposals, rankings and budget decisions	• Make Results Team documentation—ranking sheets and tollgate memos—available for agencies to review. • Finance department will better connect final budget decisions with Results Team ranking through the preliminary budget document.
• Process lacked commitment from mayor and senior staff • No buy-in from agency heads and key staff from the start	• Establish an agency head advisory group convened by the chief of staff to improve communication throughout the process, prevent misperceptions, and dispel rumors. • Each Results Team will include a deputy mayor or key senior staff member.
• Process lacked real commitment to performance measurement; not integrated with CitiStat	• Fully integrate service performance measures with CitiStat metrics, with regular reporting monitored through CitiStat and discussed at CitiStat meetings. • New, quarterly CitiStat meetings by Priority Outcome to monitor progress. All city agencies with services funded under the Priority Outcome participate.
• Results Teams didn't fully understand what agencies do and how they do it	• All agencies will have the opportunity to make presentations to Results Teams.
• Agencies need more technical assistance with proposal and performance measurement development	• Budget and CitiStat analysts trained on how to provide technical assistance to agencies.
• Finance micromanages agency budgets	• Agencies with approved budget execution plans will be able to hire and spend with less finance oversight.

Figure 2.4 Mayor's Memo

NAME & TITLE	Sheila Dixon, Mayor	CITY of
AGENCY NAME & ADDRESS	Office of the Mayor 250 City Hall	BALTIMORE
SUBJECT	OUTCOME BUDGETING	*MEMO*

To: Agency Heads

Date: September 15, 2008

My job as Mayor is to ensure that City resources are used strategically and cost-effectively to make Baltimore a better place to live. Last spring, I asked the Finance Department to develop a budget process that more clearly links resources to the results I have promised citizens and builds on our successful CitiStat program to give me more information about how City programs are performing. Today, I am pleased to announce the kickoff of Outcome Budgeting and explain how it will be implemented over the next two budget cycles.

Outcome Budgeting is a significant departure from traditional budgeting. It is built around objectives instead of organizational units, and it starts with next year's goals instead of last year's spending. The benefits of this new approach are numerous. It will drive creative thinking about how to get the most from limited dollars; integrate strategic planning, CitiStat, and the budget; and put the budget in terms citizens can relate to.

Outcome Budgeting is not a gimmick or a fad; it is a new way of doing business. As such, it is guaranteed to create some discomfort in your organizations. Fiscal staff will struggle to present budget requests differently. Program managers will be queasy about setting performance targets that make them more accountable for outcomes they do not fully control. Senior executives will be flustered by losing the predictability of a budget process that, for the most part, made marginal adjustments to the previous year's numbers.

Making outcome budgeting work will require your deep commitment and engagement, and I expect no less. I firmly believe that building our budgets around the results we care about will help us achieve those results. I look forward to working with you to move Outcome Budgeting forward.

An overview of how we will implement Outcome Budgeting is attached, and detailed guidance about Outcome Budgeting is forthcoming from the Bureau of the Budget and Management Research. If you have questions about Outcome Budgeting, please contact Andrew Kleine, the City's Budget Director, at 396-4941.

SD:nh

Attachment
Cc: Chief of Staff
          Deputy Mayors
          Edward Gallagher
          Helene Grady
          Andrew Kleine

Visit Our Website @ www.baltimorecity.gov

Source: Baltimore Bureau of the Budget and Management Research

managers will be queasy about setting performance targets that make them more accountable for outcomes they do not fully control. Senior executives will be flustered by losing the predictability of a budget process that, for the most part, made marginal adjustments to the previous year's numbers."

No agency head ever said to my face that we should stop Outcome Budgeting. The resistance was less direct. My two favorite examples come from public works directors.

Al Foxx led Baltimore's transportation and public works departments for twelve years, before leaving city government in early 2014. A retired colonel in the US Army Corps of Engineers, he brings to mind the great defensive-tackle-turned-minister Rosey Grier—a gentle giant whose double-bridge eyeglasses and ready smile make

Photo 2.1 *Rosey Grier's Needlepoint for Men* Source: Grier, Rosey. *Rosey Grier's Needlepoint for Men*. New York: Walker, 1973.

him less intimidating. I'm not sure if Colonel Foxx is into needlepoint like Grier, but I guess I could have asked him when he took me out to lunch one day in 2012. I was just too speechless.

The invitation surprised me, only because I was usually the one asking agency heads out to lunch, not the other way around. He had chosen a white tablecloth restaurant near the Inner Harbor, and we chatted about our low carb diets before ordering salads. After getting past the pleasantries, he said to me, "I heard that you came to Baltimore to experiment with Outcome Budgeting so you could write a book about it. Is that true?" Oh, the irony. The question is hilarious now, but at the time I had no thoughts of writing a book and was insulted by the rumor. It was his way of telling me that Outcome Budgeting was nice in theory, and now it was time to get back to old-school budgeting—or something like that.

When Colonel Foxx retired, he was replaced by Rudy Chow, an engineer who has spent his career operating water and wastewater utilities. Director Chow is a proud man who doesn't like to be second-guessed. I am also proud, and I like to ask questions. When the two of us got together, we didn't play patty-cake. Our back-and-forth at a CitiStat meeting in the fall of 2016 exposed a philosophical disagreement about the purpose of outcomes in city management.

The CitiStat director was reviewing data on the city's street sweeping service. In 2014, Director Chow had convinced the mayor that he could sweep 90 percent of neighborhood streets on a monthly cycle—a huge service increase—without additional funding. In reality, the new sweeping schedule had cost millions for signage, sweeper purchases and repairs, and shifting staff from other duties.

The data before us was tracking the number of street miles swept and the number of tons of debris collected per mile. As you can see in the chart in figure 2.5, the amount of street debris collected (as measured by tonnage-per-mile trend) had decreased over the previous five months. My question was, "If the tonnage per mile trend continues in that direction, at what point do we ask if we should sweep streets less often?" My unstated point was that the city should not spend resources sweeping clean streets and that we could either save

Figure 2.5 Street Sweeping

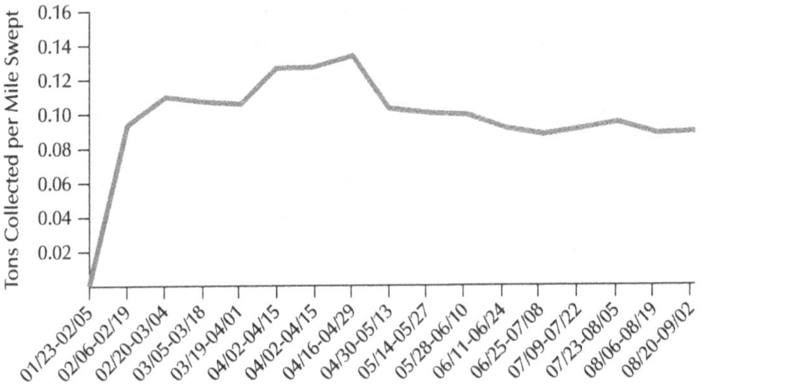

Source: Baltimore CitiStat

those resources or redirect them to dirty streets. I did say aloud that we should care about the outcome of cleaner streets, not the number of miles swept. Director Chow would have none of it, insisting that street sweeping is a service, not an outcome, and that his job is to deliver the service timely and efficiently.

If you want to know why I think Outcome Budgeting is important, it is because without it, many agency heads will go on running their services without questioning, or being questioned about, whether those services—however timely and efficient they may be—are leading to the outcomes we want.

The Human Side of Budgeting

Colonel Foxx and Director Chow would probably enjoy Scott Lazenby's book *The Human Side of Budgeting: Budget Games & How to End Them.* Like me, Lazenby is a critic of traditional budgeting. But where I advocate an outcome-first alternative, his solution is agency-first. Anyone thinking of changing how they budget should know about Lazenby's ideas. In my mind, they are in many ways compatible with Outcome Budgeting.

Lazenby, a longtime city manager in Oregon, traces traditional budgeting back to the reform era of the early twentieth century, when Frederick Taylor's "scientific management" concepts were applied to government bureaucracy. At its core, scientific management assumed that human beings are lazy and stupid, so it reduced work to instructions and rules that would keep employees in line and working efficiently. MIT professor Douglas McGregor, who wrote *The Human Side of Enterprise* in 1960, called this view of management "Theory X." He proposed "Theory Y" management, based on a more enlightened understanding of human nature. Theory Y assumes that organizations perform best when employees are given more freedom in how they work and are held accountable for results.

Theory X budgeting has survived decades of new management theories from McGregor, Peter Drucker, Tom Peters, and others. It is a top-down system in which agencies engage in a zero-sum competition for funds and spending is controlled down to the line-item level. In Lazenby's words,

> In this process, the key budget decisions are reserved to the CEO and central finance staff, and the governing body. The operating managers are players in the game, but share little of the responsibility for balancing the budget. Once the budget is adopted, the rules of the game set up an adversarial relationship between the operating managers and the central finance staff, in which the operating managers are assumed to be profligate spenders, and the finance department is there to rein them in.

Lazenby lists 21 budget games that operating managers play in Theory X budgeting to try to fool the central finance office and get the money they need, everything from padding obscure line items ("The accountants made me do it," #18) to getting approval for an expensive piece of equipment and then purchasing a less expensive item ("The old switcheroo," #13). For each trick, there is a finance office response to sniff it out or prevent it from working in the first place.

To end the budget games, Lazenby gives us Theory Y budgeting. Under Theory Y, there are no budget requests. Agencies keep the revenue they generate and are given a predictable allocation of the city's general revenue. Agencies can move dollars freely between line items and across services, and any surpluses are carried over to the next fiscal year for one-time expenses. In exchange for this freedom, agencies are expected to accomplish goals set by leadership and be responsible for keeping their spending within available funds, without babysitting from the central finance office. According to Lazenby, Theory Y aligns the budget process with how humans are wired. Empowered managers will make good decisions, be creative, and stop playing games.

A few years ago, I selected *The Human Side of Budgeting* for Baltimore's Good Government Book Club. At the book club meeting, one participant was incredulous. "I can't believe you chose this book," she said to me. "Theory Y is the exact opposite of Outcome Budgeting!"

No, it isn't. It's not the same, either. Unshackling agency heads and their managers from onerous budget controls is consistent with the philosophy of Outcome Budgeting, which is that we should bend the rules to get the best results.

Where I part ways with Lazenby is over the purpose of the budget process. For him, policy is largely fixed and the objective of budgeting is to run day-in-and day-out services as effectively and efficiently as possible. In his experience, the governing body's goals are mainly "milestones" like planning projects, major capital improvements, or new services and programs. "An elaborate process in which the governing body specifies outcomes would be a waste of time," he writes.

I'm sure that government's role is simpler in places like Sandy, Oregon, where Lazenby was manager. In Baltimore, we were confronted with complex problems on a large scale: violent crime, water pollution, heroin addiction, homelessness; the list goes on and on. If I cut out the competition for resources and put the budget on autopilot, as Lazenby suggests, I could not make the most strategic use of the city's resources to solve these problems. Why should code enforcement keep all of its citation revenue when a portion of that revenue could be better spent on an initiative to reduce infant mortality? What is more important, empowered operating managers or improved quality of life for residents? I ask this question rhetorically; I don't really think we need to choose one or the other.

Beyond Budgeting

Lazenby ends his book with a radical notion that perhaps government doesn't need to budget at all. In the Information Age, budgets could be replaced with rolling five-year forecasts, key performance indicators, fast-track approval of new investments as needed instead of on an arbitrary fiscal year schedule, and real-time monitoring of the organization's fiscal health.

These ideas come from the Beyond Budgeting Roundtable, a London-based institute whose website (bbrt.org) says,

> Beyond Budgeting is about rethinking how we manage organizations in a post-industrial world where innovative management models represent the only sustainable competitive advantage. It is also about releasing people from the burdens of stifling bureaucracy and suffocating control systems, trusting them with information and giving them time to think, reflect, share, learn and improve.

That's a lot of management speak. What caught my attention was the Roundtable's explanation of what it means by "budgeting."

> The word "budgeting" is not used in its narrow sense of planning and control, but as a generic term for the traditional command and control management model (with the annual budget process at its core).

In other words, the budget process has come to be the very definition of bureaucracy. Whether through Outcome Budgeting, Theory Y budgeting, or Beyond Budgeting, the time is now to go in a new direction.

I have made the point in this chapter that Outcome Budgeting only works if agencies write thoughtful, informative, and above all creative service proposals. The next chapter is about how to bring these kinds of proposals to life.

FIVE TAKEAWAYS

1. **Services are the building blocks of Outcome Budgeting.** Before you start Outcome Budgeting, define your services in a way that makes sense to residents and gives you units of analysis for budget decision-making. You know a service is well defined if (1) you know how much it costs, (2) its performance story can be told with five or fewer measures, and (3) you know who to talk to if the service isn't performing well.

2. **Outcome Budgeting allocates dollars to outcomes instead of agencies as one of the first steps in the budgeting process.** This is a job for the leaders of the organization, and they should take it seriously. They will probably find that the existing budget allocation, the result of years of incremental budgeting, does not match up with current priorities and challenges. Shifting the allocation signals change and begins the exciting work of figuring out how to invest the dollars for each outcome to get the best possible results.

3. **Allocating dollars by outcomes instead of agencies encourages both collaboration and competition.** First, it breaks down silos. No agency "owns" any outcome; agencies have to work together (and with other partners) to make progress toward the end goals. Second, it puts all available money into play. Agencies can't take their funding for granted anymore; they have to earn it.

4. **When managing change, the most important thing you can do is listen to the people who are affected and make adjustments that respond to their input.** Some of the focus group feedback about Outcome Budgeting was harsh, but it made the process better. Resistance to change is oftentimes passive-aggressive, which means that if you want honest opinions, you need to give people "safe spaces" to speak their minds, such as focus groups or anonymous surveys.

5. **Outcomes should be the center of attention for everything government does, not just budgeting.** As the street sweeping example in this chapter illustrates, sometimes managers obsess about doing things right (in a timely and efficient way) and lose sight of whether they are doing the right things.

FIVE QUESTIONS

1. Find a local government budget document online. Choose an agency and examine its programs/services. Do they meet the definition of a service explained in this chapter? If not, propose a new set of services.
2. What are the trade-offs between "targets" and unlimited service funding levels for budget proposals?
3. Based on Baltimore's experience, how can a budget office make the first year of Outcome Budgeting a more positive experience for agency heads?
4. Compare Scott Lazenby's "Theory Y" budgeting and Outcome Budgeting. What are the benefits of each? What organizational challenges does each approach present? In what ways are they similar to one another?
5. You've already read about several methods of budgeting, from the traditional approach to not budgeting at all. See if you can design your own new budgeting method for government.

FIVE RESOURCES

1. You can find information about all of Baltimore's services in its annual Agency Detail budget publications at budget.baltimorecity.gov/budget-publications.
2. Reports from the Baltimore Community Survey can be found at budget.baltimorecity.gov/citizen-survey.
3. Babak ("Armi") Armajani, who helped Baltimore implement Outcome Budgeting, was a prolific thinker and writer on making government services more cost-effective and customer friendly. Thankfully, Governing.com still maintains a web page with his articles at www.governing.com/authors/babak-armajani.html. Armi also wrote a book with Michael Barzelay called *Breaking Through Bureaucracy: A New Vision for Managing in Government*, about funding and managing internal functions such as data processing, printing, revenue collection, and so forth.

4. Lazenby, Scott. (2013). *The Human Side of Budgeting: Budget Games and How to End Them.* CreateSpace Independent Publishing Platform. This book is described in this chapter as a different perspective on how to change the traditional budgeting process. Lazenby is also the author of what may be the only city management novel ever written, *Playing with Fire.* It's a good read, and you can order it via his website, www.scottlazenbybooks.com.

5. Chrisinger, Jim, "Smart Management and the Turnaround of a City," *Governing*, June 1, 2011. This article describes Michael Braverman's innovative strategies for targeting Baltimore's blight elimination resources to leverage private investment.

3

Budget Proposals That Sing

■ ■ ■

SCOTT LAZENBY IS not alone in his opinion that trying to bring rationality to budget decisions is a waste of time. Ken Miller, in his book *Extreme Government Makeover: Increasing Our Capacity to Do More Good*, calls rational budgets "a myth . . . as rare as a unicorn or a U.S. World Cup soccer championship." Here's his explanation:

> About every two years, the public sector is greeted with a new budget fad: zero-based budgeting, budgeting for results, outcome-based budgeting, the price of government, and on and on and on. They all have slightly different names, with different lead singers, but the songs sound remarkably the same. What they're singing about is a careful, logical, data-driven approach to allocating scarce resources. By deftly explaining each program's purpose, measuring whether it's achieving its purpose, and then calculating the program's cost-benefit ratio, elected officials will abandon all partisanship, ideology, and constituent loyalties and either ax or grow a government program. This is simply not how the budget works, or will ever work. Elected officials use a lot of things to make their very difficult decisions, but logic and data are not chief among them.

While Miller acknowledges that these so-called fads are earnest attempts to do better than across-the-board cuts, he concludes his rant by lamenting, "Across-the-board cuts just plain suck, but they're not going away."

Miller isn't just cynical, he's wrong. Wrong that across-the-board cuts are inevitable. Wrong that elected officials won't make decisions based on rational analysis. Especially wrong that the budget process is only about allocating resources.

Sure, the budget is a political document. There's no denying that it is influenced by give and take with vocal advocates, parochial council members, big-dollar campaign contributors, unyielding labor unions, etc. Baltimore has proven that when budget trade-offs are presented with clear priorities and solid evidence about performance and impact, elected officials will listen to reason and across-the-board cuts will be a thing of the past.

Outcome Budgeting will probably change how you allocate funding, but that is not the only way it gets you better results.

Program managers are afraid to set ambitious performance goals because they believe that the penalty for falling short is a budget cut. I tell them that if their service is important enough, missing a performance target might actually get them more money. What I don't tell them is that it might also cost them their job.

In Baltimore, we found that where a service is not getting the results we want, funding is just one of many possible reasons why. Maybe the service is poorly managed (thus the possibility of heads rolling). Maybe its design is flawed. Maybe factors beyond its control are interfering with its performance. Program managers are quick to point the finger of blame at the budget, procurement, and HR shops—easy targets all—but the problems usually go deeper.

The romantic in me likes to think of the budget process as a heroic quest to discover ideas that will improve results and find the root causes of bad results. Poetically, the quest starts with a request.

REQUEST FOR RESULTS

If you want to ditch across-the-board cuts, you have to be able to sort services according to how they help you achieve your outcomes. Sorting starts with strategy. The better you can explain what you are trying to achieve, the better the budget proposals you will get from your agencies or other "bidders."

I use the word "bidders" because, as I said in chapter 1, budgeting is about purchasing results. In the same way that city procurement offices issue a Request for Proposals to buy goods and services, budget offices should issue a Request for Results (or RFR) to buy lower crime rates, cleaner air, faster commute times, and so forth.

Later in the book, I describe Baltimore's OutcomeStat program, which uses "Turn the Curve" strategic planning to power performance management, including the budget process. In this chapter, I focus on how to ask for great budget proposals and get them.

We want to know how each city service can contribute to achieving the big outcomes, the ones that require partnership, collaboration, ingenuity, and foresight. We also want to know how each service can improve its own performance, for example, by missing fewer trash pickups, approving requisitions more quickly, and making customers happier.

The best way to show you how to ask for great budget proposals and get them is to tell you about Bill Vondrasek, who I would induct into the Budget Proposal Hall of Fame if such a thing existed.

FROM PHYSICS TO FLOWERS

As soon as he opens his mouth, you know where Bill Vondrasek is from. His nasal pitch marks him as a Chicago native. Bill grew up on the far south side, near Graver Park. For high school, he took a bus and two trains to get to and from Whitney Young Magnet, one of the best high schools in Illinois, where he was one year behind Michelle Obama.

A self-described math and science geek, Bill went on to the University of Chicago with hopes of becoming a scientist. After he struggled to pull a D grade in his first physics class, his professor suggested he consider a different career. The first inkling of what that career might be came to Bill as he rode his bike from Hyde Park to his job as a lifeguard at Rainbow Beach, four blocks from the US Steel South Works plant. His route took him through Washington Park and Jackson Park, both Frederick Law Olmstead designs, and he daydreamed about being a landscape architect.

Bill's path would lead back to parks, though not as a landscape architect. Out of college, his girlfriend got him a job at a family-owned flower wholesaler, where he worked for seven years before taking his horticultural talents to the Chicago Botanic Garden. Love led him to Baltimore, where he took over the city's beleaguered conservatory. When he arrived, the historic landmark had dirt floors and three of its greenhouses were empty. Bill led a renovation that turned the neglected building into what one critic called "a brilliant symphony of curved glass and light."

Does Money Grow on Trees?

By the time Outcome Budgeting got started, Bill had risen to Director of Parks. He was disillusioned by the traditional budget process, which gave him "a little more or a little less" each year, with no apparent logic to the funding levels. He welcomed the opportunity to compete for his funding based on results. He had recently hired a city arborist named Erik Dihle, who was newly retired from taking care of the trees at Arlington National Cemetery. They were full of ideas

Photo 3.1 Rawlings Conservatory *Source: Jimi Jones, Baltimore Landscape Photographer.*

and saw Outcome Budgeting as an outlet for showing how Urban Forestry could make Baltimore a more attractive and sustainable city.

They were in luck. Cleaner, Greener Baltimore was Mayor Dixon's calling card, and one of her Priority Outcomes for the Fiscal 2011 budget process was "Make Baltimore a Cleaner, Greener & More Sustainable City." Two of the Key Indicators were right in Bill and Erik's wheelhouse: percentage of tree canopy cover and greenhouse gas emissions. The RFR for the Cleaner, Greener outcome asked for service proposals that, among other things, "prevent pollution," "conserve energy," "increase the coverage of the tree canopy," and "provide cost-effective maintenance for Baltimore's landscape." I have included the full RFR at appendix A, so you have an example to start from if you want to try Outcome Budgeting yourself.

One thing that all of Baltimore's RFRs have in common is a set of criteria to remind Bill and other people writing service proposals that same old, same old thinking doesn't cut it in Outcome Budgeting. The criteria, which are listed in box 3.1, encourage collaboration, long-term planning, use of data and evidence, and innovation.

The basic elements of an Outcome Budgeting service proposal haven't changed much since that first year. Proposals are asked to answer four big questions:

1. How will you get more results per dollar spent?
2. How will you support the mayor's Priority Outcomes?
3. What evidence do you have to support your proposal?
4. How will you measure your performance?

Bill's answers to these questions for the Urban Forestry service made the service more cost-effective and won it more resources during a period of chronic budget shortfalls. Let's take a look at how he made money grow on trees.

How Will You Get More Results per Dollar Spent?

Bill's early Urban Forestry proposals focused on making the service more cost-effective. The Great Recession had wreaked havoc on the city's budget, and he knew that even with fewer dollars, the mayor would expect him to keep up with the thousands of tree maintenance requests he gets from residents.

Box 3.1 | Request for Results Criteria

Value. Proposals that demonstrate good value tell us what we can expect to be delivered per dollar spent. Value is a measure of both efficiency and the effectiveness of a service.

Strength of alignment with the Priority Outcomes, Key Indicators, and strategies.

Innovation. Innovative proposals demonstrate new solutions or the degree to which the service improves or reengineers the way a service is currently delivered. Even high-value services as they are currently delivered have areas for improvement.

Multiple Priority Outcomes. We seek proposals that demonstrate the ability to address multiple Priority Outcomes concurrently.

Leverage. We seek proposals that demonstrate the ability to leverage other funds or resources for service delivery and/or collaborate with other internal or external entities. Partnerships can also be with neighborhood groups or other non–service providers.

Evidence-Based. We seek proposals that deliver a service that is proven effective through empirical data or professional best practices. This can be an agency's data gathered through CitiStat or some other performance measurement effort or reliable data gathered by another organization.

Part of a Strategic Plan. We seek proposals that advance an existing or emerging strategic plan. Strategic Plans outline clear goals and objectives with specific action items, funding sources, individual roles, and time lines. Examples include the Sustainability Plan, Comprehensive Master Plan, Ten-Year Plan to End Homelessness, Birth Outcomes Plan, and so forth.

Customer Service Focus. We seek proposals that focus on providing excellent customer service. Think of customers broadly and include internal customers, such as other city agencies or city staff members, and external customers, including citizens and users of city services.

Historically, the Department of Recreation and Parks relied mainly on in-house crews to perform tree work. Tree work is physically demanding, and the reality Bill faced in the early 2010s was that as his laborers aged, they became less productive. In his service proposals, Bill laid out a multipoint plan to do more with less.

First, he decided to contract out tree planting. He figured that even though the up-front cost would increase from $210 to $220 per tree, the new strategy would pay off in the long run because the contract would include a one-year replacement warranty. It so happens that infant mortality is a problem for trees, too, and the new contract would reduce the rate.

Second, he partnered with the nonprofit TreeBaltimore to enlist more volunteers to plant trees. Over time, the city and TreeBaltimore would join forces to form the TreeKeepers and Weed Warriors programs, volunteer efforts to care for trees after they're planted and remove invasive plants that threaten tree health.

Third, he changed the way he paid for contract tree maintenance. Instead of paying for tree work by the hour, he shifted to "unit cost" contracts that would give the crews an incentive to work quickly and efficiently. This was an idea that Erik brought with him from Arlington. As in-house laborers have retired, more and more tree work is being done by contract crews.

Fourth, he began planting trees in geographical clusters, starting with the most tree-starved neighborhoods. This approach has many advantages over responding to tree planting requests in the order received. Trees are cheaper to plant and maintain in clusters, they survive longer, and they make residents feel better about where they live. Clustered tree planting was followed in later years by a proactive pruning initiative, which has expanded to fifteen neighborhoods. Cyclical pruning is far more efficient than sending crews all over town to respond to service calls, and with each neighborhood added to the cycle, the call backlog shrinks.

Finally, Bill took a simple step to make his in-house crews more efficient: send an inspector to check out urgent service requests before dispatching the crew. The inspectors prioritize the jobs using a new hazard rating index, which leads to better time management and scheduling for the crew.

Maybe what Bill is doing isn't physics, but it is a more scientific approach to city government.

How Will You Support the Mayor's Priority Outcomes?

Bill's Urban Forestry proposals made the case for how a larger and healthier tree canopy supports every one of the Priority Outcomes. Now, the environmental benefits of trees are well known. Trees consume carbon dioxide to clean the air and absorb polluted rainwater that would otherwise flow into the Chesapeake Bay. Their shade cools streets and homes. It is not hard to connect the dots on how money spent to plant and maintain trees will help us "Turn the Curve" in the right direction on our water quality and energy usage indicators.

Some of the other connections Bill made were unexpected. For example, he made the case that regular tree pruning helps fight crime by making street lights and crime cameras more effective. He also explained that street trees reduce asthma-related emergency-room visits, increase neighborhood walkability, and even boost retail sales in well-landscaped business districts. All of these benefits relate directly to specific indicators.

What Evidence Do You Have to Support Your Proposal?

Bill's proposals cited studies showing that trees reduce heating and air conditioning costs by 15 to 50 percent, improve air quality, reduce stormwater runoff by up to 15 percent, lengthen the road repaving cycle from ten years to twenty years, and increase property values by 5 to 25 percent.

This question also goes to how a service uses data to improve results. A few years ago, Bill was funded for an enhancement to gather data for a tree inventory. Knowing the number, species, and condition of street trees will allow Urban Forestry to target its resources more effectively to maintain, remove, and replace trees.

How Will You Measure Your Performance?

Many books have been written about performance measurement, and the terminology around performance measurement is all over the place. The simplest approach I have seen to measuring a service's performance comes from Mark Friedman's book *Trying Hard Is Not Good Enough: How to Produce Measurable Improvements for Customers and Communities*. He boils it down to three basic questions:

> How much did we do?
> How well did we do it?
> Is anyone better off?

Figure 3.1 Performance Measure Matrix

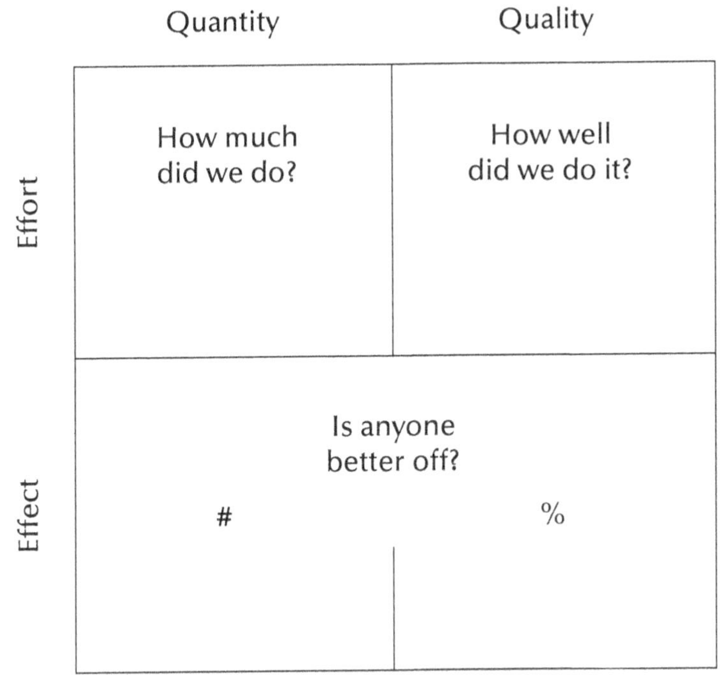

	Quantity	Quality
Effort	How much did we do?	How well did we do it?
Effect	#	Is anyone better off? %

Source: *Trying Hard Is Not Good Enough*, Mark Friedman

The chart in figure 3.1 puts these questions into quadrants and shows the types of measures that answer each question.

I wish I had read Mark's book before I started Outcome Budgeting. What we asked our agencies for was a set of five performance measures for each service, including at least one of each of the following types of measures: Output, Efficiency, Effectiveness, and Outcome. We wrote examples of each type of measure, which are shown in box 3.2, but even my budget analysts sometimes had trouble distinguishing one type from another. The good news is that there is a pretty straight line from Mark's questions to our measures:

Output = How much did we do?
Efficiency and Effectiveness = How well did we do it?
Outcome = Is anyone better off?

Box 3.2 | Types of Service Performance Measures

How Much?
Output:
- Number of people/calls/inquiries served.
- Miles of road cleaned/paved.
- Number of potholes repaired.
- Number of inspections done.
- Number of incidents responded to.
- Number of website hits.
- Number of books checked out.

How Well?
Efficiency:
- Cost (time and materials) per pothole fixed.
- Number of volunteer hours for invasive plant removal.
- Refuse collection cost per household.
- Cost per vaccination/inoculation.
- Cost per mile of roadway construction.

How Well?
Effectiveness:
- Percentage of service requests closed on time.
- Number of complaints or callbacks due to poor service.
- Percentage of calls answered "accurately."
- Average lead time for stump removal.
- Percentage of customers rating the service as "outstanding."
- Number of red-light-running violations.

Better Off?
Outcome:
- Number/percentage of clients who attain program goal (employment, smoking cessation, high school graduation, etc.).
- Crime rates, poverty rates, health status in areas targeted through service delivery.
- Air and water quality in designated areas.
- Commuting times/traffic flow times in designated areas.

In doing research for this book, I unearthed a document from March 2009 with Bill Vondrasek's first cut at Urban Forestry performance measures. You can see Bill's math and science brain at work in one of the Outcome measures, called Environmental Services Contribution. Box 3.3 explains how he described the measure:

It's not exactly $E=MC^2$, but it is a serious attempt to overcome a common performance measurement challenge, which is that two

---

Box 3.3 | Environmental Services Measure

Environmental Services (ES) are dependent on species planted, as different species contribute in different ways. The way we measure the contribution of the species we plant each year is by the sum of environmental contribution (EC) times the survival rate (SR) of the species. The formula would be:

ES = EC × SR, which could then be used to calculate the cost/benefit (CB), where CB = ES – (PC + MC)
PC = Planting Cost
MC = Maintenance Cost

At the end of each fiscal year, we can perform the cost/benefit analysis to evaluate the real value of planting trees in Baltimore.

---

units of service are not always the same. In this case, no two tree species have the same impact on the environment or the same cost. Similarly, the city's purchasing office weights procurement actions based on their complexity, such that the two capital project contracts Purchaser Bob is working on this month count as a larger workload than Purchaser Rita's five office supply contracts.

Environmental Services Contribution didn't make it as one of Urban Forestry's five "headline" performance measures, which are shown in table 3.1.

As you can see in the table, we asked our agencies to set performance targets each year—not estimates, targets—and we reported how they actually did. Urban Forestry has consistently improved its performance for most of its measures. Trees are getting healthier, proactive pruning is reducing service calls, and the canopy is holding its own against development, disease, and disasters.

Figure 3.2 shows what it would look like if we put Urban Forestry's measures into Mark Friedman's matrix.

For Bill Vondrasek, Outcome Budgeting has been a chance to use his great ideas to compete for funding that wouldn't have been available under traditional budgeting. For other agency heads, Outcome Budgeting has brought about a new way of thinking about how to plan for and achieve better results, which is reflected in their service proposals.

Table 3.1 Urban Forestry Performance Measures

Type	Measure	FY13 Actual	FY14 Actual	FY15 Actual	FY16 Target	FY16 Actual	FY17 Target	FY17 Actual
Output	Total # of trees planted by City crews	N/A	700	750	750	425	750	750
Efficiency	% of tree maintenance that is proactive	N/A	N/A	7%	22%	24%	33%	33%
Effectiveness	% of trees remaining healthy two years after planting	72%	73%	78%	85%	94%	85%	85%
Effectiveness	# of tree maintenance service requests received	13,190	10,881	10,734	10,555	9,783	10,500	10,500
Outcome	Baltimore's urban tree canopy	27%	27%	27%	28%	27%	28%	28%

Figure 3.2 Urban Forestry Performance Measures Matrix

	Quantity	Quality
Effort	How much did we do? # of trees planted	How well did we do it? % of tree maintenance work that is proactive % of trees remaining healthy two years after planting
Effect	Is anyone better off? # of tree maintenance service requests received	% of urban tree canopy cover

Source: Baltimore Bureau of the Budget and Management Research

CHANGING THE WAY AGENCIES THINK

To look at them, Steve Sharkey and Gary Holland—the director and chief of staff of Baltimore's Department of General Services—seem an unlikely duo. Steve is the stereotypical "All-American Boy," with blonde hair, blue eyes, and a football player's build. At thirty-eight, he is a bit too old to be called a millennial, but his uniform is casual oxford shirts and khaki pants. Gary is some thirty years older, a grandfatherly African American who favors tailored suits and accents them with colorful suspenders and pocket squares.

What they have in common is a strong public service ethic. Steve's was formed early in life. A Long Island native, he started reading *Newsday* at age seven. "Every section, not just Sports," he says. "I was always into the news, especially about government and politics."

Gary's father was a boilermaker at the Patuxent River Naval Air Station in southern Maryland, a "doer" who showed Gary what hard work looks like. As an undergrad at Morgan State University in Baltimore, Gary took a sociology class taught by Parren Mitchell and later worked on Mitchell's successful 1970 campaign to become the first African American elected to Congress from Maryland (in fact, he was the first African American congressman from south of the Mason–Dixon line since Reconstruction).

Gary credits Mitchell with inspiring him to pursue a master's degree in public administration at Ohio State, where he got added motivation from legendary football coach Woody Hayes, who exhorted Buckeyes to "pay it forward." He has done so over a forty-year career that includes leading public safety agencies in Cleveland and Columbus, eight years on the Columbus school board, and managing operations for Maryland's labor department.

Steve started his government career as an analyst in Mayor Martin O'Malley's CitiStat program, where he became a true believer in its tenets: accurate and timely intelligence shared by all, rapid deployment of resources, effective tactics and strategies, and relentless follow-up and assessment. After stints with the Bureau of Solid Waste and Police Department, he was asked to take over the Department of General Services (DGS). Having twice been rejected by the city's elite Mayoral Fellows program as a graduate student, Steve was now a member of the Mayor's Cabinet. He quickly hired Gary as his partner in leading the agency.

What Steve and Gary found at DGS was an organization that had suffered from years of indifferent management. Morale was "garbage," according to Steve. There was no strategy or desire to improve. Employees were spending all of their time fighting fires and blaming each other when things went wrong. Steve cancelled a strategic visioning retreat that was on the calendar when he arrived and replaced it with red-carpet customer service training. It was a signal that he wanted to start by getting the basics right, then build from there.

Steve and Gary embraced Outcome Budgeting as a tool for strategic management: establishing priorities, measuring performance, and focusing on long-term improvement, not just troubleshooting. When I ask Steve how he approached the budget process, he quickly replies, "I approach it every day. We identify where we need to improve, develop a data-driven solution, and keep looking long-term." He describes "jam sessions" in the bullpen office space he created, where he and his team of young analysts (including three poached from my office) kick around ideas and update each other on their cool projects.

Steve and Gary have turned the mess they inherited into what is probably the most energized, sophisticated, and forward-thinking agency in Baltimore city government. The evidence can be seen in DGS's service proposals and the results that have come from smarter budgeting.

When asked what result he is most proud of, Steve points to the dramatic increase in the percentage of building maintenance that is preventative as opposed to complaint-driven. Preventative maintenance jumped from 6 percent of DGS's work to 46 percent in just two years. This jump in performance was preceded by a hop and a skip, both of which happened in the Outcome Budgeting process.

The brain behind the maintenance breakthrough is Steve's CFO, a stylish, convivial Turkish immigrant named Berke Attila. I hired Berke into city government as a budget analyst. My deputy favored another candidate who had better writing skills, but I was intrigued by Berke's business mind.

When he applied for the budget job, he was working for a custom counter and tile company, where he had used barcoding and new technology to speed up the countertop production process. In his relentless search for efficiencies, Berke didn't just help his company's bottom line, he also found love. When he cut out the middleman to buy stone directly from a Brazilian quarry, the woman on the other end of the phone line was a seller with the rather fabulous name of Bruna Baldez Siqueira Carvalho, who would become his wife.

I wanted to bring Berke's way of thinking into the budget office, but I was careful to manage his expectations. I told him that the satisfaction he would get from improving city services falls somewhere between shaving a few cents off a countertop and wedded bliss. He ultimately chose city government over a competing job offer with more pay because of Outcome Budgeting. Coming from the private sector, Outcome Budgeting's use of data to make resource decisions seemed "natural" to him, and he saw how his skills could be helpful.

After two years at DGS, Berke was even more sold on Outcome Budgeting. "The work we do in DGS is not as sexy as firefighting or affordable housing, but Outcome Budgeting levels the playing field for us versus the large agencies. It awards dollars based on merit, not politics."

Program managers in DGS didn't share Berke's faith in Outcome Budgeting; they saw it as a paperwork exercise. As a result, they weren't measuring the right things, much less using performance measurement to improve their services. It was a target-rich environment for a CFO who Steve Sharkey had empowered to help him change the agency's culture.

In reviewing DGS's performance record, the first thing that stood out to Berke was the time it took for facilities maintenance to complete work orders. Work-order durations were getting longer, not shorter, and nobody seemed to know why. The facilities director was dismissive. He spent every minute of every day troubleshooting customer complaints and didn't see the value of spending even one minute on data analysis. As far as he was concerned, work orders took too long because he didn't have enough staff.

Berke knew better. He pulled work-order data from the past year and quickly found that half of the overdue orders were for heating, ventilation, and air conditioning (HVAC) repairs. A little more digging revealed that buildings in the municipal complex around City Hall got the fastest service, while work orders for outlying facilities took way too long.

When Berke and the facilities director went over the data, they had an "aha!" moment. The problem was that their technicians at outlying facilities did not have easy access to the tools and parts they needed to fix HVAC systems. The solution they came up with was a mobile repair unit, which was not only funded but won the Outcome Budgeting award for best evidence-based service proposal.

The mobile unit has cut work-order time, which in turn has boosted customer satisfaction and enabled DGS technicians to spend more of their workdays doing preventative maintenance. It also made a believer out of the facilities director and other program managers who watched how data was turned into better performance and more money for the agency.

"I HATED IT"

Alvin Gillard hated Outcome Budgeting when it started. He thought it was unfair to agencies like his—the Office of Civil Rights—that lacked the capacity to write great service proposals and could not be measured by "how many widgets they produced." He fought the process that first year, but in the second year decided to stop fighting and figure out how to make it work. The result is a great example of how Outcome Budgeting can motivate organizations to reinvent themselves.

Alvin was born in 1954, the year of the Supreme Court's *Brown v. Board of Education* decision. Now the executive director of Maryland's Commission on Civil Rights, he has spent nearly forty years working to fulfill the promise of that landmark decision, fighting discrimination and ensuring equal opportunity for all people.

Growing up on the east side of Baltimore, in what is now called the Clifton Park neighborhood, Alvin saw things change rapidly after the school desegregation order. White families moved to the suburbs. His elementary school was nearly all black, and he remembers that in the aftermath of the 1968 riot, his diverse classmates at Herring Run Junior High were sharply divided along racial lines between Nixon and Humphrey for president.

The neighborhood held on, thanks to people like Alvin's father, who never missed a day of work at the Bethlehem Steel mill at Sparrows Point, just southeast of the city on the Patapsco River. He and his wife showed their three boys the importance of faith, responsibility and relationships, and saw them become successful adults. Occasionally, Alvin drives through his old neighborhood on the way home from work. "It's not even the same place," he says. White flight and the disappearance of blue-collar jobs (the steel mill closed years ago) eventually took their toll. What Alvin remembers as a "self-contained community," with corner stores, small businesses, and arabbers selling fresh fruits and vegetables from horse-drawn carts, is now a wasteland of vacant lots, shuttered storefronts, and neglect. "There's no community pride left," he sighs.

Having spent his formative years in the midst of the civil rights struggle, it's no wonder that Alvin joined the cause with passion in 1980, when he signed on as an investigator with Baltimore's Community Relations Commission. He recalls that in those days, there were as many Jews as African Americans doing civil rights work. There are not enough whites in the field anymore, he says, and the people he hires nowadays are just looking for a job, not answering the call. "People no longer see public service as the best way to make a difference."

With the urgency of the civil rights movement fading into history, Alvin says his agency had become "comfortable" and was never challenged to reexamine its mission and how it did business. Outcome Budgeting forced Alvin and his team to confront some hard truths. As they started to measure their performance, they realized that they had taken on more nice-to-do programs and initiatives than they could manage with their resources. They were spread too thin and not doing anything well, including the core work of investigating and resolving discrimination complaints.

In its service proposal for the second year of Outcome Budgeting, the Office of Civil Rights set ambitious targets for improving the timeliness of its case work. According to Alvin, paring down the mission to its core freed the staff to focus on improving service delivery, and measuring performance gave them the "discipline and focus" to reach for ambitious goals.

In thinking about how to do a better job of resolving cases, the team got creative. Cutting back on competing priorities was only part of the solution. It would help get more cases done more quickly, but timeliness was not the only measure of success, or even the most important one. The team wanted to resolve cases in a way that strengthened communities and made a lasting impact on human relations, so they decided to acquire new skills in conflict resolution to mediate disputes. Resolving more cases through negotiation, as opposed to adjudication, became a measure of successful outcomes.

The chart in figure 3.3, from Baltimore's Scorecard performance management system, shows that Alvin set an audacious target of more than doubling negotiated settlements in one year. The Office of Civil Rights got more realistic in succeeding years but didn't stop working to get better, notching a 40 percent improvement over three years.

One of Alvin's mentors was the late Clarence "Du" Burns, a long-time Baltimore City Councilman who became the city's first black mayor when William Donald Schaefer was elected as governor of Maryland. Alvin interned for Burns as a student at Morgan State. He calls Burns "the most practical politician I've ever known." "He knew he needed to be a cut above the white politicians, and while he may not have been as educated or articulate, he knew how to get things done." Getting things done in a practical way is how Alvin turned around the Office of Civil Rights. "Du" Burns would have been proud.

Figure 3.3 Percentage of Complaints Closed through Negotiated Resolution

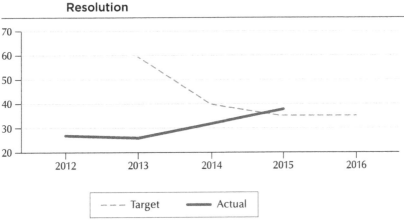

Source: Baltimore Bureau of the Budget and Management Research

ALL I REALLY NEED TO KNOW
I LEARNED IN KINDERGARTEN

In his best-selling book of life lessons, Robert Fulghum lists sixteen simple things to do to lead a meaningful life and make the world a better place, all of which, he writes, are learned "not at the top of the graduate school mountain, but there in the sandpile at Sunday School." The first item on the list: "Share everything."

Along the way, many of us forget those early lessons. Local government sometimes resembles the game Risk, where the objective is to capture territory from other players and ultimately dominate the world. I am exaggerating, of course, but I have worked with agency heads who are bent on building their empires and lose sight of the citywide outcomes that no agency can accomplish on its own. They array their armies to defend against proposals to reallocate funding, consolidate functions, eliminate duplication, or target scarce resources. They resist the prying questions of analysts looking to find ways to improve service efficiency and effectiveness. One Baltimore agency head even managed to convince the mayor to discontinue her agency's CitiStat sessions, arguing that it was a waste of time to regularly review her performance data.

I will never forget refereeing a meeting between our Departments of Recreation and Parks and Public Works about a Results Team recommendation that Public Works crews collect trash from the city's parks. At the time, Recreation and Parks had its own trash collection crews, but its loadpackers were in need of replacement and the Results Team made the case that adding parks to existing Public Works collection routes would be more efficient. On one side was our friend Bill Vondrasek from Recreation and Parks, the unassuming Midwesterner with his nasal accent. On the other side was Valentina Ukwuoma, a regal Nigerian whose rise to the top of the Bureau of Solid Waste had earned her the nickname "Diva of Debris."

This wasn't your typical prizefight, because both sides were battling a common enemy: change. Bill didn't want to give up his trash crews and Val didn't want to pick up his trash. Bill admitted that his crews were not doing a good job, but he didn't trust Val to do better. Val knew she could do a better job, but she thought she was being handed more work without any more money, with some crappy trucks thrown in as part of the bargain. They were both more animated than I had ever seen them, with most of their anger directed at me. Honestly, I didn't understand everything that was said in that meeting, but I can assure you it wasn't constructive.

In a warped way, our "discussion" was a great example of interagency collaboration. The problem was that Bill and Val had joined forces to defend the status quo. These were two of the best and brightest of Baltimore's bureaucrats who couldn't shake free from their territorial impulses to find a new and better way of doing business. In the end, the new way was forced upon them.

Blessedly, I have also seen examples of real collaboration to solve problems. One of the best is called Operation Care. It is a partnership between Baltimore's Fire and Health Departments that assigns nurses to help so-called frequent flyers of the city's 911 ambulance service. A data analysis by CitiStat had found that 5 percent of patients accounted for 30 percent of ambulance transports, most of them unnecessary.

Operation Care nurses work for a nonprofit called Health Care Access Maryland. They connect patients with more appropriate levels of care by making home visits, escorting patients to behavioral or primary care doctors, referring them to social services, and enrolling them in health insurance plans. This intensive intervention started with a ten-patient pilot. In the first twelve weeks, their transport calls dropped by 32 percent and nontransport calls by 80 percent, resulting in a net savings of $20,000.

No surprise, Operation Care was scaled up. In 2016, the program made more than 1,300 patient visits, resulting in a 59 percent reduction in 911 calls from those patients. Operation Care's success motivated Fire and Health to look for more ways to work together. Fire needed help to stem rapidly growing 911 calls that stretched the emergency medical service (EMS) beyond its ability to meet response standards. Health saw the EMS service as a conduit for connecting patients with appropriate care and improving public health overall.

Ambulance runs to the emergency room (ER) are no longer the default response to 911 calls. Medics are trained to treat non-emergency patients on-site and put them in touch with community health resources. A new stabilization center—funded with help from local hospitals—will be a lower-cost alternative to the ER for drug overdose patients. Even when ER transports are needed, they are more cost-effective than they used to be. Lean business process review has made ER turnaround times faster so ambulances can get quickly on to the next call, and a loan from the City's Innovation Fund is upgrading technology to capture patient data for ambulance fee billing and other purposes. You will find more about Lean and the Innovation Fund in chapter 7.

Collaboration among agencies and with community partners is central to the Outcome Budgeting theory of change. Starting the budget process by focusing on the ends instead of the means is all about encouraging creative thinking and teamwork. This way of solving problems and getting better results doesn't come naturally to Balkanized bureaucracies that are geared toward protecting themselves from budget cuts and accustomed to being judged on individual versus group performance. Which is why Results Teams are such an important part of Outcome Budgeting. These teams of civil servants and citizens exist to survey the landscape of government and community and find fusion points that agencies can't see. Chapter 4 takes an inside look at the work of Results Teams and how they turn the budget process into a give-and-take about getting maximum value from limited resources.

FIVE TAKEAWAYS

1. **Outcome Budgeting is not just about allocating dollars.** Yes, it will almost surely change how your organization spends its money. Just as importantly, it will shed light on other issues holding you back from better performance and results, such as poor management, flawed program design, and useless (or unused) measures.
2. **Budgeting should be thought of as a process of purchasing results.** The way to maximize value—results per dollar spent—is to specify

the results you are looking for and broadly solicit proposals. This is how well-run governments procure goods and services every day. Are results really any different?

3. **A service should be able to tell the story of how it's performing in five measures or fewer.** The measures need to answer three questions: How much are we doing? How well are we doing it? Is anyone better off?

4. **Performance measures give clues to how well or poorly a service is performing, but not much more.** Following the clues to get to the bottom of performance problems and come up with solutions sometimes requires digging into the data behind the measures. Data analytics is one of the latest buzzwords in public management. It sounds complicated, but oftentimes all you need is a little curiosity and determination.

5. Achieving an outcome is like climbing to the top of a tall mountain; you can't do it alone. Collaboration among agencies and with external partners doesn't always come naturally, because planning, budgeting, and performance measurement have traditionally been siloed. **The budget can be a powerful tool for encouraging and rewarding collaboration.**

FIVE QUESTIONS

1. Ken Miller argues that there is no such thing as a rational public budget because the process is so political. Explain one way Outcome Budgeting can help overcome political hurdles and make the process more rational.

2. Take another look at the Urban Forestry service performance measures on page 64. Do these measures tell you what you need to know about the performance of the service? If not, what is missing?

3. Research a service in your local or state government. Does it have published performance measures? If so, do they answer the three basic questions: How much did we do, How well did we do it, and Is anyone better off? If they don't, try to think of additional or better measures for the service.

4. The chart in figure 3.3 shows that the Office of Civil Rights set a very ambitious performance target for increasing the percentage of human relations cases resolved through negotiation, then lowered the target to the point where it was about the same as actual performance. What guidelines would you put in place about setting performance targets?

5. If you were running a city government, what would you do to get agencies to collaborate more with each other and with outside partners?

FIVE RESOURCES

1. Miller, Ken. (2011). *Extreme Government Makeover: Increasing Our Capacity to Do More Good*. Washington, DC: Governing Books. While I may be more optimistic than Ken Miller about the prospects for making budgets more rational, I'm a big fan of this book. It identifies broken systems, not bad people, as the reason why government is such a mess, and the book is full of wisdom about how to "straighten the pipes" of government services that waste resources and confound and infuriate customers.

2. Stansbury, Margaret Haviland (author), and Simpson, David (photographer). (2010). *Glass House of Dreams: Baltimore's Victorian Glass Palace in the Park*. Baltimore, MD: Palm House Studios. This book celebrates Baltimore's historic Conservatory in words and photographs. Bill Vondrasek, who you met in this chapter, helped bring the Conservatory back to life.

3. A Parren J. Mitchell tribute video can be found at www. cityontheline.com. Mitchell was a mentor to Gary Holland, one of the heroes of this chapter. In addition to being Maryland's first African American congressman, Mitchell was a decorated World War II veteran and integrated the University of Maryland graduate school.

4. Pietila, Antero. (2010). *Not in My Neighborhood: How Bigotry Shaped a Great American City*. Chicago, IL: Ivan R. Dee. Alvin Gillard, whose work to advance civil rights is profiled in this chapter, inspired me to spotlight this book, an extensively

researched narrative on the history of residential segregation in Baltimore.

5. Rinke, M. L., Dietrich, E, Kodeck, T, and Westcoat, K. (2012). "Operation Care: A Pilot Case Management Intervention for Frequent Emergency Medical System Users." *American Journal of Emergency Medicine*, 30(2): 352–57. This study showed the effectiveness of Operation Care, the collaborative effort of the Baltimore City Health and Fire Departments. Based on the study's findings, the initiative was scaled up.

4

Making the Magic Happen

■ ■ ■

WE KNEW THAT standing up a new and radically different budgeting process would be a tall task, so we decided to bring in some hired help. The competition to be our consultant came down to a David versus Goliath face-off.

"Goliath" was Public Financial Management (PFM), a firm with five hundred employees and offices throughout the country. "David" was Public Strategies Group (PSG), a tiny outfit from St. Paul, Minnesota, whose founders included David Osborne and Peter Hutchinson, the authors of *The Price of Government*, the book that had introduced me to Outcome Budgeting.

We held the final interviews in the CitiStat room, which is located in the sixth-floor "attic" of City Hall. At the front of the high-ceilinged room is a podium flanked by two large screens. Facing the podium is a long, semicircular table where the mayor and senior administration officials sit to grill agency heads about their perform-ance data. Behind the table is a control room, where CitiStat analysts cue up slides showing charts and graphs about police overtime, stump removal, and any number of other services.

PFM went first. It had sent a team of eight consultants, including some hired specifically for this job. They all wore suits and took turns at the podium talking through slides about the firm's expertise and their own personal experience with Outcome Budgeting. PFM's proposal was to deploy a group of analysts to assist us with every aspect of the budget process, including writing the budget publications at the end. It was a polished and professional pitch, and we were duly impressed.

PSG sent only one person, a man named Jim Chrisinger. A ruddy-faced Iowan whose soft yellow hair calls to mind corn tassels, Jim's approach was anything but corporate. He brought no slides and walked past the podium so he could be right in front of us.

Of all the things Jim told us that day, there are three that I haven't forgotten.

The first was that he would be brief, in the spirit of French scientist and theologian Blaise Pascal, who wrote, "I would have written a shorter letter, but I did not have the time."

The second was that PSG would not do Outcome Budgeting for us. Jim and his partner Babak Armajani would train and coach us as we went through the process for the first time, but we would have to do the dirty work. "If we are successful," he said, "you will not need us for Year Two."

The third was his explanation of Results Teams, which are the "buyers" in Outcome Budgeting's exchange of ideas about how to get more value from each tax dollar. When Outcome Budgeting is at its best, Results Teams are pushing agencies (the "sellers" or "bidders") to up their game, get more creative, even start over with a blank sheet of paper to break free from the status quo.

In Jim's words, the give-and-take between Results Teams and agencies is "where the magic happens."

You can probably guess who won the contract.

READY FOR RESULTS

This chapter is about the work of Results Teams in the Outcome Budgeting process. If you skipped chapter 1 and came straight here (to where the magic happens), you need to know that in Outcome Budgeting, there is a Results Team assigned to each Outcome. These teams, made up of employees and community members, are responsible for soliciting and reviewing service proposals and recommending how to spend available dollars to get the best possible results.

Results Teams bring a whole new perspective to budgeting. In a traditional budget process, spending proposals are reviewed by overworked budget analysts who are more concerned about the numbers adding up than how dollars will be turned into outcomes. Results Teams are given budgets, but their focus is on the value offered by the service proposals they receive.

In Baltimore, Results Teams are composed of eight to ten members, many of whom are selected through a competitive application process. For Fiscal 2018, 150 employees applied for about fifteen open slots on Results Teams. Keep in mind that these people are vying to spend six weeks doing two jobs: their regular job plus the Results Team work. Experience has shown that the double duty is no deterrent, because 99.9 percent of Results Team members want to do it again.

The members are the following: a chair, a budget analyst, a CitiStat analyst, three to five agency representatives, and two community members. In putting the teams together, our goal was to have a mixture of subject-matter expertise and unconventional thinking. Sometimes we got both in one person.

A GENTLE RADICAL

Beth Strommen could easily fool you. On the surface, she was casual, with a mop of dark, curly hair, an outdoorsy wardrobe, and a wry sense of humor. Underneath, she was equal parts artist and engineer— free-spirited but logical, and tough when she needed to be. When asked to name a hero, she picked Columbo, the scruffy TV detective who drove a pickup truck and solved mysteries by "keeping at it until he got the answers."

Beth, who died of cancer in 2018, is one of my heroes of Outcome Budgeting. She chaired Results Teams for the first five years of the process, starting with the Cleaner, Greener team and later the Stronger Neighborhoods team.

Beth brought to her Results Team work the missionary zeal she learned from her father, whom she described as a "radical UUC minister" who registered black voters in the South, helped integrate public swimming pools, and started the first gay church in Cleveland. "He was always marching for something," she said, which included taking her to Martin Luther King Jr.'s "I Have A Dream" speech as an infant.

She also brought to it her love for Baltimore. She moved to the city in 1988, after working on the Sky Mound project that turned a gigantic New Jersey landfill into a work of environmental art. She recalled that when she arrived, the only crane in the sky was building a jail, but she was smitten. As someone who restored antique furniture as a hobby, she knew that you sometimes have to scrape off the old paint to find the hidden beauty.

As a Results Team chair in the first year of Outcome Budgeting, Beth scraped a lot of paint off of agency service proposals to get to something she could work with. "Many of the agencies were just shitting us that first year," she remembered. "Some didn't know what they were doing and others were trying to game the system. They were afraid of losing control."

One of the team's community members was ready to "slash and burn" the services that didn't seem to take Outcome Budgeting seriously. Beth's instinct was to help agencies develop better proposals, but she was willing to confront agency officials to get the results the team wanted. In one case, she cornered the deputy transportation director, who had instructed his staff to be uncooperative with the Results Team. That conversation was the first of many between the two, resulting in a proposal to contract out the mowing of the city's roadway medians, which saved $2 million and allowed the Department of Transportation (DOT) to redeploy some of its crews to higher-priority work.

"We had to get past what I call a 'Honey Do List' mentality that I saw in a lot of the agencies," Beth said. "They want bodies around to take care of odd jobs, and they don't care about efficiency."

Beth saw the magic happen when her teams worked together on reviewing service proposals. They recommended strategies for performing graffiti removal with fewer crews and training neighborhood volunteers to help. They also encouraged the Department of Recreation and Parks to shift more tree maintenance to piece-work contracts, because they saw that aging laborers were becoming less productive. Beth was pleasantly surprised when these and other ideas won approval from the mayor.

CITIZEN CAN

Beth's "slash and burn" community member was Inez Robb, who may well be Baltimore's most involved citizen. Even though her comrades took a more diplomatic approach than she wanted, Inez gave the team the courage and credibility to recommend moving the dividing line between the roles of government and the community.

Inez grew up on Baltimore's east side and graduated from the all-girls Eastern High School, which sat across the street from Memorial Stadium, where the Colts and Orioles won their many championships. She went straight from high school to the Social Security Administration, starting as a file clerk and spending forty-two years in the IT department, with a front-row seat to watch the progress from punch cards to mainframes to the internet.

She traces her civic activism back to 1987, when she bought a row house condo in the westside Sandtown-Winchester neighborhood. The row house had been renovated by The Rouse Company as part of a $100 million effort to reclaim blocks of abandoned houses and give hope to residents who the company's founder, Jim Rouse, believed were "alienated from the rest of America." In the wake of the unrest that followed Freddie Gray's death, which was centered in Sandtown-Winchester, one of the media storylines was that Rouse's grand plan had come to nothing. The truth is more nuanced, as it usually is; Inez and her neighbors live in a safe, stable section of Sandtown-Winchester that they have fought hard to maintain for the last thirty years.

For Inez, the fight has included pressuring the condo developer to fix sagging beams and uneven floors in several units, chairing the western district police community relations council for ten years, convincing city officials to beautify her street, and educating people about "sustainability"—keeping debris out of the storm drains, recycling, and reducing energy use (which is how she ended up on the Cleaner, Greener Results Team).

As a veteran of many community improvement efforts, Inez has made the process work for her, and she gets tired of hearing residents complain about City Hall. "These people want to play the victim, when they should be stepping up to be part of the solution," she told me. "City government should empower residents, not do everything for them." Her philosophy can be seen in her Results Team's recommendations, which asked residents and businesses to play a larger role in keeping the city clean, so that core trash collection and disposal services would not have to suffer.

"I'm not intimidated. Never have been," Inez declares. When the job is to take on the Iron Triangle of politicians, bureaucrats, and residents trying to preserve the status quo, this kind of fearlessness is what's needed, which is why community members are the guts of Results Teams.

DRILLING FOR VALUE

In chapter 3, I described the Requests for Results (RFRs) that Results Teams issue to agency "bidders." RFRs are strategic roadmaps for achieving outcomes, and they signal to agencies what the Results Teams are looking for in the service proposals they receive. The first RFR from Beth's Cleaner, Greener team can be found in appendix A.

Approval of RFRs by the mayor is the first of three "tollgates" to pass in the Outcome Budgeting process. The second tollgate is the presentation of Results Team recommendations to the mayor. What happens between these tollgates is many hours of Results Team meetings to rank proposals and put them in priority order for funding. Jim Chrisinger used the image of a drilling platform to show us that focusing our limited dollars on the highest-priority services meant that other services would fall below the water line (figure 4.1).

The drilling platform leaves no confusion about which services are being funded, or "purchased," and which ones are not. Making the trade-offs this clear is a breakthrough in public budgeting.

Figure 4.1 Drilling Platform

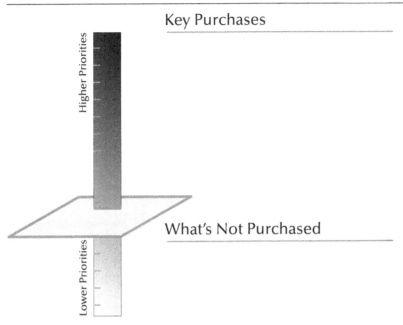

Source: *The Price of Government,* David Osborne and Peter Hutchinson

No city has budgeted for outcomes more openly than Fort Collins, Colorado. In a 2007 article called "Your Budget: From Axe to Aim," Fort Collins city manager Darin Atteberry wrote, "An editorial in the *Fort Collins Coloradoan* . . . summed up what many in the community felt about the process . . . Not everybody agree[s] with the specifics of what was funded in the end. But the advantage of budgeting for outcomes is that it makes city government more transparent in its budgeting decisions."

What if a city budget publication read less like an accounting manual and more like a pop-up book, where the choices jump off the page? At a time when citizens' trust in government is at an all-time low, budgets that are easy to understand can help rebuild trust—something money can't buy. Fort Collins's budget book is the closest I've seen to that kind of transparency. Take a look at the small excerpt shown in figure 4.2. It tells you not only what is funded, but also which proposals were left on the cutting-room floor.

Figure 4.2 Fort Collins Budget Excerpt

ECONOMIC HEALTH

115.2   ENHANCEMENT: Midtown Corridor/College Avenue Boulevard Transportation Study - Unfunded

2011 - $85,000
2012 - $85,000

This offer provides funding for a College Avenue Boulevard study in an effort to support redevelopment scenarios identified in Midtown Corridor study. The Study will include developing a functional, safe, context-sensitive boulevard for pedestrians, cars and bicycles, and providing improved connections to the Mason Corridor along College Avenue/US287, from Prospect Road south to Harmony Road. Transportation Planning will be the lead department, partnering with staff from Advance Planning, PDT, and Economic Health as well as with the Colorado Department of Transportation (CDOT) to conduct the College Avenue Boulevard study as the first step toward improving the Midtown Corridor and preparing the area for future redevelopment opportunities. This offer assumes that Planning staff remains at 2010 levels and could do the majority of project work. The $85,000 would fund additional outside support.

115.3   KFCG - Railroad Quiet Zone Phase II Study - Funded

2011 - $0
2012 - $100,000

Transportation Planning will manage the Phase II Railroad Quiet Zone Study along the Burlington Northern Santa Fe (BNSF) railroad corridor from Mulberry Street south to Trilby Road. The study will identify the needed improvements at 10 railroad crossings to establish a Quiet Zone per Federal Railroad Administration (FRA) regulations. The goal of these improvements is to enhance safety and the quality of life for residents and businesses, and support economic growth along the Mason, Midtown, and South College corridors. The Study area also includes Colorado State University, and existing neighborhoods near the railroad. The Phase I Study, or the Downtown Railroad Quiet Zone Study, is underway and will be complete by first quarter, 2011. The Phase I Study area overlays the Downtown Development Authority's boundaries.

160.1   GID #1 and Downtown Sidewalk Replacement - Funded

2011 - $497,923
2012 - $303,179

This offer is for the General Improvement District #1 (GID). The GID receives revenues of about $300,000 per year from a mil levy on taxable property in the Downtown commercial area within a specified boundary, along with interest on reserves and an auto-specific ownership tax. GID revenues are used to fund public policy, pedestrian and beautification improvements. Expenses may include construction, maintenance and operation of GID-funded improvements. Example improvements are streetscapes, medians and corner plazas, Oak Street Plaza, and the Oak/Remington parking lot. In 2011, funds will be used to continue the sidewalk replacement work started in 2010. Projects for 2012 are yet to be determined. Improvements are generally determined under a capital improvement program with an evolving list of projects. The GID is administered by the Advance Planning Department in collaboration with other departments as appropriate, often including Parks and Engineering.

174.2   ENHANCEMENT: Historic Preservation - Reinstate Planner - Unfunded

2011 - $63,981
2012 - $65,748

This offer requests reinstatement of the lost 1 FTE Historic Preservation Planner position eliminated as part of the 2009 reductions. In 2009, Historic Preservation Program staffing was cut by more than 50%. Quality of service has noticeably suffered. This offer requests reinstating the lost 1 FTE in staffing, resulting in a return in value far exceeding the costs of salary and benefits.

Source: Fort Collins, CO, Budget Office

I like to say that what a Results Team presents to the mayor is an investment portfolio for maximizing results per dollar spent, also known as value. Inside the portfolio are all sorts of trade-offs: more money for services that demonstrate high value, less for lower-value services, nothing for poor performers that aren't aligned with a Priority Outcome.

One such trade-off has had a profound impact on one of the city's most visible services. In the Fiscal 2011 budget process, the Build Strong, Healthy and Educated Children and Families Results Team was wrestling with a $13 million gap between its budget allocation and the previous year's funding level for the services it was reviewing. The Great Recession had gut-punched Baltimore's revenues, and the choices ranged from hard to impossible.

The chair of the Families team was Dr. Jackie Duval-Harvey, a deputy health commissioner who had recently been lured to city government after ten years managing Johns Hopkins Hospital's community mental health services.

Jackie is a native of St. Lucia, the small Caribbean island that changed hands between the French and the British fourteen times before the British took definitive control in the early 1800s. The youngest of four children, she moved with her mother to New York City when she was fifteen, after her father died. She got interested in psychology while working at Bloomingdale's to pay her way through Nassau Community College. "We had very wealthy customers, including [soap opera star] Susan Lucci, who would buy hundreds of dollars' worth of clothes, then return them a week later and buy more," she recalls. "I became very curious about human behavior, what makes people tick."

She eventually earned a PhD in clinical psychology from Penn State and spent a decade working with children in Metropolitan Hospital, near Spanish Harlem. She started with Johns Hopkins as a school-based clinician. She knew from day one that it would be the most challenging and fulfilling clinical experience of her career. When she arrived at City Springs Elementary School in east Baltimore, she was urgently summoned to the principal's office, where a child was on the floor, being detained by a police officer. "My work with the children at that school was in the moment," she explains. "I had an immediate impact on very difficult families."

An across-the-board cut to all of the services in the Families portfolio would have meant axing nearly 20 percent from the Fiscal 2010 funding levels. The team's job was to figure out how to get the most possible value out of $59 million for an outcome that encompassed kindergarten readiness, homelessness, public health, and quality of life for seniors. They had thirty-five service proposals and every one of them was for helping the city's most vulnerable people (and animals, for that matter).

Jackie's child psychology expertise came in handy in leading a Results Team loaded with smart, passionate members, each with different priorities. She was skilled at validating people's feelings, channeling their energies, and sharing knowledge, without being bossy. It also helped that she made a delicious curry chicken, which she fed to the team when its work dragged into the evening hours.

The team looked to its RFR to choose among the competing priorities. Jackie describes writing the RFR as "hard, painful" work, but nearly ten years later, she still refers to it. "City agencies were too caught up in the day-to-day details of running their programs," she says. "The RFR helped us shift our focus to outcomes and get specific about what we needed to change."

One of the strategies in the RFR was to "provide structured recreational programming for children and youth." What the team learned as it reviewed service proposals was that the city's recreation centers were in disarray and directionless. At the time, the city was operating fifty-five recreation centers, more per capita and square mile than anywhere else in the country. Staff was stretched thin, programming was a patchwork, and the buildings were in disrepair. Half of the centers were tiny—less than 5,000 square feet in size—and underutilized. After years of neglect, the need for a new approach was clear, but the Department of Recreation and Parks didn't offer anything new.

Jackie would chair five Results Teams and become legendary for running them efficiently. Her secret was that she focused her teams' time on the big decisions and areas of disagreement. The Families team spent a lot of time debating what to do about recreation centers. "We obsessed over it," Jackie says. Ultimately, the team could not justify continuing to pour money into a failing service. Without any evidence of how recreation centers impacted children, the team couldn't be sure they weren't doing more harm than good.

The team's recommendation was dramatic. It cut the recreation center budget in half and repurposed those dollars to protect funding for services that had demonstrated measurable results for children, such as libraries, summer jobs, and maternal and child health. It suggested that programming at recreation centers be provided by community organizations and schools, and that consolidation of centers be on the table.

The team's findings moved Mayor Rawlings-Blake to take action. She approved a smaller budget reduction and appointed a task force to study the recreation centers further. The task force emphasized "quality over quantity," a vision that led to the closure of nine underperforming centers, the establishment of nine "charter centers" run by community organizations, the adoption of six centers by the public schools to which they were attached, and a plan that has so far built three new model centers, with more on the drawing board.

Jackie told me that in the Caribbean, there is no sense that regular people can make a difference, which is why she was so gratified by her Results Team experience. "I felt like our contributions were valued," she says. "Outcome Budgeting put reason over authority in making decisions about how to spend the city's money."

Jackie's team wasn't the only one whose work in that first year of Outcome Budgeting has rippled across the years. The Make Baltimore's Government More Innovative, Efficient and Customer-Friendly Team was charged with reviewing proposals from the city's "support functions": human resources, finance, information technology, building maintenance, fleet, and so on. These are the functions that every operating agency would blame for its performance failures, sometimes with good reason. The Government Team wanted to find out why it took so long to hire an employee, why contracts weren't awarded to the best value bidders, and why so many vehicles were out of service. If the team had stopped there, it would have done its job, but it went further, because it realized that the expectation for more innovative, efficient, and customer-friendly government must extend to each and every agency, not just those behind the scenes.

WHERE'S THE BEEF?

The Government Team had a not-so-secret weapon for its attack on the bureaucracy. Its community member, David Rudow, had been pushing City Hall to use taxpayer dollars more wisely for two decades.

David is a son of Baltimore. As a 1952 graduate of City College, he is part of a friendly rivalry with the city's other selective high school, Baltimore Polytechnic Institute. Their annual football matchup dates back to 1889 and is thought to be the longest-running in the country. Many City and Poly alums wear their class rings to the grave; David gave his to his future wife when they were courting.

After earning an accounting degree from the University of Maryland, David worked as an IRS agent while simultaneously taking law classes and studying for the CPA exam every night but Sundays. He joined his father-in-law's law firm in 1960 and still works there fifty-eight years later. When I asked him if he had reduced his hours any, he told me, "A few years ago, I cut back to full-time." At the age of eighty-three, he still carries his tall, slender frame with ramrod posture, so he must know something about growing old gracefully.

David's civic activism started in 1988, when he received a letter informing him of a huge increase in the assessed value of his house in Roland Park, a neighborhood of large, handsome homes built in the late nineteenth and early twentieth centuries. He told his wife that at the city's high property-tax rates, he wasn't sure they could afford to stay.

Instead of fleeing the city like so many before them, David and his neighbors in the Roland Park Civic League took action. They started by forming a committee with like-minded homeowners from other neighborhoods, which David chaired. The kickoff meeting was held at Grace United Methodist Church, and leaders from one hundred civic associations showed up. "Everyone was upset about property taxes," David said. The keynote speaker was Tim Armbruster, president of the local Goldseker Foundation. He had recently published a report called *Baltimore 2000: A Choice of Futures*, which documented the city's quarter century of population loss and economic decline and recommended bold solutions, including school vouchers, regional government, and a property-tax cap.

Sufficiently fired up, the group sent "busloads" of people to the city's Taxpayers' Night, an annual meeting at which city leaders listen to resident input on the budget. Mayor Kurt Schmoke got the message, and he proposed property-tax rate reductions in each of the next four years.

After proving that you *can* fight City Hall, the homeowners coalition could have kept fighting, but instead it decided to work with the mayor and city council. In 1998, it formed the Baltimore Efficiency & Economy Foundation, known as BEEF, to conduct independent studies of city government management, operations, and fiscal and tax policy. BEEF's first study recommended reforms to the city's employee and retiree health plans that saved tens of millions of dollars. Another report led to an initiative called Selling City-Owned Property Efficiently (SCOPE), which engaged private brokers to clear a backlog of hundreds of vacant houses that were languishing in the city's understaffed and red tape–choked disposition program.

You might say that BEEF was Baltimore's original Results Team, so David came to Outcome Budgeting with a good understanding of how city government worked (or didn't work, as the case may be). As a community member of the Government Team, he recalls feeling like he had "no constraints, no muzzle." "I could ask questions that the city employees on the team couldn't ask," he said.

David's independence was crucial, because as the team dug deeper into issues, information was harder and harder to get. This was especially true when it came to human resources. The team had many questions about job classification, hiring, and compensation policy, but, in David's words, "the HR director had been there a long time and didn't want to change." With David leading the way, the team nudged HR to review the classification system and migrate to "pay for performance." It also prioritized funding for a web-based recruiting, testing, and hiring tool. The team's recommendation memo was clear about how much these reforms mattered: "We believe there is [nothing] as important to the future performance of the city as [attracting] the best employees." In a dense, seven-page document, it was the only sentence underlined.

The team also urged consolidating operations into fewer buildings and charging agencies for utility costs to encourage conservation, and it funded a new finance unit to find and fix erroneous and fraudulent tax credits—steps that have saved the city millions of dollars.

David supported one of Mayor Rawlings-Blake's opponents in the 2011 election, so he wasn't asked back for Results Team duty, but he left his mark by demonstrating that informed residents are a must for Outcome Budgeting to reach its full potential.

CAUSE AND EFFECT

The Government Team's ambitions were evident in its Cause-and-Effect Map. The map is the first step in writing a Request for Results. To create the map, the team had to identify the primary factors that will lead to the Outcome and the secondary factors that will make the primary factors happen. Box 4.1 explains the step-by-step instructions given to Results Teams for cause-and-effect mapping.

The map shown in figure 4.3 is full of great ideas that the Government Team came up with for making city government more innovative, efficient, and customer-friendly. I have highlighted two of them that changed how Baltimore does business: "Funds for Innovation" and "Process Improvement & Lean." You will learn more about what became of these ideas in chapter 7.

Box 4.1 | Steps in Cause-and-Effect Mapping

1. Write the Priority Outcome in a circle in the middle of your white board.
2. Brainstorm what you individually know or believe to be the factors that lead to or produce your Priority Outcome. Individually write your ideas on the "sticky notes" provided —one idea per sticky note. Capture your factors in a word or a few words and write in big enough letters that the group will be able to read the sticky note from ten or so feet away. Brainstorm all significant factors, whether the city currently addresses it or impacts it or not. As an example, important factors leading to public health might include safe water, clean air, safe food, access to health care, knowledge of healthy behaviors, the behaviors themselves, and risk factors. See the "Tips about Causal Factors" below.
3. Compare your individual brainstorms by sticking them all up on a large blank wall, around the Priority Outcome in the center. Post all the stickies. Seeing others' factors may prompt you to think of more. Put them up too.
4. Then collectively look for natural groupings. Which ones logically go together? Group them and create a new sticky note characterizing the higher-level factor that characterizes each group of stickies.
5. Now create a draft Cause-Effect Map on the wall. Build out from the Priority Outcome in the center. Each grouping of stickies represents a primary factor. Strive for two to five primary factors. Then use those stickies associated with a given primary factor and distill from them two to five secondary factors. The secondary factors are the ones that make the primary factors happen. You may find yourselves writing new stickies to fill in blanks or responding to "aha!" moments as you work. Your map now shows the primary and secondary factors that achieve your assigned Priority Outcome. There are, of course, third- and fourth-level factors too, but stopping at two levels is sufficient for this work. Be prepared to describe the cause-and-effect routes, as backed by evidence.
6. Rank the primary factors. Decide among yourselves which factor is the most powerful in achieving the Priority Outcome. Which factor generates the most "bang for the buck"? Label it with a "1." Then identify the second-most powerful and label it with a "2." And so on until all the primary factors are ranked. You do not need to rank the secondary factors, though you may wish to highlight any secondary factors that you feel are particularly powerful for agency proposals.

7. Be ready with your "theory of what matters most" and for friendly challenges from competing theories. Discuss and rework your map as needed.
8. Identify any follow-up research assignments or other questions to which you would like to answer before you finalize your map. You may also want to "soundboard" your map with others for further input. Make plans for any needed follow-up meeting or communications to complete your map.
9. Finally, please have someone in the group sketch out your final work product on a sheet of paper, or capture it electronically.

Tips about Causal Factors:

- Show all the significant factors, whether government provided or not. This will help you differentiate between what you can control versus what you must influence to produce the intended outcome.
- Follow the evidence where it leads, even if contrary to business as usual. This is not the time for ideology or your *favorite* source of evidence. Seek out sources that most residents would be able to trust. If evidence doesn't exist, use logic and professional judgment.
- Causal factors are different from organizational or budget structures. Hold back from discussing current departments, programs, and activities. Use this time to consider what factors matter in producing your result—and which ones matter more than others.
- Causal factors tend to be nouns, not verbs. Avoid listing what we currently "do" to make the result happen. For this purpose, please focus on the result outside the context of your day-to-day work. We don't want to limit our thinking to what we currently do.

Figure 4.3 Cause-and-Effect Map

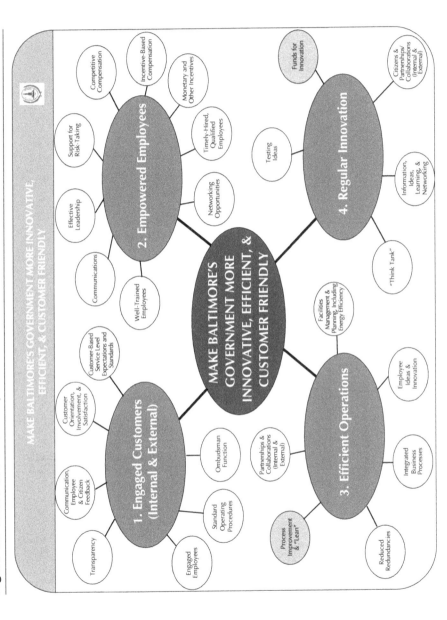

Source: Baltimore Bureau of the Budget and Management Research

THINKING BEYOND THE PROPOSALS

Where I see Results Teams struggle is in keeping their eye on what the RFR says is needed to make progress toward the outcome, and how the service proposals before them do or do not fit into a coherent strategy for getting there. Teams often get lost in the time suck of reading and scoring individual service proposals, and their thinking becomes constrained. This problem was worst in the first few years. Results Teams were asking the budget office for line-item detail of service budgets, including prior-year actual spending. In some cases, they were trying to find savings to shift to their higher-value services. In others, they were just trying to fit more services into the budget by, in effect, lowering their water line.

Figure 4.4 Proposal Evaluation Tool

FISCAL 2017 – PROPOSAL EVALUATION TOOL

Service Number: 305	Service Name: Healthy Homes
Agency: Health	Outcome: A Healthier City

Fiscal 2017 Funding Recommendation
click a box below to select

CLS	PROPOSED	BELOW THE LINE	OTHER *(and explain)*
☐	☒	☐	☐ Click here to enter text.

Scoring: 0 = missing this component 1 = poor 2 = good 3 = excellent

Performance-Priority Evaluations

Questions	Rating	Explanation
Evaluation of Priority (reference question 4):		
The service demonstrates clear alignment with one or more of the Mayor's Priority Outcome indicators and/or strategies.	3.0	This service area directly impacts the Healthier City Outcome indicator on asthma and the Better Schools indicator on school attendance.
The service addresses other specific community needs or problems (i.e. not just related to a Priority Outcome). *Team should consider Citizen Survey results where applicable.*	3.0	This service area also impacts childhood lead exposure, a major community need.
Evaluation of Performance:		
The measures are straightforward and easy to understand. Would be meaningful to the public.	2.8	The measures are easy to understand and core to the service's central mission.
The measures measure something of central importance about the services provided. Are meaningful to management in decision-making.	2.8	All five measures are central to measuring the effectiveness of the service area. Are there people who need the Lead program who can't get it, or does the reduction solely reflect a drop in need? How many people need the asthma program? Does the program measure days elapsed between alert and lead home visit?
The service achieved annual performance targets (this should be an objective yes or no, averaged across all measures for the service. *Score: 0- no, 1- close, 2- yes+)*	1.0	Two measures met their targets; one was close; two did not meet their targets. Provided key reasons as to why certain service targets were not met.
The Stories Behind the Curve...		
...discusses at least 1-2 factors that led to good/improved performance in prior years.	1.8	1 of 2 measures showing good/improved performance discusses factors leading to improvement. Best practices w/ the asthma program are mentioned but not named.
...discusses at least 1-2 factors that hindered	2.2	3 of 3 measures showing decreased performance discuss hindering factors. Is the program tracking the # of attempts to contact the family?

	Rating	Explanation
performance in prior years.		
...addresses if the identified factors are ongoing or one-time influencers of performance.	2.0	4 of 5 measures discuss implicitly whether factors are ongoing or one-time. Symptom improvement for children in the asthma program - how did the calculation change? Will this affect future years? Is the program keeping data on complicated asthma cases to inform strategy?
...clearly explains why their target was or was not reached in FY15.	1.9	4 of 5 measures explain why their target was or was not met. Why did Lead program not meet their targets despite having fewer cases?
The service's FY17 target is achievable and realistic under the FY17 proposed funding level	2.2	It is not clear if all measures have realistic, achievable goals for FY17. Some possibly require more funding/staffing.
Total for "Performance-Priority Evaluations" *out of 29 possible points*	**22.7**	

Generating Results

Questions	Rating	Explanation
Proposed Operating Plan (reference question 1):		
The service proposes **new** strategies to improve or maintain performance (i.e. not just "same old" approach if that is not generating desired results).	2.0	Healthy Homes proposes new strategies to track lead cases, and target areas where testing should be increased. Mentions increasing pediatric provider outreach, collaboration for increased testing, community outreach, quality improvement, and geocoding. Asthma proposes to continue their approach.
Proposed steps are targeted to address performance challenges identified in Stories Behind the Curve, or capitalize on factors identified as helping to improve performance.	2.2	Proposed steps, while impressive, did not tie directly to the challenges/improvement factors identified in the Stories Behind the Curve. Data collection strategy must be outlined. What triggers a referral to one of these programs? Are we capturing nearly all who need them?
Proposed steps identify possible innovative actions or process improvements.	1.9	Innovations in tracking and targeting areas where lead cases may be concentrated were proposed.
Proposal demonstrates commitment to improved (or maintain if working) customer service.	2.2	Proposal demonstrates commitment to providing services to areas of the city in greatest need.
What Works & Partners (reference questions 2-3):		
Clearly articulates 3 key partners (or potential partners) and their role(s) in providing the service.	2.9	Partners and roles were clearly articulated.
Clearly articulates evidence (cited, research-based) backing up proposed plan for operations in FY17.	2.8	Cites CDC on childhood lead poisoning prevention and evidence-based CAP on asthma.
Surfaces and challenges outdated assumptions about "what works."	1.9	Proposal does not directly address status quo; however, proposal does mention primary prevention for lead cases of 5-9 blood levels, which is not required under state or national law.
Total for "Generating Results" *out of 21 possible points*	**15.9**	

Total Score All Sections *out of 50 possible points*	**38.6**

General Feedback on Service Proposal

Proposal is well-written. It would be beneficial to hear more about what the program is doing above and beyond the evidence-based practices that have been instituted, such as the work with children with blood lead levels of 5-9. The team wanted to know more about what is innovative vs. best practices/standard of care. It seems like there are key data missing from the picture. How is the program measuring its target population? What % of the target population is reached? Are their needs measured? What needs are met/not met? Reduction of ER visits is a good outcome measure – are there other outcomes measured? Given limited resources to allocate across services, the team recommends Proposed level funding.

Source: Baltimore Bureau of the Budget and Management Research

Either way, they were nickel-and-diming everyone and burning time and energy that should have been spent on bigger-picture thinking.

To get the Results Teams' heads out of the nitty-gritty numbers, we stopped giving them detailed budget reports and developed a value rubric for scoring proposals. The rubric, an example of which is shown in figure 4.4, is meant to guide teams through a series of questions that get at the priority and performance of a proposed service. As you can see, the rubric explores many aspects of a service's value: its alignment with the Priority Outcome; how well it measures its performance, performs against its targets, and understands what went right or wrong; its operating plan to improve performance; and evidence of the impact it has on the community. The rubric includes a set of questions about the service's "Story Behind the Curve," which you will learn about in chapter 8.

The value rubric is the brainchild of Laura Larsen, an analyst who coordinated the Outcome Budgeting process for three years. Laura was part of the first wave of millennials who came from near and far and brought new energy and idealism to the budget office. Her journey was the longest, from a small town on the western edge of Nebraska that couldn't have been more different from Baltimore. She got the public service bug when working part-time in a State Game and Parks Commission field office during college. The biologists who staffed the office were doing what they loved, and having fun.

Laura says that she got into budgeting "by accident" (how else would you get into budgeting?). After college, she worked on a few political campaigns, which left her seeking "less theater and more substance." She found what she was looking for in the public administration school at the University of Nebraska Omaha, where a professor steered her toward local government, and specifically to my posting on the alumni job board.

Even though she had always wanted to leave Nebraska, Laura was very nervous about moving from the cornfields to *The Corner*. (For those who are not familiar, *The Corner* is a book and HBO miniseries about a family living in poverty amid the open-air drug markets of West Baltimore. It is the creation of David Simon, the former *Baltimore Sun* reporter who later produced *The Wire*.) Her three sisters had all stayed in their hometown, and her parents couldn't stand the idea of her living halfway across the country in what must have seemed to them like a scary place.

Laura took to Baltimore quickly, renting an apartment in Federal Hill with three women she found on Craigslist, learning how to ride the bus, and diving headfirst into her work. As a member of the Stronger Neighborhoods Results Team her first year, she was blown

Figure 4.5 Funding Choices

CLS	PROPOSED	BELOW THE LINE	OTHER (and explain)
☐	☒	☐	☐ Click here to enter text.

Source: Baltimore Bureau of the Budget and Management Research

away by the honesty with which her teammates evaluated services in their own agencies. At the same time, she was concerned that some of the dollar amounts assigned to services in the drilling platform were not well documented. In scrambling to "make the numbers work," the team had penciled in cuts that it would be hard-pressed to explain later. For someone who was raised to take pride in doing quality work, this kind of improvisation was disquieting. It was as if the black box was still lurking about.

Laura saw the value rubric as a way to shift Results Teams' focus from dollars to value, and also to, in her words, "close the feedback loop with agencies wondering why their services were funded the way they were funded." The first thing you notice when looking at the value rubric is the four checkboxes at the top, each representing a different funding level (see figure 4.5).

The checkboxes simplify the task of setting funding levels, without taking away Results Teams' discretion to recommend alternative funding levels where they can make a rigorous case. "CLS" stands for Current Level of Service, which is the amount that would allow a service to continue functioning as is, with adjustments for pay raises, inflation, and so on. "Proposed" is the amount requested by the agency, which could be higher or lower than the CLS. "Below the Line" means zero funding. "Other" could be any other funding level and has to be explained by the team. Beth Strommen's team would have checked this box for its plan to contract out median mowing.

Using scores from the value rubric, teams are able to populate a matrix like the one shown in Figure 4.6, from the Safer Streets team. It condenses the scoring of thirty-two service proposals—six weeks of the Results Team's blood, sweat, and tears—into one powerful visual that focuses the mayor and her senior staff on what they need to discuss.

Figure 4.6 Performance/Priority Matrix

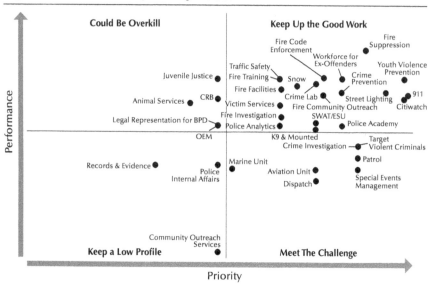

Source: Baltimore Bureau of the Budget and Management Research

Services in the upper right quadrant are high priority and performing well. This is the "Keep Up the Good Work" category. Below them, in the lower right quadrant, are important services that are low-performing. They need to "Meet the Challenge" by figuring out how to get better results. The upper left quadrant is the "Could Be Overkill" category. These services are performing well but are less critical to achieving the Priority Outcome. Here we might be willing to give up some performance in exchange for savings to repurpose, perhaps to the lower right quadrant. Then there's the dreaded lower left quadrant, which we call "Keep a Low Profile." These services would like to escape notice, but they can't in Outcome Budgeting. They are candidates for reduction or even elimination.

I can't resist telling you about the service at the very bottom of the matrix, even though it doesn't show Outcome Budgeting's best side. Community Outreach Services is perennially ranked "below the line." Its purpose is to assist families during emergencies, relocate police informants, resolve community conflicts, and provide information about city services. The problems with the service are that its performance measures are unclear, it lacks basic data about its activities, and it duplicates functions of several other services. One Results Team after another recommended to cut, consolidate, or eliminate the service, with only limited success. The reason it survives is its director, Reggie Scriber, one of the savviest (and best-dressed) bureaucrats in city government. Reggie has made himself indispensable to mayors and city council members by being the go-to guy to get help to hard-luck constituents. A former emergency management chief would often say, "If you need a shovel, a ladder, and a chicken, Reggie's your guy." Reggie hated Outcome Budgeting, and he hated me for it. The only compliment he ever gave me was for a colorful pair of socks I wore to a budget hearing.

The lesson from Community Outreach Services is that when you change things, there will always be sacred cows. I choose to focus my energies on the rest of the herd—the champions who embrace the change and the fence-sitters who just need some persuasion. I had enough of them to more than make up for the ones I couldn't win over.

BudgetCon

Every August, the Baltimore Convention Center hosts BronyCon, a conference for adult male fans of the animated TV series My Little Pony, a show geared to young girls. I always knew when BronyCon was happening, because on my drive to work I would see grown men walking along Pratt Street wearing colorful wigs, pony ears, wings, and sometimes dresses.

I don't know what goes on inside BronyCon, but I'm guessing it isn't half as serious as the Results Team agency conferences that are part of the Outcome Budgeting process. Agency conferences are face-to-face meetings between Results Team members and the agency officials who wrote the service proposals under review. The conferences were started in response to focus group feedback from agency heads after Year One. They felt that written communication alone was not enough for the teams to fully appreciate their proposals and wanted to be able to pull back the curtain a bit and make sure the people behind it weren't missing anything.

Figure 4.7 Cradle-to-Career Continuum

Maternal and Child Health	Schools/Out of School Time	Youth Recreation	Youth Violence Prevention	College & Career Readiness/Adult Literacy
Cradle ←				→ Career
• Health: Maternal and Child Health • Family League Home Visiting • MOHS: Head Start • Health: School Health Services	• Health: School Health Services • Family League Community Schools/ Out of School Time • MOHS: Head Start • HCD: Dawson Center • Library	• Rec/Parks: Aquatics • Rec/Parks: Youth & Adult Sports • Rec/Parks: Recreation Centers	• Health: Youth Violence Prevention • MOCJ: Juvenile Justice • MOED: Youth Opportunity Centers (YOI)	• Health: Youth Violence Prevention • MOCJ: Juvenile Justice • MOED: Youth Opportunity Centers (YOI) • Library

Source: Baltimore Bureau of the Budget and Management Research

Like most aspects of Outcome Budgeting, the agency conferences have evolved over the years. What started as individual meetings with agencies spread out over several weeks became full-day outcome "summits," each with a series of issue-themed panels. In the Fiscal 2018 cycle, the Thriving Youth & Families Results Team convened five panels, each with four to five services. The topics were Maternal and Child Health, Out of School Time, Youth Recreation, Youth Violence Prevention, and Career Readiness. These are points on the Cradle-to-Career continuum that guided the team's recommendations to the mayor. Figure 4.7 is from the team's tollgate presentation to the mayor and shows how the team saw its services fitting within a larger youth development strategy.

The chair of the Youth & Families Team was John Kirk, a cerebral Recreation and Parks employee with both an MBA and Peace Corps service on his resume. He told me that his inspiration throughout the Results Team process was a quote from the great abolitionist and author Frederick Douglass, who as a young man worked as a slave in Baltimore, where he learned to read and write. Douglass wrote, "It is easier to build strong children than to repair broken men."

From his experience as a Results Team member the previous two years, John was aware that Results Team conferences put agency officials on the defensive, for a couple of reasons. First, they knew that Results Team recommendations carried weight with the mayor, so they nervously stepped around landmines that might drop their ratings, such as data showing that a service was underperforming.

Second, they didn't much like being poked and prodded by outsiders. John thought that having multiple agencies around the table would be less threatening and encourage open dialogue about how agencies could collaborate to get better results. Structuring the conferences this way also forced the Results Team to do more cross-service thinking and stay focused on outcomes, not just individual service ratings.

"The Results Team is not a firing squad," John says. "Our job is to spur discussion about solving real problems, to listen, and give fair, honest, constructive feedback. I see it as free consulting."

John wanted agencies to "embrace limited resources" and bring positive energy to figuring out how to do more with less. It was not an easy sell, but John came out of the conferences with a sense of accomplishment. He talks excitedly about new ideas generated at the conferences, such as enrolling repeat graffiti "taggers" in art classes and training recreation leaders to assess children for asthma and connect with school health nurses and Family League home visitors for follow-up. One recurring realization throughout the panel discussions was that the libraries were not well integrated into youth development programs run by other agencies, including after-school activities, career readiness, and GED prep. Another was that "trauma-informed care," which the health department cared a lot about in the wake of the Freddie Gray unrest, required virtually every agency to (1) realize the widespread impact of trauma in the community, (2) recognize the effects of various types of trauma in their clients, and (3) respond through changes in policies, procedures, and practices.

In its recommendations to the mayor, the Youth & Families Team rewarded services that were part of citywide, collective impact strategies along the Cradle-to-Career continuum. Examples are the B'More for Healthy Babies maternal and child health initiative; the B'More, Read More grade-level reading campaign; and the Youth Health and Wellness Strategy. What these strategies have in common is that they are data driven and rely on partners from government, the nonprofit community, philanthropy, and other sectors. They are exactly the kind of collaborative efforts Outcome Budgeting seeks to promote.

Each year, as budget season approached, my staff and I would have long debates about how to best use the time and talents of Results Teams. We gradually moved the teams away from attaching an exact dollar figure to each service and toward giving the mayor more strategic advice on how services should be funded, whether up, way up, down, sideways, zero, and so on, and how they could perform better. Yet, even the best Results Teams have a hard time focusing on the larger strategy for achieving their assigned Priority Outcome and recognizing when the collective service proposals they are reviewing are insufficient, or insufficiently coordinated, to get the kinds of results we want. This gap in strategic focus became one of the inspirations for OutcomeStat, which you will learn about later in the book. Before we get there, I want to discuss how Outcome Budgeting shifted the budget debate in Baltimore, which is the subject of chapter 5.

FIVE TAKEAWAYS

1. Results Teams are at the heart of Outcome Budgeting. They are at their best when empowered by leadership to ask tough questions about agency service proposals and get answers. **The magic of Outcome Budgeting happens when Results Teams encourage, inspire, and cajole agencies to think more creatively about how to deliver more value from city services.**

2. Results Teams should include a mixture of subject-matter experts and people who can bring a fresh perspective and ask the "dumb questions" that challenge the status quo. **Above all, Results Teams need community members who are not intimidated by senior agency officials and know how government and community can work together to solve problems.**

3. **The job of Results Teams is to make budget trade-offs as transparent as possible for city leaders and residents.** Using the image of a drilling platform, the teams rate and rank service proposals and show which ones are above and below the "water line" of funding availability, and why. Ideally, agency service proposals and Results Team rankings are shared with the public so that there is no mystery about the logic of what's in the budget.

4. **Cause-and-Effect Mapping is a helpful tool for Outcome Budgeting.** By understanding the primary and secondary factors that influence an outcome, Results Teams are able to guide agency service proposals and decide which proposals are most likely to achieve results.
5. **Results Teams can spend so much time reviewing and scoring individual service proposals that they lose sight of how (or whether) the proposals collectively advance the Priority Outcome and Key Indicators.** The ideal Results Team can recognize when the proposals in front of them are insufficient and recommend to leadership how to fill the gaps.

FIVE QUESTIONS

1. One of the challenges of Outcome Budgeting is that some agencies take their funding for granted and don't make the effort to increase the value of their services. How would you motivate these agencies to strengthen their service proposals?
2. The line separating what government needs to do for communities and what communities should do for themselves is often fuzzy. Think about some services your local government provides, like sanitation, public safety, health and welfare, and community development. Do you think communities are overly reliant on government, or that government isn't doing enough? If the line is in the wrong place, how would you move it?
3. How transparent do you think government should be about its budget process? Are there dangers in sharing predecisional information—like agency service proposals and Results Team rankings—with the public? If so, are there benefits that outweigh those dangers?
4. Research a service in your local or state government and determine which quadrant it would fall into on the Priority–Performance matrix. Explain your determination.
5. Select an outcome that you care about for your community and draw a Cause-and-Effect Map of the primary and secondary factors that influence the outcome.

FIVE RESOURCES

1. Chrisinger, Jim, "Results from Baltimore's Budget," *Governing*, December 7, 2010. Jim was the lead consultant who helped Baltimore implement Outcome Budgeting. Here he shares his observations about how things went in Year One.
2. Marx, Paul. (2007). *Jim Rouse: Capitalist/Idealist*. Lanham, MD: UPA. Jim Rouse is the developer who built Baltimore's Inner Harbor and the acclaimed planned community of Columbia, Maryland. In the early 1990s, many years after retiring as CEO of his eponymous company, Rouse invested $100 million in an ambitious effort to revitalize one of Baltimore's most blighted neighborhoods, with mixed success.
3. This chapter gave you a little taste of Fort Collins's budget. To see more, visit https://www.fcgov.com/citymanager/budget.php.
4. Baltimore Efficiency & Economy Foundation (BEEF) website: www.beefbaltimore.org. BEEF is described in this chapter as Baltimore's original Results Team. Since 1998, BEEF has funded research on issues including economic development, transportation, tax policy, housing, and public safety.
5. Douglass, F., and Garrison, W. L. (1846). *Narrative of the Life of Frederick Douglass, an American slave*. Wortley, near Leeds: Printed by Joseph Barker. Frederick Douglass is quoted in this chapter. He worked as a slave for a ship carpenter in Baltimore from age seven to fifteen. It is where he learned to read and write, and began to yearn for freedom. He also built a group of five row houses in the Fells Point area of Baltimore as rental housing for blacks. Douglass Place is now on the National Register of Historic Places.

5

Shifting the Debate

■ ■ ■

IN CHAPTER 1, I explained that one of the ways Outcome Budgeting disrupts the status quo is by shifting the budget debate from "What to Cut" to "What to Keep." In traditional budget debates, interest groups and elected officials wrestle over incremental cuts from, or additions to, a large base of funding that goes mostly unquestioned and untouched. Outcome Budgeting looks to justify all available funding in terms of how it contributes to achieving the community's goals.

At its best, an Outcome Budget describes the results residents can expect from the dollars allocated to each service. If there is disagreement, it should be over the amount of results, not the amount of money. This new perspective is reminiscent of one of the central ideas from the classic book on negotiation *Getting to Yes*, by Roger Fisher and William Ury, which is to focus on interests rather than positions—what people really care about versus the hard-and-fast demands they make. When the argument is over a dollar amount, there are only two options: fund it or don't. When the argument is over results, many more options open up, including targeting funding to areas of greatest need, improving interagency collaboration, and asking the community to step up. If at the end of the day there is a desire to spend more money on one kind of result, the trade-off of giving up other results should be clear to everyone at the table.

In Baltimore, before we could shift the budget debate, we first had to shift the budget culture. This chapter is about four shifts—to the mission of the budget office, the role of the budget director, the mayor's focus, and the city council's deliberations.

SHIFT 1: THE BUDGET OFFICE

Driving the Bus

I came to City Hall in 2008 with big plans. I knew that transforming the budget process was going to be hard and that I would meet a lot of resistance along the way. For some reason, it didn't occur to me that the first line of defense for the old way of doing things would be my own staff.

Don't get me wrong. The budget analysts who welcomed me to the Bureau of the Budget and Management Research (BBMR) were experienced, well-meaning, nice people. It's just that most of them were near the end of long careers spent doing traditional budgeting. They knew the line items backward and forward and could crack the whip to keep agency spending in line, but they had never been asked to think about service performance, much less citywide outcomes.

In some ways, teaching these old dogs new budget tricks was easier than trying to reshape work routines and attitudes and build a cohesive team. My first directive was for everyone to open their office doors. Closed doors were symbolic of how the analysts preferred to do their work—in isolation from one another. They also hid some bad behaviors. One analyst was running an eBay business selling sports memorabilia; another had an alcohol problem. When I suggested an office potluck to get to know people better, I was told that those had been discontinued after someone discovered cat hair in a casserole. It wasn't surprising that two young analysts hired by the previous director had gotten out as soon as they could.

The book that influenced me most about how to be a manager is *First, Break All the Rules: What the World's Greatest Managers Do Differently*, by Marcus Buckingham and Curt Coffman. The authors led two research studies by the Gallup Organization—one a survey of more than 1 million employees, the other in-depth interviews with more than eighty thousand managers—to find out what separates the best managers from the rest.

The lesson that stuck with me from *First, Break All the Rules* is that in staffing a high-performing team, talent trumps experience, and you can't teach talent. By talent, Buckingham and Coffman mean characteristics that by adulthood are more or less hardwired into us. They put talents into three categories: striving, thinking, and relating. Striving is about a person's motivation, thinking is about how a person processes information, and relating is about how a person interacts with others.

Neuroscience tells us that we each have unique mental pathways that define our talents. Take the relating talent, for example. As the authors put it, one person's mental pathway for empathy may be a "four lane superhighway," while another's is a "barren wasteland." There are limits to how much a person's talents can change, or be changed. Training, coaching, and encouragement might turn a barren wasteland into a narrow path, but not a superhighway.

For a manager, matching people's talents with the work to be done can be tricky. Business writer Jim Collins likens the manager to a bus driver. Before you go anywhere, he says, you need to (1) get the right people on the bus, (2) get the right people in the right seats, and (3) get the wrong people off the bus. In my case, I had a group of analysts whose talents were well suited for the routine of the old budget process, but ill-suited for the one I aspired to create. I needed strivers who could think strategically, embrace teamwork, and win over skeptics in their assigned agencies. Civil service rules being what they are, I would have to start driving the bus without all the seats filled the way I wanted, but I made two early moves that got the trip off to a good start.

One move was to get a few people off the bus, including one who I twice had to remind that sweatpants are not appropriate office attire. Their lack of effort was obvious to everyone on the team, and as long as they stayed in their seats, I could not make headway on establishing a new culture.

More important than getting them off the bus was bringing my first hire onboard. Kristin Dawson was a "poach." I lured her away from another city agency, the Department of Housing and Community Development. When I called her supervisor as a courtesy before making the job offer, the reaction confirmed to me that I had picked a winner. It wasn't quite wailing and gnashing of teeth, but I felt a little guilty when I hung up the phone.

Awesome Dawson

Kristin was exactly what I needed. Like a beacon in the fog, her irrepressible spirit signaled the direction I wanted to take the budget office. She would be my right hand in making Outcome Budgeting a reality, and her uninhibited enthusiasm for the mission (and for life in general) had everyone asking, "Where did this woman come from?"

Not far, as it happens. Kristin was raised about an hour north of Baltimore, in York County, Pennsylvania. Her parents were working class. Her father ran a body shop and her mother worked for a company that made tanks for the military. She grew up fast. "Kid stuff bored me," she remembers. "If there weren't child labor laws, I would have gone to work when I was six years old."

Dying to be useful, she would straighten grocery shelves on shopping trips with her mom and help an elderly neighbor by mowing his lawn, cleaning his garage, and fixing his car. Even her play was about working. She loved to pretend she owned a restaurant. By twelve, she was babysitting and had a paper route. "I always had more than one job," she says. "I didn't care about the money, I just wanted to be in adult conversations."

Kristin's parents weren't political ("I'm not sure my dad has ever voted," she muses), but she is, and after working on Bill Clinton's presidential campaign, she signed up for his new AmeriCorps national service program. She spent two years leading a volunteer team that traveled by van across the Southeast, working on projects of all sorts, from trail cutting to disaster response to running after-school programs.

The experience brought her face to face with entrenched poverty that until then she had only read about. At the end of an eight-week project at a Boys & Girls Club in North Little Rock, Arkansas, she sat in the gym and sobbed, thinking, "these kids are never going to get out of here." It also reinforced her innate belief in herself, that she could do anything. She wanted to change the world, and she decided to do it through public service. She used the education award she earned from AmeriCorps to get a master's degree in public policy from the University of Minnesota, then was drawn back to Baltimore. "I liked what Martin O'Malley was doing with CitiStat," she says, "and I didn't feel like Minneapolis needed me."

Kristin was undeterred by the budget office environment she stepped into. "I don't need cheerleaders," she told me. The budget analysts were tired and bored after many years in the same hamster wheel; our challenge was to bring out whatever they had left to get Outcome Budgeting going. I gave directions and Kristin gave the place a new vibe.

To their credit, the analysts did what was asked of them, including a lot of dirty work to reorganize the service structure and build budgets from scratch. That was enough to keep Outcome Budgeting on the rails, but to make it fly would take a new kind of analyst. Looking back many years later, Kristin is spot-on in her assessment of what was missing. "The old-school analysts were trained to be gatekeepers, not teammates," she says. "Outcome Budgeting calls for analysts who can give agencies coaching, consultation, care, and collaboration—who can be force multipliers."

Wonder Ys

Kristin left after two budget cycles to pursue her dream of traveling around the world. While she was with me, we began to replace retiring analysts with the kind she described, some of them straight from graduate school. Outcome Budgeting was a magnet for people who wanted to do interesting, meaningful work. We got hundreds of applications for our job postings, which was unheard of for budget analyst positions. Every person we hired told us the same thing: "I took this job because I want to be in a place that is innovating."

Go to any professional conference these days—it doesn't matter what industry—and you are almost sure to find a panel session about "managing millennials." Members of this mysterious generation (also called Generation Y), born between the early 1980s and late

1990s, have taken their share of potshots from baby boomer bosses. To a boomer, the typical millennial is lazy, self-absorbed, and entitled, waltzing into the workplace looking for a beanbag, a flexible schedule, and a pat on the back. Leadership guru Simon Sinek is more sympathetic toward millennials, who he sees as victims of overweening parents who handed out participation medals and gave their children the idea that they could do anything they wanted without having to try real hard.

I guess you could say that I found the beauty in millennials. The ones I hired had the confidence to question me when they thought I was wrong, the tech savvy to simplify their work (they're not lazy, they're just smarter than the rest of us), and an idealism that reminded me why BBMR's slogan, "Budgeting for a Better Baltimore," still resonated.

The truth is, I didn't have to change my management style for millennials, because my style was a good fit for them. For that, I have Rick Kowalewski to thank. When I was the age of the young people I was now hiring, Rick was my role model. He was a Coast Guard officer on loan to the Secretary of Transportation to implement the new Government Performance and Results Act (GPRA), which required federal agencies for the first time to set goals, write strategic plans, and report on their progress.

As you might expect from a military officer, there was nothing out of place about Rick. He wore a helmet of gray hair, neatly trimmed mustache, and off-the-rack suits that fit him to a T. He was calm, cool, and collected, with the emphasis on calm. He led not by barking orders but by asking penetrating questions, presenting interesting ideas, and giving thoughtful feedback. His only impatience was with conventional thinking.

A few years after we worked together on GPRA, Rick hired me into my first management position. He had retired from the Coast Guard to be the Deputy Administrator of the Bureau of Transportation Statistics, and he brought me on as the agency's first CFO. As I assembled my staff, Rick gave me advice that has stuck with me ever since: let people pursue their interests within the parameters of what needs to get done. He let me do that, including a semi-successful experiment

Figure 5.1 Logic Model

Outcome	Intermediate Outcome	Output	Activity	Input
Increase # of healthy families	_How?_ → Increase # of families using healthy food practices	_How?_ → 200 families complete an educational workshop	_How?_ → Conduct four educational workshops per month	_How?_ → • Funding • Program staff • AmeriCorps Members • Volunteers • Research

with something I called Logic Model Budgeting. I asked program managers to build their budgets by starting with the outcomes they wanted to achieve and working back to inputs by asking "How?" I've included a simple example in figure 5.1. I'm sure I owe my life to Rick, because a lot of the program managers wanted to kill me.

I can draw a straight line from my GPRA work with Rick to Outcome Budgeting in Baltimore and to the kind of manager I became. I throw ideas at my staff and expect them to throw ideas back. When they come up with a good idea, I tell them to run with it. Sometimes I let them run with ideas they think are good, even if I don't. I like to make decisions collaboratively, which means listening and being willing to justify myself to people half my age. I give them pats on the back for a job well done. For those, I have high standards, but no quotas.

What millennials want is to have a voice in the workplace, room for initiative, and flexibility in how they do their work. They don't have much use for traditional power relationships, but they aim to please and take as much pride in their work as any generation I've worked with. My millennials were leaders in their Results Teams, invented new ways to engage residents with the budget process, produced management research reports that a consultant would have charged six figures to write, and seemed to have fun doing all of it. They were the core of the most talented, dynamic team in city government.

To my delight, I wound up on the receiving end of several phone calls like the one I made when I hired Kristin Dawson. My analysts were promoted into the top fiscal and administrative posts of several of the city's largest agencies, where they spread the BBMR gospel of using data and evidence to get better results.

Since retiring from public service, Rick has become a yoga instructor and taken up water painting and the guitar. He calls himself an "artist, teacher, and life practitioner," and the mustache is now a goatee. Still my role model after all these years.

SHIFT 2: THE BUDGET DIRECTOR

Leadership on the Line

Besides his example and advice, another gift Rick gave me was sending me for a month to the Senior Executive Fellows Program at Harvard's Kennedy School of Government, a chance to step away from day-to-day responsibilities and learn about leadership in all its dimensions. One of our lecturers was Marty Linsky, coauthor (with Ronald Heifetz) of *Leadership on the Line: Staying Alive through the Dangers of Change. Leadership on the Line* inspired the title of this book, because its lessons guided me as I sought to transform Baltimore's budget process in the face of resistance, indifference, and crisis.

Heifetz and Linsky define leadership as going beyond your authority to get people to tackle the problems at hand, to make them face what they do not want to face. They write, "To act outside the narrow confines of your job description when progress requires it lies close to the heart of leadership, and to its danger."

I was pushing the boundaries of the budget director's role. The easy route would have been to treat the challenge of balancing the city's budget as a math problem. How large is the deficit? How much does each 1 percent across-the-board cut save? How much revenue do we get from each 1 percent increase in the tax rate? This is the traditional role for a budget director—the technician, crunching the numbers, counting the beans. No offense to accountants, but it always bothered me to be mistaken for one. I guess being bald and bespectacled doesn't help, but I have always seen myself as more like a traffic cop, standing at the intersection of politics, policy, program management, and finance, pointing people in the right direction. In Baltimore, it was a busy intersection.

As you know by now, I was not taking the easy route. I wanted to create budgets that allocated dollars based on merit, not math. In the abstract, this made sense to everyone. When it came to making the hard, real-life choices that Outcome Budgeting demands, those in the wrong quadrant of the priority–performance matrix—those who stood to lose funding—put up whatever roadblocks they could.

The budget wasn't the only envelope I was pushing. My analysts were taking deep dives into sensitive management issues, encouraging agencies to make their business processes more efficient, demanding data and evidence, and urging innovation. You will read more about some of these efforts in chapter 7. We were disturbing people, maybe at a rate faster than they could absorb.

"Stay in Your Lane"
Heifetz and Linsky caution that while exceeding your formal authority might pay off for your organization, "you will be characterized as being out of place, out of turn, or too big for your britches." I found this out when I took on the police department.

One of the most provocative recommendations from Results Teams was that resources should be shifted from law enforcement to longer-term crime reduction strategies like youth development, job training, and drug treatment. Baltimore is a violent city, and it has one of the largest police forces in America, but, as I've pointed out, there was no correlation between the number of police officers and the crime rate. All the same, the police department was consuming more than a third of the discretionary general fund budget, crowding out dollars for many underfunded services.

Advocates outside of City Hall, and even some on the city council, had long called for a change in spending priorities. Until Outcome Budgeting, specific trade-offs between the police department's budget and alternative options had not been seriously debated in front of the mayor. The Results Teams teed the trade-offs up, and it was my job to get the mayor to swing at them. Usually, I was the one who got swung at.

The list of options for cutting police spending was a long one: curb overtime use; take more property crime reports by phone; disband the largely ceremonial mounted unit; ground one of the four helicopters, which assist on only a small fraction of arrests; staff the marine unit seasonally; civilianize administrative positions; change how patrol officers are deployed; and abolish long-vacant positions.

I argued for these cuts, and the new investments they would make possible, every chance I got. In one session, the police commissioner and I sat across from each other at the head of the executive conference table, flanking Mayor Rawlings-Blake. After listening to us go back and forth for the good part of an hour, the mayor finally turned to me and said, "You are in charge of the money, he is in charge of police operations. You two need to work this out." Afterwards, the mayor's chief of staff pulled me aside and put it more bluntly: "Stay in your lane."

I was furious. Stay in my lane? If we were going to reorient the budget toward the Mayor's Priority Outcomes, I needed to swim in the whole pool. We were making progress, but if I couldn't crack into the police department's base budget, Outcome Budgeting's potential was limited. I had to remind myself of Winston Churchill's words: "Success is not final, failure is not fatal: it is the courage to continue that counts."

Leadership can be lonely, whether you are at the top of the organization or closer to the middle, where I was. Even with the mayor's support and a team that believed in the cause, I was sometimes on my own to fend off the naysayers and fight for budget decisions that moved money to where it would do more good.

Be the Change

I don't mean to sound like a martyr. I survived with my life and livelihood intact and learned valuable lessons along the way about leading change. Here are a few of them:

First and foremost, be persistent. Even if you do a good job of explaining and preparing people for change, opposition will come at you in many forms. Opponents will try to confront, marginalize, co-opt, and ignore you; they will give you every reason to quit. If you have Churchill's "courage to continue," you will gradually win your opponents over, wear them down, or outlast them. I outlasted the "stay in your lane" chief of staff and ultimately scored police department savings that was repurposed for crime prevention initiatives.

Second, listen. In chapter 2, I described the focus groups we conducted after the first three cycles of Outcome Budgeting. We heard a lot of feedback about what was wrong with the process, and we made adjustments. As useful as the focus groups were, there is no substitute for one-on-one conversations. I lunched frequently with agency heads, including those who I thought weren't fully committed to Outcome Budgeting. These meetings could have been more effective, but agency leadership was constantly turning over, which meant I was doing more talking and less listening than I wanted.

Third, nurture a network of champions. It is tempting to focus your change management energies on converting foes. I chose to spend more of my time finding and fostering friends, many of whom you are meeting in this book. With enough friends, you can overwhelm the resistance. Outcome Budgeting opened up the budget process to so many new people that it actually shifted the power center of budget decision-making, which is the subject of the next chapter.

SHIFT 3: THE MAYOR

The Black Box, Revisited

Mayor Dixon had called the budget a "black box." Because of her scandal, she never got a chance to open up the box and look inside. The pleasure of Outcome Budgeting's "Christmas morning"—when Results Teams presented their recommendations for the first time—was instead enjoyed by Dixon's successor, Mayor Rawlings-Blake, on her very first day in office.

"Pleasure" is surely an overstatement. As I've described, Mayor Rawlings-Blake was thrust into office in the middle of a fiscal meltdown, a pension crisis, and, just for good measure, a series of blizzards that came to be known as Snowmageddon.

We were only a little past the halfway mark of the current fiscal year and had already been through two rounds of budget reductions. The numbers for the next fiscal year were way out of balance. Bringing them into alignment was going to require us to prioritize spending, find efficiencies, and raise revenue. The new mayor would have to make a whole bunch of unpopular decisions, right out of the gate. The Results Teams' job was to give her the information she needed to put together the smartest, most strategic budget possible. There would be no across-the-board cuts, we would not tap reserves, and the property tax was off limits. It was time to make choices, and trade-offs.

Over two days, the mayor was filled in about each and every service in city government. She learned how it was performing, how it fit into the city's outcomes, and how it should be funded. Snowmageddon had nothing on the way the Results Teams buried the mayor in data. No mayor had ever dug into (or out of) the budget like this before, but she just kept shoveling.

Mayor Rawlings-Blake's first budget was remarkable in many ways.

On the advice of the Results Teams, she protected and even enhanced funding for services that demonstrated results, including job training, maternal and child health, and small business development. This was possible because she also did something most thought was impossible: she eliminated services that couldn't show value and repurposed their funding.

Even with a $120 million budget shortfall, taking out a whole service was no mean feat. Baltimore is a cash-strapped city, and while you didn't have to look hard to find fat, we also didn't have any nominees for the Golden Fleece Award (some of you may remember this award, given out by the late Senator William Proxmire for what he considered wasteful federal spending, such as an army study on how to buy Worcestershire sauce).

What Outcome Budgeting spotlighted was not waste, per se, but well-meaning services that weren't working. One of those was a prisoner reentry service called Baltimore Rising. The service was spending $250,000 a year and yet, according to the Safer Streets Results Team evaluation, it did not have evidence of an impact of key measures of employment, substance abuse, and recidivism. The team recommended that Baltimore Rising become a nonprofit organization so that it could more readily attract grant dollars, and it redirected the savings to a youth violence prevention program that had been evaluated by Johns Hopkins University and was leveraging outside funding.

Baltimore Rising didn't go down without a fight. At Taxpayers' Night, a brigade of protestors in matching T-shirts sat in the first three rows. Children of prisoners spoke movingly about the mentoring they received from the service. Afterward, I braced myself for the mayor to tell me to find the $250,000 savings somewhere else, but she didn't. The mayor stood by the Baltimore Rising cut, as well as the elimination of a neighborhood development service, an arts grant program, and a community liaison office. The reason is that she understood why these services had fallen "below the line" and that their demise was part of a larger plan to make what progress we could on her Priority Outcomes within severe resource constraints.

Beyond the Black Box

I like to brag that no city managed the Great Recession better than Baltimore, but Outcome Budgeting alone was not enough to get spending in line with our collapsing revenues. After prioritizing services, wringing out inefficiency, and hiking taxes, we were still short of where we needed to be. So, like most other cities, we resorted to budget Band-Aids, temporary gap-fillers until the economy got better. We froze hiring and pay, furloughed employees for up to two weeks, deferred capital projects, and closed fire companies on a rotating schedule.

Mayor Rawlings-Blake could see that the city's budget was on an unsustainable path. As revenues were slowly recovering, the fixed costs of government—pensions, retiree health, debt service—were continuing to grow faster. She had strong-armed the city council into overhauling the dangerously underfunded fire and police pension system (a reform that is still being litigated eight years later); she knew she had more work to do.

In their book *Informed Decision-Making through Forecasting: A Practitioner's Guide to Government Revenue Forecasting*, Shayne Kavanagh and Daniel Williams make the case that nontraditional budget formats, ones that have a planning orientation, allocate resources based on performance, and take a structured approach to making resource trade-offs, tend to encourage long-term financial forecasting. The mayor had pointed her annual budgets toward her vision of growing the city's population by ten thousand families over ten years, and now she wanted a multiyear financial plan of action.

She called the plan "Change to Grow," and it was the first of its kind for Baltimore. The planning process started with a ten-year forecast of the cost to maintain the current level of city services versus the revenue we could expect to bring in. The result was sobering: a $750 million cumulative operating budget shortfall, which didn't go away even with an optimistic set of economic assumptions. We also found that our baseline capital spending was $1.1 billion below what would be needed to maintain our assets in a "reasonable" state of repair, and our unfunded pension and retiree health care liabilities had ballooned to $3.2 billion.

By itself, fixing the structural operating budget deficit would have been an ambitious goal for the plan, but people don't move to a city for its balanced budgets. As you can see in figure 5.2, structural balance was just one of four cornerstones of the city's fiscal foundation that we sought to strengthen. To make Baltimore a more attractive place to live, we also had to lower the property-tax rate, invest more in our aging infrastructure, and get pension and health-benefit costs under control so they wouldn't crowd out basic services in the budget.

The plan was bold, by design. It had something for everyone to oppose. Among its hundred initiatives were restructuring pension and health benefits for current, future, and retired employees; a new fire-fighter schedule; limits on payouts for unused leave; larger payments

Figure 5.2 The Four Cornerstones of Baltimore's Fiscal Foundation

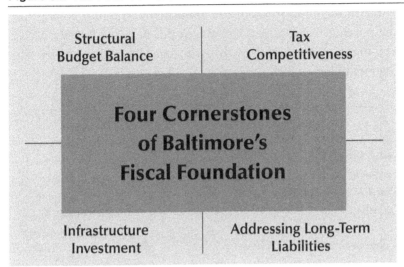

Source: Baltimore Bureau of the Budget and Management Research

to the city from nonprofits; and new levies on billboards and taxis. We consulted with stakeholders but were not seeking consensus. The mayor insisted on a plan that would accomplish all the goals, and she didn't want it watered down by compromise.

The mastermind behind the plan rollout was the mayor's spokesman, a big, self-assured Irishman named Ryan O'Doherty. Ryan's strategy was simple: scare the crap out of people. We would release the dire financial projections first, then announce our solutions a month later, when the city council, the unions, and the public would be ready to swallow tough medicine.

The strategy worked, almost too well. The day after the projections went out, an *Associated Press* headline bellowed, "City of Baltimore Is on a Path to Financial Ruin." The *Baltimore Business Journal* led with "Baltimore Could Go Bankrupt by 2023." The bond rating agencies were spooked, and I had to spend an hour on the phone reassuring a Standard & Poor's analyst that the city's finances were sound, and we would soon outline the steps needed to keep them that way.

Mayor Rawlings-Blake presented "Change to Grow" to a large audience in the auditorium of the Walters Art Museum. In contrast to the museum's antiquities, the mayor put on a modern show, her speech highly choreographed with whizbang PowerPoint slides. She opened with these words:

> This is an important moment for Baltimore's future. "Change to Grow" is a first-of-its-kind long-term fiscal plan to help achieve our goal of growing Baltimore by 10,000 families over the next decade. It is born from a belief that our work to get Baltimore growing again must be first grounded in stable city finances. With such a plan in place, Baltimore can finally end the chronic cycle of deficits that have eroded services and constantly put Baltimore on defense instead of investing in its renewal.

The next day, the *Baltimore Sun* was effusive. In an editorial titled "Mayor Takes a Risk," the paper praised Rawlings-Blake's "remarkable willingness to take on politically unpopular causes" and concluded that "if she succeeds, she will accomplish what none of her immediate predecessors have managed: Change a vicious cycle of exodus and disinvestment into a virtuous cycle of growth and redevelopment."

And succeed she did. In its first five years, "Change to Grow" cut the structural budget deficit by more than half; lowered property-tax rates for homeowners by eight percent; pumped $250 million in new capital investment into roads, blight elimination, recreation centers, and IT; shrank unfunded pension and retiree health liabilities by 25 percent; and grew the city's rainy day fund by nearly half. The plan also enabled the city to support a $1.1 billion school modernization program and resulted in a bond rating upgrade to AA, which is extraordinary for a city with Baltimore's economic profile. I have shared some lessons learned from the planning process in box 5.1.

After stabilizing, and even growing modestly, Baltimore's population has slipped in recent years. Development has been robust, with huge new waterfront projects under construction, widespread conversion of office buildings into apartments, and row house rehabs in neighborhoods near downtown, but crime, gentrification, and other factors have pushed residents out.

Box 5.1 | Long-Term Financial Plan Lessons Learned

Be Bold. A long-term plan is no place for half-measures. In most jurisdictions, incremental changes to the status quo are not enough to achieve the vision of a better, safer, and stronger community. While stakeholder input is critical in the planning process, don't get hung up on having consensus around every initiative if it means the plan, even on paper, falls short. Initiatives will inevitably be debated and negotiated in the implementation phase; you want to make sure that half a loaf is enough to sustain your progress.

Build a Baseline. A baseline revenue and expenditure projection is the starting point for your financial plan. More than that, it sets the context for change. In Baltimore's case, the prospect of growing budget shortfalls and deferred capital investment was a call to action for political and civic leaders. A common excuse for not doing long-term planning is that "we don't know what tomorrow is going to look like, much less five or ten years from now." Uncertainty is exactly why planning is so important. Tackle it by developing at least three alternative economic scenarios.

Think Beyond the Horizon. Baltimore thought a decade ahead, instead of the usual three to five years. The fact is that we thought beyond the ten-year horizon and included in our plan a number of initiatives that wouldn't generate serious savings until many years into the future. Turn the ticking fiscal time bombs you inherited into ticking gift boxes for the next generation.

Maintain a Cushion. Simply put, use conservative savings and revenue projections for the initiatives in your plan and, if possible, include extra initiatives beyond what you need to achieve your goals on paper. These steps are important for political and practical reasons. Politically, you won't bat a thousand in getting your initiatives implemented, no matter how brilliant you think they are. Practically, as you implement your plan, you will discover technical issues, misunderstandings, and even errors that change the impact of initiatives. Further, long-range revenues and expenditures will inevitably vary from even the best forecast, such that contingencies may be needed to adapt to the changing circumstances.

Commit Fully to Implementation. Plans don't implement themselves. Success will require sustained leadership commitment and a lot of plain old elbow grease. Baltimore kept two highly capable staffers—and our consultant, Public Financial Management (it won this contract)—more than busy coordinating working groups, writing legislation and policy, negotiating labor agreements, diving deeper on initiatives in the pipeline, tracking and communicating progress, and, in some cases, reselling plan initiatives inside and outside City Hall. Be mindful that implementation begins while the plan is under development. A plan that is carefully researched and well understood by key officials will have the smoothest ride after rollout.

Mayor Rawlings-Blake didn't get much love in the postmortems written about her time in office, but one thing the press couldn't deny was her fiscal leadership. Although her legacy is scarred by the Freddie Gray unrest, "Change to Grow" will have a lasting impact on Baltimore's ability to deliver services and make life better for its residents.

SHIFT 4: THE CITY COUNCIL

The Godmother of Outcome Budgeting

In my first few months in Baltimore, I made the rounds to city council members to tell them about Outcome Budgeting. My first visit was to Councilwoman Helen Holton, the chair of the Budget & Appropriations Committee. She represented the 8th district, a mostly middle-class ward that hugs the city's western edge and contains most of Gwynns Falls/Leakin Park, the city's largest green space.

An ordained minister and CPA, Holton is a small woman with an outsized presence. Her long gray hair is always elaborately braided and she speaks like she is in the middle of a windstorm, even in her tiny office.

You can imagine my surprise when the first words out of the councilwoman's mouth were, "I am about to introduce a resolution requesting that the administration adopt outcome-based budgeting." She had just returned from a National Association of Counties conference in Portland, Oregon, where she learned about this new way of budgeting, and she was excited about bringing it to Baltimore.

The resolution wasn't passed until a year later, but the timing seemed perfect, as we were gearing up for our first Outcome Budgeting cycle. It was titled "A Request for Constructive Change—Budgeting for Outcomes" and read, in part, "As fiscal resources continue to shrink . . . adopting a policy of Budgeting for Outcomes is appropriate. Baltimore City taxpayers who bear the largest burden in financing Baltimore City government should be permitted a larger voice in deciding where their hard earned dollars are spent and what services are most important to their families and their communities."

The Baltimore City Charter gives the city council little say in the details of the budget. The council cannot add to items of appropriation in the mayor's proposal or move money around. It can make cuts, but the mayor can veto them.

Its limited authority notwithstanding, I saw the council as an important ally. I envisioned the mayor and council working hand in hand to make progress toward Priority Outcomes.

My hopes were never realized. Holton resisted my pleadings to organize her budget hearings around outcomes instead of agencies, and most council members did not make the effort to understand the budget in its entirety. They came to budget hearings with one or two pet issues to grandstand about when the cameras were rolling, and those issues didn't necessarily have anything to do with the budget.

The resolution wasn't worth the paper it was printed on. That said, there's no question that Outcome Budgeting changed the council's budget discussions for the better.

The Wolf and the Sheepdog

Before Outcome Budgeting, most council budget hearings were a match of wits between me and the Budget & Appropriations vice chair, Jim Kraft. Kraft is a preppy lawyer who represented Baltimore's Gold Coast, the prosperous neighborhoods extending east from the Inner Harbor. He was the only council member who studied the voluminous budget documents in detail, and about the only one who cared about the city's high property-tax rate. Kraft would show up to the hearings looking like a retired Vineyard Vines model. He didn't appear intimidating in his pastel pants and docksiders, but he cross-examined me like I was an accused murderer.

One thing you have to learn quickly as a budget director is not to take criticism personally. If you have thin skin, you better get out of the business or it will make you crazy. After going toe to toe for hours at a time, Councilman Kraft and I would often leave the hearing room together, joking that we were like Ralph Wolf and Sam Sheepdog in the old Warner Brothers cartoon. Ralph and Sam would clock in together at 8:00 a.m., do battle all day, then clock out at 5:00 p.m., exchanging pleasant chitchat.

Kraft's questioning was less about priorities and more about technicalities. He was playing "gotcha," probing for errors that he could use to embarrass the administration. I can hardly blame him. He had a lot of time to kill over the many hours of scheduled hearings, and the budgets in those days weren't much more than tables of numbers, just asking to be ticked and tied (that's accounting slang). Enter Outcome Budgeting.

What to Keep?

The mayors I worked for didn't have much appetite for consulting with councilmembers about the budget. They preferred to use their power to the fullest, controlling how funding was allocated and more or less telling the council to take it or leave it. Typically, they could buy votes for pocket change —$50,000 for new street lights for one member, $75,000 for the animal shelter for another. It was not the right relationship for Outcome Budgeting, which thrives on cooperation around a common set of goals.

For at least one councilmember, Outcome Budgeting made the mayor's spending plan even more suspicious. Mary Pat Clarke, a liberal crusader who has served on and off since the mid-1970s, considered me a bean counter and demanded to know who was on these "secret tribunals" that were making budget decisions she didn't like. She talked about the Results Teams (whose names were published in the budget books) the way Sarah Palin talked about "death panels" of bureaucrats deciding who was worthy of medical care.

Clarke was an outlier, though. Most members, though they remained myopic about the budget, suddenly started asking more questions in the budget hearings. Now, instead of just tables of numbers, they had in front of them service descriptions, performance measures, and an itemized list of changes from one budget to the next. Even if they hadn't done their homework, they could see at a glance if a service was or wasn't meeting its performance targets and ask agency heads for an explanation.

I could tell that the councilmembers felt empowered by this new information. At first, the agency heads were caught off guard by performance questions, which made for some awkward moments, as they looked back at their staffers hoping that someone had the answer. When agencies were prepared, the hearings became more substantive than ever, with give-and-take about how to fix performance problems and conversation around the results being produced for the dollars spent.

One perverse effect of the council's focus on performance data was to make agencies more cautious about setting ambitious targets.

I found myself counseling agency heads to overcome their accountability fears. The council helped me by calling out agency heads who weren't striving for improvement.

The 2016 election brought a new guard to the council—younger, smarter, more progressive and aggressive. Holton and Kraft were gone, and I finally got a version of the outcome-based hearings I had always yearned for. Councilmembers appreciated being able to discuss issues with all the relevant agencies in the room at the same time. It stopped the finger-pointing and rear-end covering they were used to and forced honest assessments of progress and agreements to work together for better results.

At the council level, shifting the budget debate from a fixation on cuts to a focus on how to best spend available resources will take much more collaboration between mayor and council, on the Priority Outcomes, Key Indicators, and funding trade-offs. The mayor must decide that bringing councilmembers into the budget fold will add to the budget's legitimacy and not subtract from her prerogatives.

Collectively, the four shifts described in this chapter fundamentally changed how Baltimore thought about budgeting, made budget decisions, and planned for the future. The next chapter is about another shift, one powered by people who had never before been part of the budget process.

FIVE TAKEAWAYS

1. **Talent trumps experience, and you can't teach talent.** I fought constantly with HR to hire the people I wanted for my team, not all of whom were conventional candidates. I have always been amazed at how much one person can do to lift up, or drag down, an organization. Work your personnel rules hard to get the right people on your bus and the wrong people off, but start driving with whatever team you have (some people might jump out!).

2. **Millennials get a bad rap.** They have skills you don't, and when they are motivated, look out! Let them self-direct their work as much as possible, encourage innovation, and don't think you can praise too much, as long as it's deserved.

3. **Leadership is venturing beyond your scope of authority to influence change.** It's like jumping over a fence into someone else's yard. You might get chased away, but you have to keep coming back.
4. **Outcome Budgeting gives you the tools to repurpose funding, and even eliminate services that aren't working.** You will find these opportunities when you have clear priorities and plans to achieve them, measure service performance, demand evidence of service impact, and fund outcomes instead of agencies.
5. Outcome Budgeting can help you firm up your financial foundation, but not by itself. **If your organization doesn't have a long-term plan for financial sustainability, it should become a priority.**

FIVE QUESTIONS

1. Put yourself in Mayor Rawlings-Blake's shoes. A Results Team is telling you that a service cannot demonstrate results. At the same time, clients of the service are making emotional appeals to save it from being cut. What information would you want to have about the service before making a final decision? How would you communicate your decision?
2. Which of your talents are "four lane superhighways," which are "barren wastelands," and which are somewhere in between? Choose one talent you'd like to improve. How would you go about doing it?
3. In what ways do workplaces need to evolve to get the most out of younger workers? The millennials will soon be followed into the labor force by a new generation. How is the new generation different?
4. What is something you'd like to change that is outside of your control? What should be your first steps to influencing this change?
5. As a class exercise, simulate a city council budget hearing. Assign teams to play council members and agency officials. Use information from a city budget document to prepare. Start with a presentation from the agency head, followed by questions from the council. The questions should be tough, and the answers must be polite! See if the agency head can hold it together.

FIVE RESOURCES

1. Buckingham, Marcus, and Coffman, Curt. (1999) *First, Break All the Rules: What the World's Greatest Managers Do Differently.* New York: Simon & Schuster. I learned from this book to hire for talent over experience. It turned out to be great advice, as I built the most talented team in city government.

2. Heifetz, Ronald, and Linsky, Marty. (2002). *Leadership on the Line: Staying Alive through the Dangers of Change.* Boston, MA: Harvard Business Review Press. This book taught me that the definition of leadership is exercising influence outside the lines of your formal authority. It can be risky, but it has to be done to make real change.

3. Baltimore's Change to Grow Ten-Year Financial Plan and the mayor's presentation can be found at bbmr.baltimorecity.gov/ten-year-financial-plan.

4. Kavanagh, Shayne, and Williams, Daniel. (2017). *Informed Decision-Making through Forecasting: A Practitioner's Guide to Government Revenue Analysis.* Chicago, IL: Government Finance Officers Association. This book includes a chapter case study of Baltimore's ten-year financial plan and how using multiple economic scenarios gave the plan credibility. Kavanagh also wrote a book called *Financing the Future: Long-Term Financial Planning for Local Government*, which was an inspiration for Baltimore's plan.

5. Kleine, Andrew, Barcak, Kristin, and Nadol, Michael, "Change to Grow: Baltimore's Ten-Year Financial Plan," *Government Finance Review*, June 2014. If you want to learn more about long-term financial planning, this article is a good place to start. Liz Farmer's article "What Other Cities Can Learn from Baltimore's Outcome Based Budgeting," *Governing*, November 11, 2013, makes the connection between Outcome Budgeting and long-term financial planning.

6

Widening the Circle

■ ■ ■

OUTCOME BUDGETING ADDED many leaves to the budget table. Traditionally a backroom huddle of the mayor, senior finance officials, and a few influential agency heads, the budget discussion was opened up to people who had never before been within shouting distance.

Democratizing the budget process wasn't part of my sales pitch for Outcome Budgeting, but I soon realized that including more voices, and more diverse voices—from program managers, frontline workers, and community members—is transformational in and of itself. The scoring rubrics, matrices, and ranking sheets that make up the mechanics of Outcome Budgeting were less important than the new perspectives and ideas that came from widening the circle out from City Hall.

SHOVELS IN THE SHED

My revelation that Outcome Budgeting was changing the culture of how budgets were built at the ground level came from an unexpected source. Dave Cunningham, the chief fiscal officer for the Department of Public Works (DPW), was the very definition of a grizzled veteran in the world of Baltimore City finance. He looked grizzled, for starters. He was wiry, with a well-worn face and gray beard that was yellowed around his mouth from smoking. He took pride in his expertise (under his email signature was the sign off, "If it was easy, anyone could do it!") and never held back in telling me what I didn't know.

After the agencies had submitted their service proposals in the first Outcome Budgeting cycle, I held a fiscal officers' meeting to explain the next steps of the process. As the meeting was breaking up, I asked Dave how he felt about DPW's proposals. Some say don't ask the question if you don't want to hear the answer, but leading change requires having uncomfortable conversations. I figured this would be one of those. Dave caught me off guard when he told me, "The budget has always been put together by the fiscal staff, without much input from the programs. This year, for the first time, fiscal staff and program managers had to work together, hand in hand. It was good for us. We all learned a lot."

In retrospect, I first saw the power of inclusion in Outcome Budgeting months before my conversation with Dave, when we convened the Results Teams and they got to work on the Requests for Results. Within Baltimore's thirteen-thousand-employee workforce were hundreds (at least) of brilliant people whose wisdom, expertise, and unique viewpoints had never before been drawn upon to inform budgeting. It was like we were digging with our hands when there were shovels in the shed.

Results Team members came from virtually every level in the organization, especially after we invited all employees to apply for open slots. Two Results Teamers who exemplify the power of inclusion are Kim Grove and Shelly Payne Broadnax.

The Little Engineer That Could

Kim is one of those hyper-capable people who you wish you could put on every project. She was a math whiz as a child, so smart that she skipped the fifth grade and was taking junior-level courses at the University of Maryland by the time she was sixteen years old. Her father was an engineer, complete with short-sleeved dressed shirts and a pocket protector. "He was so geeky that he turned me off to engineering," she laughs.

It took a kick in the butt from her AP calculus teacher to get Kim to give engineering a try. She studied civil engineering at the Florida

Institute of Technology near Cape Canaveral, where the male-to-female ratio was 7:1. In her first job out of college, she worked as a soils engineer doing deep foundation inspections for a construction project. "The holes were small and I'm small, so I was able to contribute to the team," she remembers.

That first project notwithstanding, being a woman, and a short one to boot, was not easy in a male-dominated profession. "I was treated like a little girl at first," Kim says, "but I earned respect." She points to her family. "We're all short. Snark, sarcasm, and wit are our weapons."

Kim was a manager before too long, and when family issues brought her back to Maryland, she became a consultant to Baltimore's DPW. The DPW director knew a star when he saw one, and he asked her to be the chief of the Surface Water Management Division. It was a pay cut, but she said yes, having grown tired of the consulting hunt ("You don't get to enjoy what you're eating before you have to kill again.").

As the architect of Baltimore's stormwater fee, Kim found herself in the middle of a nasty legislative fight over the details of how to charge property owners for the impact of their impervious surfaces on runoff and water quality. She was frustrated to see all of her logic blown up by politics, but she reasons that it was good preparation for her role in the budget process.

Kim served on Results Teams for five cycles, including three as a chair, of both the Stronger Neighborhoods and Growing Economy teams. If I had to describe the personal qualities it takes to be a great Results Team chair, I would start with Kim's. As she says, "Engineers are problem solvers. We keep the emotion out of it." At the same time, she knows how to take care of people, which she learned from her grandmother, who never hesitated to pick up a hitchhiker and fed strangers on her back porch. She is also highly organized, a trait she admired in her mother's boss, Jerry Sachs, who was president of the Washington Bullets basketball team. "He was a human Filofax," she marvels.

Having spent most of her career in the private sector, Kim could see that many city agencies were complacent about their budgets and performance. It energized her to see how the handful of nonprofits that participated in Outcome Budgeting—the zoo, art museums, and symphony orchestra—sought to collaborate and innovate. "Government doesn't stop to think about how to do things better," she observes. "These nonprofits need to survive and earn their keep."

Opening up the budget process to outside organizations, including those that can compete with government agencies to deliver services, is a dimension of Outcome Budgeting that Baltimore did not fully explore. As long as government agencies know they are running monopolies, they don't have the incentive to be as efficient and effective as they could be, even within the personnel, procurement, and budget constraints they so often blame for their deficiencies.

Kim saw many improvements in agency service proposals over the years, but she is most passionate when she talks about the cross-agency connections she made through Outcome Budgeting and the learnings she brought back to her own agency. In one case, she partnered with another Results Team member to streamline erosion and sediment control inspections for vacant property demolitions. From reading service proposals, she picked up ideas for equipping her inspectors with handheld units to improve their productivity and using Community Action Centers to distribute stormwater billing information. She also applied Outcome Budgeting's proposal scoring rubric to prioritize DPW's capital projects, which, in her words, "gave the agency objective rankings that could be defended."

Kim is also passionate about including people at all levels in Results Teams, which she calls a "morale booster." For her, Exhibit A is Shelley Payne Broadnax, another DPW employee, who was selected for a Results Team on her second try at the application process.

The Power of Positive Thinking

The fact that Shelley didn't give up after being left out the first time tells you a lot about a person who, in my mind, missed her calling as a motivational speaker. Talking to Shelley, you can't help but be uplifted. She says she wakes up excited every day for her job as a data entry clerk at the Back River Wastewater Treatment Plant, which is so far away from City Hall that it's not even within the city limits. She speaks of finding lessons in adversity, because "I'm a champion, not a victim," and when she practically shouts, "I'm enjoying the journey," I think she really means it, even though her journey has taken some detours.

Shelley grew up in Gilmor Homes, the public housing project on Baltimore's west side where Freddie Gray was arrested in April 2015, starting the sequence of events that led to days of protests and rioting against alleged police brutality. Shelley remembers a fun, safe community where everyone looked out for one another. In the decades since, the Homes fell into disrepair, with residents' complaints of black mold, rat infestations, and other problems being ignored or, worse, used by maintenance workers to extort sexual favors in exchange for repairs. In early 2018, the city housing authority announced plans to tear down a portion of Gilmore Homes, clearing away a crime hotbed and relocating residents to better housing.

As a little girl, Shelley dreamed of being a teacher. "I had a chalkboard, and I would give lessons to my stuffed animals, pillows, and rugs," she recalls. She was always a good student, and her parents were strict, but in her teen years, peer pressure drew her off the straight and narrow path. "Be careful who you call your friends," she cautions. Hers thought teachers were "square" and were always getting into trouble of one sort or another. Shelley credits her beautiful penmanship to frequent visits to detention, where she had to write "I will not . . ." hundreds of times.

Instead of pursuing her childhood dream, Shelley went to work out of high school. When she finally made it to college thirty years later, she was eager to make up for lost time. She earned an associate's degree from Baltimore City Community College in 2014, and just kept going. She graduated from the University of Baltimore in 2017 and is now working on a master's degree in negotiation and conflict management, which she wants to use to help resolve workplace disputes that undermine labor–management relations and employee productivity.

As a Results Team member, Shelley was ever mindful of what she calls "the two Baltimores," divided between black and white, rich and poor. In one instance, she advocated for a Planning

Department proposal to engage underserved neighborhoods that are often overlooked by urban designers. In another, she found herself outnumbered as she argued against funding for a bike master plan. Invoking "spatial justice," she raised concerns that bike lanes would serve only an elite sliver of Baltimoreans while promoting gentrification and taking up limited roadway space, making long commutes even longer for those who don't have the luxury of living and working near downtown. "Most of my teammates had sold their cars," she says. "They weren't in touch with how the other half lives."

Win or lose, voices like Shelley's in the budget conversation, close to where decisions are actually made, bring focus to issues of equity and put preconceived notions about what's best for communities to the test. "Conflict can be healthy," is Shelley's philosophy. "People just need to talk."

TALKING TO THE PEOPLE

Article 6, Section 4(b) of the Baltimore City Charter requires that the Board of Estimates (BOE) hold public hearings so that "citizens shall have the opportunity to . . . speak for or against the inclusion of any appropriation in the proposed Ordinance of Estimates," which is a fancy name for the budget bill. The BOE satisfies this requirement by holding an annual ritual called "Taxpayers' Night" in the War Memorial Building, a neoclassical monument to Maryland's World War I heroes that faces City Hall from across a grassy plaza.

Taxpayers' Night is a monument to community engagement at its worst. The five members of the BOE—the mayor, city council president, comptroller, city solicitor, and public works director—sit on a dais and invite audience members to say their piece, making clear from the outset that each speaker is allotted two minutes at the microphone and the board members are there to listen, not interact. My job as budget director was to enforce the two-minute time limit. I held up a yellow paddle to signal thirty seconds remaining and a red paddle when time was up. It really didn't matter how long people spoke or what they said, because by the time Taxpayers' Night rolled around, the mayor's budget was already "baked"—the decisions had already been made.

Photo 6.1 The Baltimore War Memorial *Source: iStock/sestevens*

In the spirit of Outcome Budgeting, I was determined to change everything about how residents were involved in the city's budget, first by explaining it to them, next by showing them why they should care about it, and finally by giving them a chance to roll up their sleeves and dig into the tough choices facing the mayor and city council. With help from my intrepid millennials, I even managed to put a new twist on Taxpayers' Night.

I've talked to fellow city budget directors about why public participation in the budget process is important. The two reasons I hear most often are (1) educating residents and (2) building their trust in government. We don't expect residents to make budget decisions for us or find money under the proverbial seat cushions. Our goal is for residents to have a basic understanding of where the city's revenue comes from, how it is spent, and what results from the spending. We want them to tell us their priorities and also appreciate the challenges of meeting competing needs with limited funding. If residents are well informed and given the chance to be heard, they are more likely to be satisfied with budget decisions, even the ones that don't go their way.

Too often, public participation is dominated by special interest groups that show up to meetings to advocate for more funding for their favorite programs or to fight against proposed cuts to those programs. Behind the scenes are business interests lobbying for tax cuts and tax breaks. These interest groups get their way by using emotion and intimidation, not data and evidence, and they give only lip service to the fiscal constraints their elected officials are under. It is part of the playbook: "I know this is a very difficult budget year, but . . ."

By going beyond the traditional town hall meeting and taking the budget to the people, the budget office was able to give the mayor informed input from thousands more residents—*before* she finalized her budget. The special interests would still have their say, only now their voices were a little harder to hear above the din of others taking part in the budget debate.

I have referenced Baltimore's community survey, from which we started to find out what the average resident cares about, how they rate city services, and how they feel about the quality of life in the city. The survey was a crucial source of data to validate budget priorities, measure performance, and provide ground truth that doesn't show up in management reports and CitiStat reviews. For example, we found out that more than 30 percent of residents planned to leave the city in the next three years. It was a splash of cold water to the face, but it shaped the mayor's strategies for growing the population by ten thousand families in ten years.

For all their benefits, surveys are random and impersonal. We wanted to reach residents in ways that closed the distance between their day-to-day lives and our work in City Hall. The rest of this section describes our engagement efforts and what we learned from them.

The Curse of Knowledge

Baltimore wasn't the first city to publish a summary budget document for residents, but we did it with the most gusto. What started out as a twelve-page pocket guide soon grew to twenty-eight full-sized pages, chock full of data on everything from tax rates to capital projects to outcome indicators. It also included a fiscal report card and a full explanation of the budget process. If it hadn't been for printing costs, I probably would have crammed even more in there. I guess I had gotten out of control.

Finally, one of my young analysts intervened. She asked me, "Who reads this thing?" I stared at her for an uncomfortably long time, because I didn't have a good answer. "I think it should be four pages, tops," she declared. "People won't bother with more than that."

As I started to grieve over all the glorious details we would have to cut out to get the guide down to four pages, I was reminded of something I'd read in Chip and Dan Heath's book *Made to Stick: Why Some Ideas Survive and Others Die.* They write that the villain of effective communication is the Curse of Knowledge. "Once we know something, we find it hard to imagine what it was like not to know it," they explain. To me, making budget information simple felt like dumbing it down, so instead, I overloaded people with information they couldn't grasp. I was cursed!

To break the curse, I agreed to the four-page format. It forced us to find more graphical (and colorful) ways to display our facts. We were able to cover key accomplishments, fast facts about services, survey results, progress on outcome indicators, data on revenue and spending, budget highlights, and more.

You know where this is going. More people than ever read the guide—we couldn't keep them in stock. Instead of turning people off, the new format drew them in. In community meetings, I found myself answering questions about the budget I had never received before. I was getting to share my knowledge, now with residents who were interested and ready to listen.

Making budget information more accessible to residents didn't stop at pretty postmortem pamphlets. We also redesigned the budget documents submitted to the BOE and city council during the budget process. Instead of being organized by fund and agency as they had been for many years, the new budget books were organized around Priority Outcomes. Each Priority Outcome chapter displayed Key

Indicator charts and explained how the budget would improve results. Readers could also find details about each and every service, including performance measures, budget highlights, and a full accounting of year-to-year funding changes.

Roll Up Your Sleeves

As I've made clear, I see little value in the "Open Mike Night"–style budget forum. When the budget pie is only so big, I don't have much patience listening to someone plead for a larger slice if they can't tell me whose slice to shave. In Baltimore, our idea of engaging residents about the budget was to have them confront the hard trade-offs needed to balance a budget that was chronically out of whack.

We called our engagement events "workshops"—not town halls or meetings or listening sessions—because we were asking the participants to do some work. In their first iteration, these workshops, held in schools and libraries around the city, featured a pen-and-paper budget balancing exercise in which participants sorted through real-life spending and revenue choices in an attempt to close the budget gap. In the Great Recession years, when the gaps were huge, only a few people at each workshop were able to bring revenue and spending into alignment, and most of them explained their service cuts and tax hikes apologetically, knowing they were unpopular.

It is impossible to simulate everything that goes into crafting a municipal budget, and some participants complained that we didn't give them enough options. In a memorable 2011 workshop, most of the seats were filled by Occupy Baltimore activists, who had been camping out for weeks in McKeldin Square, near the Inner Harbor. The encampment was an offshoot of Occupy Wall Street, a grassroots movement against income inequality, corporate influence on government, and assorted other issues. Besides bringing a distinct aroma to the workshop, the Occupy crowd denounced the budget balancing exercise as illegitimate, claiming that if the city would just revoke developer tax incentives, it could be talking about increasing services rather than cutting them.

That was the first and last time I heard from Occupy Baltimore. After wrangling with the mayor for two months over the encampment's legality and safety, the occupiers were finally evicted, though not before trying to build a bicycle-powered generator when the city cut off electricity to their site.

To get more residents into the game, we put the budget balancing exercise online. Our homemade site, called Balanced Baltimore, went a step further than other city budget simulators we reviewed. The other simulators asked users to adjust spending up or down for agencies or large spending categories in percentage or dollar increments. Ours gave users actual service funding options under each Priority Outcome and tracked their progress in closing the budget gap. The screenshot in figure 6.1 shows a few of the options we gave users.

In 2017, I was contacted by Chris Adams, the president of Engaged Public, a company that offers an interactive budget simulator called Balancing Act that is easily customized and can be used online, with mobile devices, and for live community meetings. He told me that Balanced Baltimore was one of the inspirations for Balancing Act. Now Baltimore is one of his customers.

A few years into Outcome Budgeting, we shifted gears on our community budget workshops. The budget balancing exercise focused only on the financial bottom line. It didn't connect the dots of spending, service performance, and measurable outcomes. Also, it was rooted in old-fashioned incremental budgeting, with a goal of cutting your way to balance.

Our new workshop was a simulation that condensed the six-week Results Team process into three hours. Participants sat at the Priority Outcome table of their choosing, each staffed by budget and CitiStat analysts to facilitate and take notes. The groups reviewed service proposal packets with budget and performance data and funding options, then rated and ranked the proposals and assigned dollar amounts within their allocations. These sessions were intensive, and not for everyone, but those who took part said that they had never experienced such an in-depth look at city government, even if they were tired and frazzled by the end.

Among my analysts, the Results Team workshop came to be known as the "Budget Torture Chamber," meaning, I guess, that we

Figure 6.1 Balanced Baltimore

Balanced ⚖ BALTIMORE

A Cleaner City

$20M
DEFICIT

SUBMIT BUDGET

Service	Level	Service	Level
			$18M

Environmental Health: This service is responsible for conducting inspections of food establishments to ensure a sanitary environment. Annually the service performs nearly 13,000 inspections. — **$3.4M**

Public Right of Way Cleaning: This service cleans public-rights-of-way, removes graffiti, and clears debris from storm drains to protect water quality. The service is also responsible for alley cleaning efforts.

+ $500k Add staff to provide additional licensing and regular inspections of pools and institutional facilities.

- $1.8M Charge businesses for cleaning of public space in designated business districts through a fee increase for Residential Business District Licenses.

+ $300k Purchase three compact mechanical sweepers. This would allow for a long-term reduction in alley cleaning crew size (one person crew as opposed to the current three person crew).

- $500k Eliminate Graffiti Removal services, 10 positions will be abolished. Utilize and train volunteer groups to perform this service.

Source: Baltimore Bureau of the Budget and Management Research

had made it too realistic. They decided to put some fun into budget engagement by inventing the "Budget Bazaar." In the Budget Bazaar, players are given a stack of poker chips to distribute among two dozen service buckets. During the game, budget analysts circulate around the room, handing out surprises. Lucky players might find out that income tax revenue is coming in stronger than expected, and receive an extra chip. Unlucky ones are told that a blizzard exhausted the snow fund, or police overtime is over budget, and have a chip taken away.

When everyone has spent their chips, they talk about their choices and what those choices mean for the city. Is it okay to spend heavily on youth development and almost nothing on support services such as finance, human resources, and IT? Are homeless services more important than protecting the environment? What should get more money, libraries or blight elimination? One group of high schoolers had so much fun in the Budget Bazaar, they asked if they could play again.

What I love about the Budget Bazaar is that in addition to being fun, it embodies the shifting of the budget debate that Outcome Budgeting seeks to achieve. Instead of cutting from a base budget, the players decide how to make the best use of the resources they're given. The accumulated results of past budgets are nowhere to be seen, and players are free to make their own choices. Accountability comes in when the group examines its collective allocations and discusses whether it hangs together as a sensible spending plan.

Budget Live!

Between City Hall and the Inner Harbor is Power Plant Live!, an open-air entertainment complex with trendy bars and restaurants, a concert stage, and nightclubs. It was frequently the venue for budget office happy hours (yes, budget people do get to have fun sometimes). It also has a compelling vibe that we wanted to replicate in our community engagement website. Making a city budget compelling is no easy feat, so we had to get creative with our Budget Live! online portal.

The centerpiece of Budget Live! was Balanced Baltimore. Around it we added several other interactive features: Open Budget enables users to drill into multiple years of budget data, all the way down to individual line items. Crowdsourcing questions asked residents how they would divvy up $100 among the Priority Outcomes and allowed them to give feedback and respond to others. A video and infographic explained the budget shortfall. I will forever be envious of Round Rock, Texas's Purrrrr-fect Budget Video (you can find it on YouTube), but we didn't need those kind of theatrics to bring thousands of residents into the budget conversation.

Budget Pop-Up

Attendance at Taxpayers' Night always depended on what was (or wasn't) in the budget. In the depths of the Great Recession, when service cuts and tax hikes were on the table, we filled the War Memorial's one-thousand-seat "banquet hall" to overflowing. As economic turmoil receded, so did the crowds. After a Taxpayers' Night at which only one resident spoke—about funding for a skateboard park—we decided it was time to spice things up.

Kirsten Silveira was the budget office's own Leslie Knope. Like Amy Poehler's fictional character in the TV sitcom *Parks and Recreation*, Kirsten was smart, cheerful, and unabashedly dedicated to public service. She made no secret of her ambition to be a city manager one day, and she eagerly took on tasks that others shied away from, including handling the most difficult agency accounts, coordinating budget book publication, running our website, and organizing community engagement. It was Kirsten's idea to turn the first hour of Taxpayers' Night into an educational event, which she dubbed the "Budget Pop-Up."

The Pop-Up started out as a sort of budget science fair, with poster sessions about funding for each Priority Outcome. Attendees were given a passport, and if they filled it with stamps for visiting every Outcome, they got tchotchkes donated by city agencies, such as water bottles, seed packets, and reflective tape.

Over the course of five years, the Pop-Up has taken on a life of its own and given Taxpayers' Night new life. In 2018, more than thirty city agencies sponsored information tables and the event featured music by the Baltimore Symphony Orchestra and cooking demonstrations.

You might be wondering what we did with all the input we gathered from residents. Each year, we compiled it and gave a report to the mayor during budget "tollgate" meetings, when funding recommendations were discussed. We also let residents know that their feedback didn't go into a black hole. For example, the Fiscal 2013 community budget guide included a two-page spread called "Listening to Citizens." That spread is reprinted in appendix C. It shows the services that participants in that year's budget workshops most wanted to cut and keep, and the extent to which the mayor's proposed budget reflected these recommendations.

The banner above all our community engagement efforts read, "Your City, Your Budget." As long as you have a structured budget decision-making process, you can never have too many voices at the table. More voices equals more ideas, more credibility, and more trust. Just as we widened the circle of the budget debate, we also widened our thinking about how to drive innovation in city government. In the next chapter, you will learn about what we did when we realized that Outcome Budgeting wasn't enough.

FIVE TAKEAWAYS

1. Outcome Budgeting changes budgeting from a numbers game into a strategic endeavor. To do it well, you will need to **open up the budget process to more people inside the organization.** They know how services work and how to make them work better, and they ask questions that finance folks would never think of.
2. Community engagement is not outsourcing budget decision-making to an ill-informed public. **Its value is in educating residents about the government's budget and building trust in whatever decisions are ultimately made.**
3. Bringing residents into the budget process should go beyond "open mike" town hall meetings. **Put residents in the shoes of their elected officials, and let them grapple with the difficult choices needed to balance the budget and achieve better outcomes.**

4. Budget engagement is a playground for innovation. **Continually refresh your engagement offerings, in person and online, to keep residents coming back.**

5. Use the input you receive from the public. Make it part of your budget decision meetings and **report back to residents on what you heard and what you did.**

FIVE QUESTIONS

1. In your mind, what are the three most important purposes of involving residents in a local government budget process?

2. Attend a local budget engagement event or try an online budget game (for whatever city or county you want). What did you learn? If you had to make budget trade-offs, which ones were the hardest for you? How could the experience have been improved?

3. Design your own budget engagement event or tool, based on what you would consider a fun and meaningful way for residents to have input on a city budget.

4. What are the limitations to public participation in budgeting?

5. Read budget publications from two local governments and compare them. Which was more accessible and understandable and why? How could they have been more accessible and understandable to you?

FIVE RESOURCES

1. To get a look at how Baltimore's Community Guide to the Budget was transformed to break the Curse of Knowledge, check out the Fiscal 2015 and 2016 versions at bbmr.baltimorecity.gov/budget-publications. You can also check out Baltimore's other budget publications.

2. Baltimore's Open Budget site is at openbudget.baltimorecity.gov.

3. Ebdon, Carol, and Franklin, Aimee. (2006). "Citizen Participation in Budgeting Theory." *Public Administration Review* 66(3): 437–47. This is an academic perspective on community budget engagement, coauthored by Carol Ebdon, who steered Laura Larsen (who you met in chapter 4) to Baltimore.

4. To see the latest technology for public budget participation, visit www.abalancingact.com.

5. Fenton, Justin, and Hermann, Peter, "Mayor Calls Occupy Baltimore Eviction 'Respectful'," *Baltimore Sun*, December 13, 2011. This article looks back at the controversy surrounding Occupy Baltimore's three-month encampment. Dozens of Occupy Baltimore protestors participated in one of the Fiscal 2012 budget workshops.

7

The New Status Quo?

■ ■ ■

OUTCOME BUDGETING REPLACES a status quo budget process that has outlived its usefulness. So what happens when Outcome Budgeting becomes the status quo? This question started nagging me as soon as we finished the first budget cycle. So did another: Is it enough to be better than the old status quo?

I have seen my share of management initiatives (okay, "fads"), and I know that after they pick off the low-hanging fruit, they can become huge time sucks with diminishing returns. In the first go-round, Outcome Budgeting had sorted the city's services based on their value, enhanced some, purged others, and uncovered novel ways to get more results at less cost. As I looked to the future of Outcome Budgeting in Baltimore, my rationale for sticking with it was that there was more fruit within reach. I believe the budget process has power to encourage innovative thinking—about how to improve service performance and achieve important citywide outcomes.

By nature, I am not 100 percent sure of anything. I always see the other side, the counterargument, the gray area. In this case, I realized that even the best budget process in the world didn't have the power to put innovative ideas into the heads of hidebound agency leaders. Even those who wanted to innovate could use help to conceive and implement new solutions. This chapter is about some of the spin-offs from Outcome Budgeting that got the creative juices flowing in

Baltimore: the Innovation Fund, the Good Government Book Club, Lean Government, and the Idea Lab.

INVESTING IN INNOVATION

Thanks to the Government Team you met in chapter 4, Mayor Rawlings-Blake was persuaded to create the Innovation Fund in 2012. From a budget that included service reductions, layoffs, furloughs, and deferred capital spending, she carved out $2 million to start a revolving loan fund for agency projects that would improve customer service and either reduce operating costs or generate new revenue for the city. Some council members argued that $2 million could spare forty city jobs from being abolished, but the mayor insisted that the fund would more than pay for itself in the long term.

The mayor was right. In five years, the Innovation Fund has made loans totaling $6.5 million to a dozen projects, ranging in cost from $100,000 to $2 million, and the return on investment has far exceeded the up-front seed money. Nearly a third of the loans have already been repaid, and the city council has continued to appropriate new dollars to the fund every year.

When the mayor asked agency heads to submit the first round of loan applications, they replied enthusiastically, sending my office thirty-six of them. We had enlisted a loan committee made up of a retired bank president, a tech entrepreneur, and a foundation head. They were tough customers, and they green-lighted only three projects, the ones they thought were ready to implement and had a good chance of success.

The first loan to close was for putting the housing department's development plans review process online. ePlans, as it was called, cut through a slow, cumbersome series of sequential approvals by as many as a dozen different offices. I remember seeing clerks wheeling garbage cans stuffed with blueprints from one office to the next. For developers ready to break ground, time is money, and they were more than willing to pay $100 to expedite plans approval (and avoid the cost of large format printing). ePlans has sped up approvals, cut data entry and "transportation" costs, and paid for itself from submission fees.

My favorite Innovation Fund project is the smallest loan we made. Camp Small is a twelve-acre tree waste collection yard located in the Jones Falls Valley that bisects the city. Every day, city tree crews dump fresh trimmings and felled trunks at the site. In 2016, the sustainability office and Department of Recreation and Parks put their heads together and came up with a plan for turning the massive piles of waste into wealth. With $100,000 for a contract yard master and equipment rental, recreation and parks has produced mulch for sale to residents and auctioned the logs to local sawmills.

"A tree, like every living thing, is a resource in life and death," says Shaun Preston, the Camp Small yard master. Since the Camp Small Zero Waste initiative began, fallen trees have been turned into nature playspaces, whiskey barrels, art, furniture, outdoor seating, and even ox yokes. In late 2017, forty urban trees were processed into more than 15,000 square feet of kiln-dried tongue and groove boards that will be used to clad the walls of a city recreation center.

Photo 7.1a Camp Small Before *Source:* Shaun Preston, Camp Small Yard Master

Photo 7.1b Camp Small After *Source:* Shaun Preston, Camp Small Yard Master

Lots from a Little

For my money, Baltimore's most innovative agency head is its parking director, Pete Little. We share much in common, including the same last name—mine in German, his in English—and a love for reading books about leadership and management. Pete's favorite is Simon Sinek's *Leaders Eat Last*, and when he calls himself a "servant leader," he isn't kidding. When I met him at parking authority headquarters for our interview, I found out that he had turned his spacious office into a break area for staff and taken a small desk in the corner of a back room, alongside employees far below him on the org chart. Ever fastidious (he organizes his sock drawer by type of sock), Pete says of the move, "The larger your office, the more crap you collect. Having a smaller space has forced me to simplify."

One thing he will never get rid of is a picture he keeps at his desk of a young boy using crates to make his away across a big puddle. It reminds him that "if you are creative and persistent, there is always a way to get to where you want to be." I'm sure it also reminds him of all he has done to turn a corrupt, incompetent parking operation into a customer-friendly cash cow for the city. His story, including his use of the Innovation Fund, might change the minds of those who don't think government can operate efficiently and with integrity.

Pete grew up on what he describes as a "small farm slash large vegetable garden" in southeastern Massachusetts, just west of where the Pilgrims landed on the *Mayflower*. He became interested in public affairs in part because of his father's civic-mindedness. His father served on a commission to protect cranberry bogs, built trails to help preserve wooded areas of the town, and started the local recycling program. Pete remembers spending many Saturdays at the recycling center, sorting glass bottles by color, stacking newspapers, and crushing cans with a device his father had invented.

After graduating from college, Pete entered Georgetown Law School, envisioning a career in international diplomacy. Struggling to pay tuition, he left after the first semester with the intention of earning some money and reenrolling. He never went back, instead working his way up to be the manager of a sporting goods store.

The parking business was a fluke. Married with children and tiring of retail hours, Pete answered a blind ad for management. When he arrived for the interview and realized it was with a parking company, he was halfway out the door when the HR director grabbed him and offered him the job.

Pete was a vice president overseeing the mid-Atlantic region for the nation's largest parking operator when he was recruited to run Baltimore's parking authority. He had plenty of reasons to say no. For starters, the authority had already gone through three directors in its first two years of existence, and the pay couldn't match his private-sector salary. Thankfully, he had more reasons to say yes. Less travel and a shorter commute meant he could coach his kids' baseball and softball teams, and he still had the itch for public service.

It was quickly apparent that the parking authority needed a complete overhaul. Not only were employees not doing their jobs, but they were also giving away free parking to politicians, issuing no-bid contracts to friends, and stealing money for themselves. Overtime was out of control, the garages were dirty and dangerous, and vendors were threatening to walk away unless they got paid on time. When Pete tried to follow the line of accountability for this disaster, he found it went nowhere.

"I almost got fired in my first year," he recalls. "Once I started weeding out the bad actors, their political friends came after me." Pete survived by telling the authority board and City Hall leadership that he wasn't a quitter but would only stay if he could run the organization the right way. And boy, did he ever.

After shifting the authority's mission from providing affordable parking to giving taxpayers the highest return on their investment, Pete methodically cleaned up the garages, upgraded meter technology, and put a capital improvement plan in place. His list of accomplishments is almost endless, but the bottom line sums it up: In thirteen years, Pete has more than doubled garage income and quintupled meter income. More importantly to him, he has increased the availability of parking spots, which is a boon to the city's economy.

With the garages and meters working well, Pete turned his attention next to surface parking lots. Over the years, the parking authority took on management of seven lots that other city agencies had more or less neglected. The lots were in sorry condition and generated paltry revenue. Pete saw a business opportunity and went to the Innovation Fund for a loan. In four years, the parking authority spent $235,000 to remove trash and debris, resurface and restripe lots, install fencing and lighting, upgrade signage, landscape, and modernize meters. The refurbished lots attracted dozens of new monthly contract parkers, even at a higher price point, and revenue more than doubled.

Something else happened that wasn't expected. The lots changed from being eyesores that people avoided to community assets. Northeast Market, in the Middle East neighborhood not far from Johns Hopkins Hospital, had a reputation for nasty traffic and few parking options. The Innovation Fund project added capacity to a lot nearby and made parking easier and safer, much to the delight of the market's merchants.

The Waverly neighborhood got a similar boost. Located a few miles north of downtown, Waverly started as an enclave of summer cottages for the city's wealthy, but since the late sixties it has struggled against white flight, crime, and, in 2001, the demolition of nearby Memorial Stadium when the Ravens football team moved to new digs closer to the Inner Harbor. For its rebounding commercial district and popular farmers market, a more welcoming parking lot represented an opportunity. The local business association leveraged the parking authority's investment to get grant funding for beautification and signage. According to Michelle Bond, a member of the farmers market board, "The parking lot renovation showed that something was going on here. Even simple things like painting new lines made people say, 'Wow! This is a place where I want to spend my time. This is a place where I want to spend my money.'"

To see a short video about the parking authority's Innovation Fund project, you can go to budget.baltimorecity.gov/innovation-spotlight-videos.

WHAT ARE YOU READING?

Another reason I think the world of Pete Little is that when I started the Good Government Book Club (GGBC) in 2010, he was one of the dozen or so people who showed up, and then he kept showing up, missing only one brown bag over the next six years. Pete takes reading to a whole new level; he would come to the meetings with pages of handwritten notes, which he summarized to help him absorb the key points.

The GGBC exemplifies the culture of learning and continuous improvement that Outcome Budgeting needs to thrive. The books we read, which are listed in box 7.1, covered topics ranging from teamwork (*The Boys in the Boat*) to communication (*Made to Stick*) to the history of housing discrimination in Baltimore (*Not in My Neighborhood*).

Box 7.1 | Good Government Book Club Selections

GGBC Selections (in no particular order)

Extreme Government Makeover: Increasing Our Capacity to Do More Good by Ken Miller

Citizenville: How to Take the Town Square Digital and Reinvent Government by Gavin Newsome and Lisa Dickey

The Ten Faces of Innovation: IDEO's Strategies for Beating the Devil's Advocate and Driving Creativity throughout Your Organization by Tom Kelley and Jonathan Littman

Trying Hard Is Not Good Enough: How to Produce Measurable Improvements for Customers and Communities by Mark Friedman *Made to Stick* by Chip and Dan Heath

Drive: The Surprising Truth about What Motivates Us by Daniel Pink

A More Beautiful Question: The Power of Inquiry to Spark Breakthrough Ideas by Warren Berger

Many Unhappy Returns: One Man's Quest to Turn Around the Most Unpopular Organization in America by Charles O. Rossotti *Triumph of the City* by Edward Glaeser

If We Can Put a Man on the Moon . . .: Getting Big Things Done in Government by William Eggers and John O'Leary

Change or Die: The Three Keys to Change at Work and in Life by Alan Deutschman

The Human Side of Budgeting: Budget Games and How to End Them by Scott Lazenby

Moneyball: The Art of Winning an Unfair Game by Michael Lewis *A Prayer for the City* by Buzz Bissinger

The Fifth Discipline: The Art and Practice of the Learning Organization by Peter Senge

The Responsive City: Engaging Communities through Data-Smart Governance by Stephen Goldsmith and Susan Crawford

The Ethics of Dissent: Managing Guerrilla Government by Rosemary O'Leary

The Solution Revolution: How Business, Government, and Social Enterprises Are Teaming Up to Solve Society's Toughest Problems by William Eggers and Paul Macmillan

The Boys in the Boat: Nine Americans and Their Epic Quest for Gold at the 1936 Olympics by Daniel James Brown

Leaders Eat Last: Why Some Teams Pull Together and Others Don't by Simon Sinek

Peak Performance: How Denver's Peak Academy Is Saving Money, Boosting Morale, and Just Maybe Changing the World (and How You Can, Too) by Brian Elms and J. B. Wogan

Predictably Irrational: The Hidden Forces That Shape Our Decisions by Dan Ariely

Comeback Cities: A Blueprint for Neighborhood Revival by Paul

Grogan and Tony Proscio
Not in My Neighborhood: How Bigotry Shaped a Great American City by Antero Pietila
Mayor: The Best Job in Politics by Michael A. Nutter
The Color of Law: A Forgotten History of How Our Government Segregated America by Richard Rothstein

From the beginning, I knew that the book club was more than just a lunch break confab. The first book was *Extreme Government Makeover: Increasing Our Capacity to Do More Good* by Ken Miller, which I referenced in chapter 3. Its central point is that government dysfunction is not a people problem, but a process problem, and it explains how to "straighten the pipes" of complicated and inefficient services. At the inaugural meeting, one participant announced, "I've been a manager in Baltimore city government for ten years, and this is the closest thing I've ever had to management training." Another, a veteran fiscal manager who was a hard-bitten skeptic of Outcome Budgeting and generally hostile toward change of any kind, floored me when she said, "This book was a revelation for me. I can't wait to take these ideas back to my agency."

When a reporter from *Governing Magazine* interviewed me about the GGBC, she wanted to know how the book club was improving city government. I told her that *Extreme Government Makeover* was part of our journey toward Lean Government, which is discussed later in this chapter; *Citizenville* by Gavin Newsome and Lisa Dickey had encouraged us to put more citizen engagement tools online; *The Ten Faces of Innovation* by Tom Kelley and Jonathan Littman changed how our General Services department designed workspaces; and *Trying Hard Is Not Good Enough* by Mark Friedman turned out to be the missing link between Outcome Budgeting and CitiStat, which is the subject of the next chapter.

I like to think that the book club improved city government in a million smaller ways, too, by bringing people together around new ideas, showing them that change is possible, and giving a little kick to the shins of an insular organization that tends to believe that "Baltimore is different."

I asked Pete Little to name his three favorite GGBC selections (besides *Leaders Eat Last*). Here are the ones he chose:

Drive: The Surprising Truth about What Motivates Us by Daniel Pink

Drive is about a mismatch between what science knows and what business does when it comes to motivating employees to perform better. Pink reviewed the research and found that traditional "carrot and stick" incentives, like monetary rewards, are ineffective and even counterproductive for nonroutine work. The reason is that pursuing incentives for measurable tasks or benchmarks narrows our focus and thinking. We might work harder, but not smarter.

To bring out the best in the people doing most twenty-first-century jobs, Pink tells us to nurture three sources of intrinsic motivation:

> **Autonomy**—We want to direct our own lives and that includes our work.
> **Mastery**—We want to get better and better at what we do.
> **Purpose**—We want to be part of something larger than ourselves.

Pete thinks about these motivations constantly. He equipped his parking meter technicians with laptops so they could self-direct their daily work instead of being dispatched by the central office. They are accountable for meter uptime and are free to decide how best to meet Pete's standard. He emphasizes training to make sure his employees are up to date with the latest thinking in parking management. He is ever-conscious of talking to his team about the parking authority's goals and their individual roles in achieving them.

A More Beautiful Question: The Power of Inquiry to Spark Breakthrough Ideas by Warren Berger

This book would make my top three also. Berger explains that from infancy, humans use questions to learn about the world around them, but that questioning declines with age and is often discouraged in our schools and workplaces. Every innovation starts with a question. Asking "Why?" and "How?" and "What If?" can lead to unexpected insights. It sounds simple, but good questioning requires putting aside "the way things are," asking the "dumb" questions, using our imaginations, and digging deep to get the heart of the matter. A popular method for digging deep is called "The 5 Whys." As the name suggests, it involves repeating the question "Why?" to get to the root cause of a problem. Here's what "The 5 Whys" looks like for a problem many cities face:

Why is the city's recycling rate so low?
Because residents throw a lot of recyclable material into the trash.
Why do residents throw a lot of recyclable material into the trash?
Because they find recycling inconvenient.
Why do they find recycling inconvenient?
Because recycling requires separating plastic, glass, and paper.
Why does recycling require separating plastic, glass, and paper?
Because the city doesn't offer single stream recycling.
Why doesn't the city offer single stream recycling?
Hmmm . . .

The recycling problem could generate many lines of questioning; this is just one. "The 5 Whys" is a great technique for finding the new solutions we are looking for in Outcome Budgeting.

Berger has a website, AMoreBeautifulQuestion.com, where among other things he promotes Question Week, which is scheduled for the third week of March each year to correspond with Albert Einstein's birthday. A few years ago, the Baltimore budget office celebrated Question Week with a Questionstorming session, one of Berger's suggestions for kick-starting constructive inquiry. Instead of throwing out ideas, we came up with fifty questions related to how we could have more impact on the city's performance and outcomes. We later voted on the most important five questions for further work. They included, "How can we help agencies write better budget proposals?" and "Why do we have to approve routine purchase requisitions?"

Many Unhappy Returns: One Man's Quest to Turn Around the Most Unpopular Organization in America by Charles O. Rossotti

Pete found this book after calling the Internal Revenue Service (IRS) with a complicated tax problem and being delighted by the customer service he received. Rossotti was the IRS commissioner from 1997 to

2002. When he took over, the IRS had the largest number of customers and lowest approval rating of any institution in America.

"This book," writes Rossotti, "is a way for me to state my deep conviction that any organization, even a tax collection agency, can serve its stakeholders at higher levels than it ever imagined—if its leaders resolutely and passionately set out to do so." Under Rossotti's leadership, the IRS overhauled its massive 1960s-era computer systems, cut management layers, established accountability measures, reoriented itself toward its customers, and improved tax compliance at the same time. The book is chock full of vivid, detailed, and often humorous accounts of Rossotti's efforts to reshape the IRS bureaucracy, battle naysayers within the administration, gain cooperation from a fed-up Congress, and get to know his taxpayer customers.

Rossotti was the first businessperson to run the IRS. A cofounder and CEO of American Management Systems, which helped companies implement technology, Rossotti ends his book with nine principles of successful organizational change, which I will summarize:

1. Reject the idea that you have to choose one set of stakeholders over another, such as shareholders versus employees or, in Rossotti's case, taxpayers versus the Treasury.
2. Get the right people in the right jobs.
3. Get the right measures and incentives in place.
4. Update technology to meet the current needs of your customers.
5. Know what is really going on at the front lines, where real employees deal with real customers.
6. Communicate openly and honestly inside and outside the organization.
7. Make change, don't just communicate about change.
8. Understand that good governance, leadership, and direction is more important than rules and mandates.
9. Work first on the things you can control, then take on the larger issues that impact your organization. Rossotti knew that the entire tax system needed fixing, but he kept his focus on the operations of the IRS. By the time he left, customers surveyed by *USA Today* reported that they were more satisfied with service from the IRS than service from McDonald's. It was a start.

Over the years, Pete tried to persuade other agency heads to join the GGBC, but they would beg off, saying they were too busy to read.

Purveyors of speed-reading courses tell us that top CEOs read a book a week. I'm sure that's an exaggeration, but it is true that many "ultra-successful" people—Bill Gates, Warren Buffett, and Elon Musk, to name a few—make time to read for education and self-improvement. By one estimate, a book a week breaks down to forty-five minutes of reading a day. That seems like a reasonable investment of time to gain knowledge that will help you get better results for city residents. Maybe a book about time management should be part of Baltimore's onboarding program for new executives.

LEAN ON ME

I had never heard of "Lean" before I saw the Government Team's Cause-and-Effect Map that I showed you back in chapter 4, but I got up to speed quickly. It turns out that Lean started in Toyota's factories in the 1950s. By understanding their product's "value stream" from raw materials to the customer experience, and cutting out wasteful steps, Toyota modernized Henry Ford's assembly line and manufactured high-quality cars at low cost. Toyota's success explains why Baltimore's General Motors plant closed in 2005 (the site is now home to an Amazon distribution center) and why Lean business process improvement has made its way into government.

After researching Lean, I was convinced it would help agencies get more value out of their services in ways Outcome Budgeting couldn't. Outcome Budgeting gives agencies direction and incentive to innovate; Lean provides the tools. I also liked that Lean relies on the people who actually do the work to figure out how to do it better.

My first step in promoting Lean was a meeting with the city's union leaders. They were instantly suspicious that this was another one of the budget director's cost-cutting schemes, though after I assured them that nobody would lose their job due to Lean, they softened. The head of the local American Federation of State, County and Municipal Employees (AFSCME) chapter, a ton of bricks in a suit, with a permanent scowl, pulled me aside after the meeting and said, "I'm excited about what you're doing. My members have good ideas, but they are never asked for their opinions." These were unexpected sentiments from a man who had once carried a protest sign

depicting me with devil horns. He wouldn't have agreed with me pub-
licly about much of anything; here, he didn't have to.

With support from labor, I polled managers around city government to find business processes that needed the Lean treatment. The
first manager who raised his hand wound up fighting with Lean, then
finding "new religion" in its power to create change from within.

Epiphany

Gerald Grimes wasn't exactly sure what he was signing up for when
he volunteered for Lean, but he needed help. He runs the Northwest
One-Stop Career Center, a place where residents can go to find a job.
Many of Gerald's clients are ex-offenders looking to reenter society
and become productive citizens.

The One-Stop Center is always busy, but in the wake of the
Great Recession it was overwhelmed. Lines snaked out the door
daily, to the point where people desperate for services would give
up waiting and come back another time. Even those who made
it to the front desk and filled out the requisite paperwork had to
come back at a later date for orientation before they could see a
job counselor. Staff members were frazzled as their attention was
pulled back and forth between the people line and the phone line.
Entry of data from the paper forms that was supposed to be done
at the end of each day often didn't get done, resulting in a months-
long backlog.

Gerald hoped that a Lean "Value Stream Mapping" event would
be the solution to get people jobs faster. He wanted to provide same-
day service, but for most clients it was taking weeks. The event was
scheduled for four days in the city's brand-new Idea Lab.

The first morning of the event was devoted to training the team
about Lean thinking. When Gerald heard the facilitators say that
Lean is about finding and eliminating waste, he found himself getting
defensive. "I pride myself on program development," he says. "When
they started talking about waste, it grated on me. It felt like they were
telling us that what we were doing was all wrong."

"Then we did the Waste Walk," he remembers.

On the Waste Walk, Gerald was able to observe the One-Stop operation through the eyes of a Lean expert, and he had an "epiphany."

"I realized that I had to purge my own feelings," he told me. "Lean was not attacking what we had built, it was trying to make it better."

All of his life, Gerald has proved doubters wrong. He credits his faith and family. As a boy growing up in south Baltimore, he had to be resourceful. In the winter, he and his friends would sled down Federal Hill on metal wringer washer tops. In the summer, he would be lowered down by his ankles to retrieve kickballs that had bounced into the Inner Harbor. "I was the only one who knew how to swim, but honestly, the harbor was so scuzzy, it looked like you could walk on it," he jokes.

When he was seven years old, Gerald and a friend built a shoeshine box so they could make money to go to the movies. It was 1963, and Gerald remembers standing in line one day to see a surf movie starring Frankie Avalon and Annette Funicello. As he was admiring the movie poster, with beachgoers frolicking among the waves, an old lady behind him said, "That's not for you. Do you see any little colored boys on that poster?" Gerald was so crushed by these words that he ran straight home. His father found him on the back steps, sobbing and pulling at his skin.

Gerald's father always had good advice ("I've got his speeches numbered," Gerald says). On this day, he gave Gerald a simple message: "People will always make you doubt yourself, but you can do whatever you want." Today, Gerald wonders whether that old lady was a blessing or a curse. "Ever since then, I have been doing everything a little colored boy is not supposed to do." That included going away to Beloit College in Wisconsin, where he was one of 45 black students out of 1,500, then returning to his hometown to help people get jobs.

The last afternoon of the four-day Lean event was a "report out," when the team would describe the new business process and implementation plan to the department director and other senior executives. As I walked from City Hall to the Innovation Lab, I was nervous. I had sold Lean hard and had a lot riding on its success. The moment I walked into the Lab, I could feel the positive vibe. There was a cake on the table, and team members were smiling and talking excitedly. They were ready to celebrate. It turned out to be one of the best days of my career.

Gerald and his team had figured out how to give their customers same-day service, eliminate the data entry backlog, and make their jobs less stressful, all with a few commonsense process changes. They would split the line in two, one for new and one for returning customers. A greeter would check customers in and give them a number. Staff at the front desk would enter customer data on the spot; no more paperwork. The security officer would handle the phone. They would make an orientation DVD so customers wouldn't have to come back for the weekly live session, which was often booked solid. Their first rough sketch of the new process is shown in figure 7.1.

The new process worked so well that Lean thinking has permeated the Office of Employment Development (OED). OED has revamped its case management system, sped up registration for the youth summer jobs program, and more.

"A lot of what we do in government is bureaucratic nonsense," Gerald says. "Lean makes us ask ourselves why we do things and if they are really necessary."

If you'd like to see a short video about Gerald's Lean project, you can find it at budget.baltimorecity.gov/innovation-spotlight-videos.

HOME OF BRAVE THINKERS

To get Lean going in Baltimore, I enlisted the help of my counterparts in Human Resources, IT, and CitiStat. We all agreed that if we were going to lock people in a room for four straight days to revamp a business process, it couldn't be a drab, windowless conference room with bad lighting and mismatched chairs. The Idea Lab was born.

The Idea Lab started as a space designed for Lean events and other creative gatherings, like brainstorming sessions, strategic planning powwows, and Outcome Budgeting conferences. We equipped it with everything you need to get the right side of the brain activated: wall-to-wall whiteboards, a butcher paper dispenser, a lifetime supply of sticky notes, a basket full of stress balls, and, of course, a coffee maker.

The Idea Lab became something more than a cool meeting room. It became a brand, representing how the city's various management initiatives can work together. We envisioned CitiStat data reviews

Figure 7.1 One-Stop Center Process Drawing

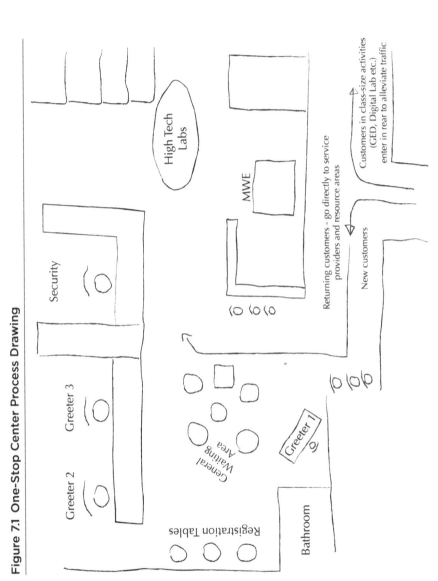

High Tech Labs

Security

Greeter 3

Greeter 2

Registration Tables

General Waiting Area

Greeter 1

Bathroom

MWE

Returning customers - go directly to service providers and resource areas

New customers

Customers in class-size activities (GED, Digital Lab etc.) enter in rear to alleviate traffic

Source: Baltimore Bureau of the Budget and Management Research

Photo 7.2 Idea Lab logo *Source:* Baltimore Bureau of the Budget and Management Research

zeroing in on business processes in need of Lean, and Lean events leading to Innovation Fund proposals. We also saw the opportunity to apply Lean more broadly. Lean is usually associated with streamlining manufacturing operations or administrative procedures, but its problem-solving methods can be applied to citywide outcomes, like reducing domestic violence, improving urban mobility, and expanding affordable housing. I will build on that thought in the next chapter.

Our logo for the Idea Lab, shown in photo 7.2, is a mini history lesson about Baltimore. In the middle is the Battle Monument, which was completed in 1825 as a memorial to soldiers who died in a series of War of 1812 battles in and around Baltimore during September 1814; their names are listed on the cords that bind the monument's column. The monument has been depicted on the city's seal since 1827.

The most famous battle that September was the Battle of Baltimore. The pentagonal star around the monument on the logo represents Fort McHenry, which withstood the British Navy's bombardment and protected Baltimore Harbor on September 13 and 14. Watching the battle from a truce ship was Francis Scott Key, a Washington lawyer who was negotiating the release of prisoners of war. Seeing an oversized American flag waving over the fort on the morning of September 14 inspired Key to write a poem, "Defence of Fort M'Henry," which was later set to music and became "The Star-Spangled Banner," America's national anthem. The Idea Lab's slogan, "Home of Brave Thinkers," refers to the last line of the anthem's first stanza, the one we sing at ball games.

Baltimoreans still celebrate the war victories with a September 12 Defender's Day holiday, and whenever a star is added to the American flag, the new flag is first flown over Fort McHenry.

The logo's background is the field of Baltimore's flag. The black-and-gold design is from the coat of arms of the Calvert family, which chartered the Maryland colony in 1632 as a haven for English Catholics in the New World. The city is named after Cecil Calvert, second Lord Baltimore, who inherited the charter from his father George, but never set foot in Maryland, instead sending his younger brother Leonard to manage things. As rent, the Calverts paid the king "two Indian arrowheads annually and one fifth of all gold and silver found in the colony."

"PROTECT THIS HOUSE"

For the etymologists out there, Baltimore is an anglicization of the Irish name Baile an Tí Mhóir, meaning "town of the big house." Today, "Protect This House" is the marketing tagline of Baltimore-based sports apparel company Under Armour and rallying cry for the Baltimore Ravens professional football team. Though maybe coincidental, "Protect This House" echoes from the city's origins and its War of 1812 glory.

"Protect This House" ought to be painted on the City Hall dome, because it reflects the parochialism, even jealousy, of many of the leaders inside. Baltimore's boosters take pride in calling it "America's largest independent city." This is a trivial distinction, meaning only that Baltimore is not part of a county, but it expresses a conviction that the city can take care of its own business and suspicion of ideas from the outside. I saw these attitudes over and over again.

When I presented data benchmarking Baltimore's sanitation service against other cities to the CitiStat panel, I was pilloried for suggesting that Baltimore could be compared with any other city.

The city council president dug in his heels against selling four city-owned garages, even though the proceeds would be used to build new recreation centers. He couldn't stand the idea of outsiders buying city assets, despite numbers showing that it would be a good deal financially.

When the unrest started after Freddie Gray died in police custody, Mayor Rawlings-Blake was reluctant to ask for the governor's help in getting control of the situation. He sent in the National Guard and played the role of hero; her political career was ruined.

In his 1996 book *Baltimore Unbound: A Strategy for Regional Renewal*, David Rusk makes a bleak assessment of Baltimore's future, writing that it is "programmed for inexorable decline . . . because it must house a disproportionate share of the region's poor blacks." He writes that Baltimore, along with many other postindustrial cities, is "past the point of no return"—trapped within its political boundaries and isolated, socially and economically, from its ever-expanding suburbs. His solution is bold: a metropolitan governing body covering the city and six surrounding counties that would implement, among other things, (1) a uniform regional property-tax increment to fund scattered site public housing and a regionwide revenue-sharing program and (2) a "fair share" housing program requiring that 15 percent of new housing units be available for moderate- and low-income families, with the goal of deconcentrating poverty.

It shouldn't surprise you that Rusk's ideas went nowhere. Getting a city and its suburbs to willingly join hands in this way is almost unheard of. Suburban leaders don't want to shoulder urban problems, and city leaders don't want to cede power to anyone. The reason I bring Rusk up is that around the time *Baltimore Unbound* was published, a lawsuit was filed against the US Department of Housing and Urban Development, charging that Baltimore's public housing unfairly clustered black residents in the most impoverished, segregated parts of the city. The case eventually led to the Baltimore Housing Mobility

Program, which has voluntarily relocated thousands of poor families from the city to mixed-income suburban neighborhoods, with thousands more on a waiting list.

Instead of celebrating a solution that has dramatically improved outcomes for children who otherwise have the worst odds in the nation of escaping poverty, I have heard politicians grouse that the program "steals" kids from Baltimore and cuts the city's census count.

When "Protect This House" means protecting the way things are and repelling needed change, building a culture of innovation takes perseverance, ingenuity, and some fight. I didn't want Outcome Budgeting to be a "one-off" management initiative that came and went like so many before it, so I decided to double down by marrying it to its older cousin, CitiStat. It's not as creepy as it sounds. Read on.

FIVE TAKEAWAYS

1. Outcome Budgeting thrives on innovative ideas; without them, it is a lot of work spent sorting through the same old stuff. **In Baltimore, we never stopped looking for new ways to encourage innovative thinking.** You learned about some of them in this chapter, and there were more. For example, the TECHEALTH initiative enlists teams from Baltimore's tech and design community to help solve pressing public health problems. The first cohort of projects included a neighborhood asthma-monitoring system and an opioid overdose notification and outreach system. The winning teams received investments from the Innovation Fund to take their project from concept to implementation.

2. **Baltimore's Innovation Fund has invested in a dozen projects that improve customer service and return budgetary savings, new revenue, or both.** If you start this kind of fund in your organization, be sure to use rigorous criteria to approve investments. Also, let agencies share in the savings they produce. Before I left City Hall, I was working on an extension of the Innovation Fund I called "Shark Tank for Government." The idea was for private investors to provide seed funding for city efficiency projects and lend their expertise for project implementation. The more successful the

project, the greater the investor return. The local chamber of commerce was a willing partner.

3. **A book club is a great way to get people talking about new ideas, and it's easy to start one.** Choose a book that's not too long or technical, give people a few months to read it, reserve a conference room, bring a plate of cookies, and have a few discussion questions ready just in case!

4. **Lean business process review is the best way I know of to untangle the red tape that drives customers and employees crazy.** I have seen Lean dramatically improve service delivery, from fire-inspector productivity to on-time vendor payments to asthma program intake. Building a Lean culture means training employees to look at their work in a new way and strive for continuous improvement. Lean is about getting to the root cause of problems, which means that Lean and Outcome Budgeting go hand in hand.

5. Baltimore's Idea Lab is an inviting space dedicated to innovation. It is equipped with everything a team needs to hunker down and get creative: white boards, butcher paper, sticky notes, stress balls, coffee, and more. **Besides being functional and fun, this kind of space sends a message about your organization's values.**

FIVE QUESTIONS

1. Pete Little describes himself as a "servant leader." What does that mean to you? What leaders do you most admire? What do they have in common?

2. Read a book from the Good Government Book Club list (after you finish this one). What did you learn? How do you think the book can help government?

3. Try using the 5 Whys method on a problem in your community. You can start with something like, "Why does it take so long for an ambulance to respond to a call?" or "Why aren't third-grade reading scores higher?"

4. Charles Rossotti was the first business person to run the IRS. Do you think government should be run more like a business? In what ways is government like a business? In what ways is it different?

5. David Rusk argues for regional government to save struggling cities. Why do you think regional government is so rare? Can you find examples of where it is working? Are Rusk's ideas still relevant?

FIVE RESOURCES

1. Two articles have been written about the Good Government Book Club:
   Kerrigan, Heather, "Can a Book Club Improve Government?," *Governing*, February 12, 2014; and Massey, Wyatt, "Baltimore City Hall Book Club Lets Employees Share Ideas about Leadership, Teamwork," *Baltimore Sun*, June 24, 2016.
2. Lord, Walter. (1972). *The Dawn's Early Light*. Baltimore, MD: Johns Hopkins University Press. This is considered one of the best histories of the War of 1812 battles in Washington, DC, and Baltimore, including the attack on Fort McHenry.
3. Locher, Drew. (2011). *Lean Office and Service Simplified*. Boca Raton: Productivity Press. My Lean guru, John Beakes III of Operational Performance Solutions, recommended this book as a good primer on how to use Lean and build a Lean culture in your organization. Also, you can find a white paper on Lean Government at John's website: http://www.opsinc.com/pdf/OPS-LeanGovernmentWhitePaper.pdf.
4. If you'd like to learn more about the Camp Small Zero Waste initiative, the Institute for Local Self-Reliance published an article on its website at https://ilsr.org/baltimores-camp-small-zero-waste-initiative/.
5. Rusk, David. (1996). *Baltimore Unbound: A Strategy for Regional Renewal*. Baltimore: Johns Hopkins University Press. This book is described in the chapter. Rusk also wrote *Cities without Suburbs*, an influential book arguing that the solution to urban problems is to end the isolation of poor cities from their surrounding wealthy suburbs.

8

OutcomeStat

■ ■ ■

WHEN I SAT down with Mark Grimes in late 2014, he was looking for answers. Mark (no relation to Gerald from chapter 7) is a dead ringer for comedian Steve Harvey, but there was nothing funny about his dilemma. A few months earlier, he had been reassigned from being the top lawyer at the police department to running CitiStat. Mayor Rawlings-Blake had pushed out the previous CitiStat director and told Mark she wanted him to retool the vaunted management accountability program. The problem was, he didn't know how.

CitiStat was the legacy of former mayor Martin O'Malley. O'Malley took the NYPD's CompStat idea—intensive use of data to reduce crime—and applied it to a wide range of municipal services. The mayor himself ran many of the early CitiStat meetings, in which agency heads stood before a panel and were asked why it was taking so long to fill potholes, how to reduce the stump removal backlog, what was behind the high levels of absenteeism, and so forth. At least one agency head compared the meetings to the Spanish Inquisition, and when answers weren't forthcoming or performance wasn't improving, they could get ugly.

CitiStat became one of Baltimore's most popular tourist attractions. Mayors traveled from near and far to see what all the fuss was about, and they replicated what they saw back home. Today, you can find a variation on CitiStat in almost any City Hall. From PhillyStat to LouieStat to ChattaStat, data-driven government is now de rigueur.

Watching CitiStat fade into irrelevance was almost like watching another Baltimore legend, Colts quarterback Johnny Unitas, get shipped off to the San Diego Chargers at the end of his career. Some said CitiStat's confrontational style had become counterproductive, but the real problem was that there was no confrontation at all. As CitiStat was passed from O'Malley to Dixon to Rawlings-Blake, mayoral interest waned. Reviewing the same operational metrics week after week got boring, and when the mayor stopped showing up to CitiStat meetings, they lost their teeth.

While other cities were evolving the CitiStat model, Baltimore was clinging to O'Malley's version, but without O'Malley, it didn't really work. Mayor Rawlings-Blake wanted a new vision for CitiStat, and that's what I came to talk to Mark about.

You see, I was looking for answers, too. As I've explained, when we started Outcome Budgeting, the city had no strategic plan. That was still true five years later. The Requests for Results (RFRs) were (collectively) the closest thing we had to a strategic plan, but the heavy lifting on those had been done under the previous mayor, with limited input from agency heads, citizens, and other partners.

In the absence of a singular strategic plan, agencies were wandering off on their own. The Health Department produced a plan called "Healthy Baltimore 2015." The Planning Department got a grant to participate in the STAR Community Rating System, which involved developing a set of economic, environmental, and social sustainability measures. At one point, an intern in the mayor's office circulated a memo showing that there were four different sets of city-wide indicators floating around.

Naturally, agency heads were confused. A few had complained to me that management direction from City Hall was all over the map. For one thing, the indicators and performance measures used in Outcome Budgeting were not tracked by CitiStat, which had its own metrics. Many agencies had more or less given up hope of finding the "North Star." They were checking the boxes of the budget process, surviving CitiStat, and reacting to the latest orders from the mayor and her senior team, which often seemed to come out of nowhere.

I wanted to be the savior, of course. My proposal to Mark was that we "marry" Outcome Budgeting and CitiStat. Baltimore was seen as a leader in these two best practices, but we both knew they weren't coordinated. In the world of performance management, there is a virtuous circle called Plan-Do-Check-Adjust, which makes something that is incredibly complicated look simple. In this scheme, Outcome Budgeting straddles the Plan-and-Do steps and CitiStat straddles the Check-and-Adjust steps, as shown in figure 8.1.

Figure 8.1 Plan-Do-Check-Adjust

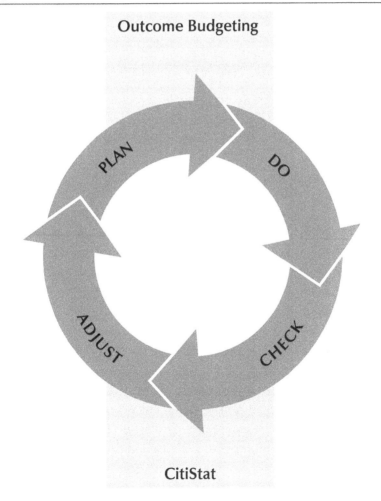

In Plan-Do-Check-Adjust, all of the steps are continuous and connected. Plans are supported by the budget, executed by agencies and partners, reviewed for measurable results, modified as needed, and round and round we go. Our circle had gaps. With no unified plan, what agencies were budgeted to do, what they were actually doing, and what CitiStat was checking were not always one and the same. The line from resources to results was broken.

At the end of the meeting, I gave Mark the book *Trying Hard Is Not Good Enough* by Mark Friedman, a recent Good Government Book Club selection that I thought provided the guidance we were looking for to complete our circle. We agreed to meet again in two weeks.

ALL THE WAY WITH RBA

For the book club meeting, we had Skyped in Mark Friedman from his home in New Mexico. Friedman spent nearly twenty years at the Maryland Department of Human Resources, including as CFO, so he knew our territory. His passion for improving the well-being of children drove him to develop a new method for achieving such improvements, which he calls Results Based Accountability, or RBA for short (in the United Kingdom, they call it Outcomes Based Accountability). Since 1996, he has worked with governments and nonprofits around the world to use RBA to produce better outcomes not only for children but also across a range of public policy issues.

What had inspired Friedman to write his book was a disconnect between resources and results very much like the one Mark and I saw in Baltimore. Friedman writes, "Fixing the formal system of government and non-profit services is not the same thing as improving the quality of life for children and families . . . We were pouring billions of dollars into social programs that claimed to be successful, and could demonstrate significant benefits, but overall social conditions for children and families were getting worse. How is it possible to have all these successful programs while conditions get worse?"

The answer is that individual government programs (or services, as we called them) are each just one part of a much larger set of solutions—going well beyond government—that need to be coordinated in order to make headway on the outcomes we care most about. These solutions can be hard to see from behind a desk in a city office building.

CitiStat wasn't helping. It was obsessed with service performance, updating hundreds of operational metrics every two weeks and asking agencies to explain the numbers, but rarely stepping back to take in the bigger picture of citywide conditions. This is why agencies could "win" at CitiStat even though the city's most pressing problems persisted. The Department of Transportation filled potholes within forty-eight hours of a complaint, while fewer than 30 percent of residents were satisfied with roadway conditions. The Department of Public Works swept thousands more miles of streets every month, but residents remained unhappy about the city's cleanliness.

Outcome Budgeting was trying to get agencies to focus on citywide outcomes. As you've learned, though, time-strapped Results Teams are overwhelmed with the task of rating and ranking the service proposals sent to them and struggle to understand how all of it fits together and what might be missing. They reward services that perform well and are logically aligned with outcomes; the question is, do their recommendations add up to a comprehensive strategy? Probably not, because nearly all the proposals they receive are from inside one organization and have only a one-year time horizon.

Outcome Budgeting and CitiStat were great leaps forward from the way city government used to be managed, when budgets were mostly self-driving and performance was not measured, much less analyzed. Friedman showed us how to take the next great leap.

The Truth about Accountability

Friedman spent his first year out of college as a high school math teacher, and in RBA, he offers a hard-headed, mathematical approach to the soft-hearted people who are trying to make communities better. Friedman calls RBA "a disciplined way of thinking and taking action"—measuring, problem-solving, and planning. Like Outcome Budgeting, it works backward from ends to means.

Friedman starts by making a critical distinction between "population" and "program" accountability. Through the lens of Outcome Budgeting in Baltimore, population accountability is government and other partners taking responsibility to improve citywide Priority Outcomes and Key Indicators. It is about reducing the number of shootings, making the water cleaner, increasing employment. Program accountability is agency heads and managers delivering services that improve the well-being of their customers.

I know I was guilty of getting these two types of accountability confused. I preached to managers that performance measurement can't stop at just those things they control. Every service (our equivalent of Friedman's "program") has a sphere of influence, which can be visualized as a set of concentric circles radiating from a core of what the service controls, like the input of how many staff are assigned to a health clinic, out to population-level outcomes such as the city's HIV infection rate. Between the core and outer reaches of the circles are measures of output (number of HIV clients treated, number of needles exchanged), efficiency (cost per HIV client treated), effectiveness (percentage of identified HIV-positive clients enrolled in care), and client outcomes (percentage of HIV clients achieving an undetectable viral load) (see figure 8.2).

My mistake was asking for services to be on the hook for measures that stretched their spheres of influence too far. In my defense, it isn't always easy to determine where service accountability ends and population accountability begins. Take police patrol for example. I think we can agree that response time to 911 calls and the number of discourtesy complaints per hundred officers are service accountability measures, but what about successful prosecution of crimes? Sure, detectives, lab technicians, prosecutors, judges, and community members also have to do their part, but the beat cop is on the front line. How about the citywide crime rate? There is no question that the crime rate is a function of many factors besides effective law enforcement. That said, policing has a large influence on crime deterrence,

Figure 8.2 Service Sphere of Influence

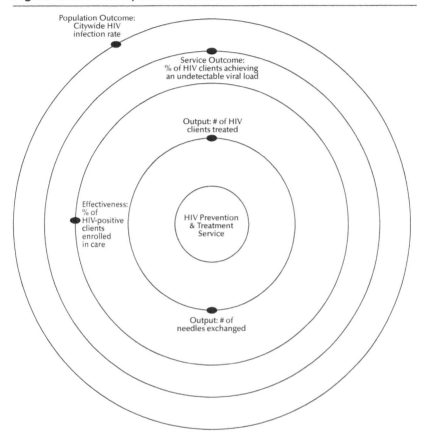

Population Outcome: Citywide HIV infection rate

Service Outcome: % of HIV clients achieving an undetectable viral load

Output: # of HIV clients treated

Effectiveness: % of HIV-positive clients enrolled in care

HIV Prevention & Treatment Service

Output: # of needles exchanged

and the police department should play a lead role in devising and implementing crime prevention strategies.

Population and service accountability are closely linked. For one thing, many city services are trying to achieve the same condition for their customers as we want for the city population as a whole, such as in the HIV example. Also, city services are key partners in the coalitions necessary to change citywide conditions on everything from crime to health to the environment, and so on. If they don't perform well, change becomes hard to achieve.

After Mark Grimes finished reading *Trying Hard Is Not Good Enough*, we met to talk about lessons learned. We agreed on two next steps. First, bring together community partners to plan for better population outcomes. Second, hold agencies *even more* accountable for the appropriate service performance measures.

Dangerous Curves

The way we would improve service performance and citywide outcomes was by using Friedman's commonsense "Turn the Curve" planning exercise. The population outcome version of the exercise is depicted in figure 8.3. Our many years of CitiStat and Outcome Budgeting had prepared us for Turn the Curve. We had what we needed to get started. For population accountability, we knew the

Figure 8.3 Turn the Curve Planning

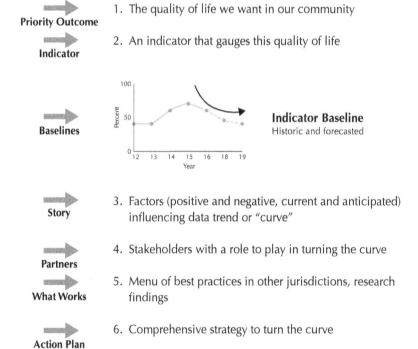

Priority Outcome — 1. The quality of life we want in our community

Indicator — 2. An indicator that gauges this quality of life

Baselines — **Indicator Baseline** Historic and forecasted

Story — 3. Factors (positive and negative, current and anticipated) influencing data trend or "curve"

Partners — 4. Stakeholders with a role to play in turning the curve

What Works — 5. Menu of best practices in other jurisdictions, research findings

Action Plan — 6. Comprehensive strategy to turn the curve

Source: Baltimore Bureau of the Budget and Management Research

Priority Outcomes we wanted to achieve and the **Key Indicators** to measure our progress. For service accountability, we had measures and targets for every service. For all of our measures, we had data.

The "Curve" in Turn the Curve is a **baseline data trend** that includes the past and the future. The past part of the curve is historical data telling us where we've been. The future part of the curve is a **forecast** of where we are going in the next five years if nothing changes. The most basic forecast simply extends the historical trend. A more sophisticated forecast takes into account what we know about how factors that influence the trend will behave in the years ahead. Forecasts are almost always wrong, but thinking about the future gives us insight about how to shape it (see figure 8.4).

Once you have plotted your curve, the question becomes, Are you okay with where it is headed? If the answer is yes, you can skip the rest of the exercise and move on to the next measure. For Baltimore's Key Indicators, the answer was invariably no; they represented the city's toughest challenges, the things we needed to make better. We

Figure 8.4 Baseline Graph

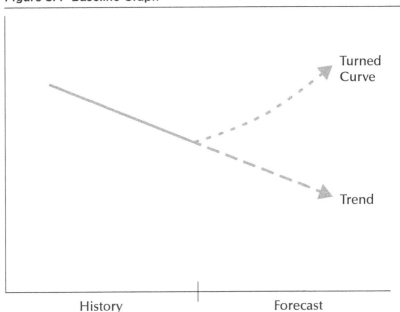

wanted to turn our curves from where they were going to a better trajectory.

Notice I didn't say turn our curves in a different direction. Sometimes, when a curve is moving in the wrong direction, the first order of business is to slow down its momentum. If our forecast is for Baltimore's drug overdose deaths to increase from 800 in 2017 to 900 in 2018, an actual result of 825 deaths would signal progress, even though it is more deaths than the year before. Some problems are like the proverbial aircraft carrier headed off course; as hard as you may work the wheel, the ship will take time to turn around.

The next step in Turn the Curve planning is to tell the **Story Behind the Curve,** which is an explanation of how you got to where you are today. What are the root causes of the rise in drug overdose deaths, for instance? This is where the Cause-and-Effect Map from chapter 4 and the "5 Whys" from chapter 7 come in handy. In writing our stories for Baltimore's Key Indicators, the array of causes and contributing factors ran from mega to micro. To take another Key Indicator, infant mortality, the factors negatively impacting the rate ranged from "High mobility rates and lack of safe, stable housing among high-risk pregnant women" to "Paper-based prenatal risk assessment, causing delays in care." Addressing the first factor might require moving Heaven and Earth, while addressing the second might require merely moving a form online.

We found that most of the thought, research, and discussion that goes into the Story Behind the Curve was already done in the forecasting step of Turn the Curve. There are bound to be disagreements in these early phases of the planning process. Some of them will be academic, such as whether high tax rates or lack of investment are more responsible for an increase in vacant and abandoned properties. Others can get personal, with root cause analysis devolving into finger-pointing about who is to blame for the city's problems. This is where Turn the Curve gets real, and that's exactly what happened in Baltimore.

Turn the Curve calls for engaging **partners** in the process, so in early 2015, Mark and I invited more than two hundred people, including city officials and external partners, to an OutcomeStat conference scheduled for September. The attendees would be organized into Outcome Leadership Teams and spend two days doing Turn the Curve planning for a total of twenty-one Key Indicators. Not to be overly dramatic, but we envisioned the conference as kicking off a revolutionary new approach to moving Baltimore forward, one that was more inclusive, strategic, and data driven. The Turn the Curve plans would inform budgeting and be monitored by CitiStat, which would open its doors for the first time to outside partners who committed themselves to helping implement the plans. Instead of one ponderous strategic plan that would gather dust, our aim was for twenty-one small, nimble, actionable plans that would be central to how the city was managed day to day.

The explosive events of April 2015 made turning curves more urgent than ever and also made our OutcomeStat work more difficult and uncertain.

On April 27, 2015, I was waiting to board a flight to Boston to speak about, of all things, voluntary payments to cities from tax-exempt nonprofit organizations, when television screens in the terminal started showing scenes of chaos on the streets of Baltimore: young men standing triumphantly atop an abandoned police car, a police van in flames, stores being looted, officers in riot gear confronted by brick-throwing crowds.

The city had been simmering for two weeks. On April 12, a twenty-five-year-old man named Freddie Gray was arrested near the Gilmor Homes public housing project on the city's west side. Eyewitnesses claimed that the police had used unnecessary force on Gray, and he died a week later from spinal injuries. Peaceful protests that started while Gray was in a postsurgery coma became disorderly after his death, culminating in the unrest on the day of his funeral that had the whole world watching.

When I returned to Baltimore a few days later, the cobblestone parking lot in front of City Hall was filled with National Guard Humvees, part of a deployment ordered by the governor to enforce a strict curfew and keep a lid on the continuing protests. On May 1, State's Attorney Marilyn Mosby stood on the steps of the War

184 ■ Chapter 8

Memorial Building and announced charges against six police officers, from illegal arrest all the way up to "depraved-heart murder." (In the end, none of the officers was convicted.)

It is hard to overstate the repercussions of the Freddie Gray unrest. It took down a police commissioner and mayor; laid bare the deep distrust of police in many Baltimore neighborhoods; cost the city tens of millions of dollars for police overtime, recovery, and legal costs, including a $6.4 million settlement with Freddie Gray's family; and precipitated a spike in murders that continues more than three years later. It also forced everyone who cared about Baltimore to ask themselves some fundamental questions, not just about policing, but also about poverty, inequality, and priorities. These questions were still fresh less than four months later when we convened for the OutcomeStat conference, as were feelings of anger and despair, which came to the surface in the Safer Streets discussions.

The thirty members of the Safer Streets Outcome Leadership Team were packed shoulder to shoulder into the dining room of a restored Civil War–era mansion on the grounds of the city's Cylburn Arboretum. Interest in the conference had swelled after the unrest, to the point that we finally had to draft a "You Can't Come" email to turn people away. The setting was lovely, but the discourse was tense as participants confronted the underlying problems that had come to a head in April.

The facilitator for the Safer Streets Team was a young consultant named Zachary Epps. A Baltimore native, Zachary grew up on the city's western edge, across the street from Baltimore County. He was not new to Baltimore politics, having interned with Mayor Dixon and been the "body man" for one of Mayor Rawlings-Blake's opponents in the 2011 election. He also felt a deeply personal connection to the issues at play in the room. As a six-year-old, he looked on as his parents were pulled from the family car and handcuffed, because police suspected the car was stolen. For much of his childhood, Zachary aspired to be an FBI agent or prosecutor so that he could deliver true justice, not just send more black men to jail. He studied criminal justice at the University of Maryland (as a Rawlings Fellow, a scholarship named for the mayor's late father) and found his calling helping public organizations work with communities.

None of his life experiences prepared Zachary for what he encountered at the conference. "It was the most contentious conversation I have ever facilitated," he remembers. Zachary explains that as a facilitator, his job is to sit "in the balcony" to get perspective on the discussion. What he saw from the balcony on the first day was ten law enforcement officials sitting together on one side of the room, setting the stage for an "Us versus Them" skirmish.

"The conversation was all about who was to blame for the unrest," Zachary told me. The participants were honest with each other, and most of their discourse was surprisingly grounded in data and research. Community members cited racial disparities in arrests and incarcerations; the police countered with statistics on crime reduction. Even still, the room was on edge. Swipes were taken at the mayor for calling the Freddie Gray rioters "thugs" (a comment she later walked back) and at a former police commissioner whose mantra was that his officers were going after "bad guys with guns."

Tempers finally boiled over when a professor from a local university stood up and yelled at the police officers, accusing them of waging a years-long war on young black men and destroying the fabric of neighborhoods. A detective rose to his feet and responded in kind, arguing that the police were in a no-win situation trying to keep order in a city rife with social dysfunction. At that point, Zachary stopped the conversation and reinforced the ground rules. His intervention shifted the tone but didn't alter the reality that the team could not reach consensus on the root causes of crime in Baltimore. Its Turn the Curve plan contained a laundry list of fine ideas, but it was not a collective action agenda.

In the months leading up to the conference, I had asked Results Team members to volunteer even more of their time to do preliminary work on the Story Behind the Curve and **What Works** steps of the Turn the Curve plan, giving the Outcome Leadership Teams a starting point. What Works is the bridge between the problem and the solution. It involves coming up with a list of possible actions that could turn the curve. The ideal What Works list runs from low-cost/ no-cost actions (my favorite kind) to "blue sky" ideas unconstrained by resource limits. It is informed by research, but not bound to what has already been tried and tested.

The Results Teams did the research. The root causes they identified in the Story Behind the Curve gave them direction. For example, the Cleaner City team determined that residents' lack of personal responsibility was one cause of the city's litter problem, so it looked into what other cities were doing to educate and motivate residents to clean up their neighborhoods. Like the other teams, they scoured the internet, trade publications, and even academic journals looking for best practices and evidence-backed interventions that Baltimore might try.

To their delight, Cleaner City Team members discovered a website that aggregates information about proven solutions to a wide range of city problems. There they found out about a Chicago initiative that had cut illegal dumping by compensating citizens who helped with neighborhood surveillance, an Indianapolis program that awarded grants to neighborhood groups for community cleanups and tree plantings, and a Houston campaign that partnered with the business community to target anti-litter messaging to neighborhoods, organize neighborhood cleanup plans, and place dumpsters in high-litter areas.

The preconference reports produced by the Results Teams were chock-full of this sort of information, about every one of the twenty-one Key Indicators. The job of the Outcome Leadership Teams was to complete the Turn the Curve plans that the Results Teams had started. This meant refining the Story Behind the Curve, brainstorming additional What Works options, and taking the final steps of (1) setting a target for where we want the curve to be in five years and (2) agreeing on an **Action Plan** for getting to that target.

You may have noticed that target setting is not part of Friedman's planning model. He cautions that unrealistic targets can breed a culture of fear and punishment around performance accountability. I agree; at the same time, I know from experience that a specific, ambitious target can focus thinking and compel action more powerfully than a general desire for improvement. Should we celebrate incremental performance gains? Sure, but incremental may not be the best we can do, and it is a disservice to Baltimore's residents to settle for inches when feet, yards, or even miles are within our reach.

Friedman offers some good advice about setting targets in a fair and useful way.

First, set targets in relation to a baseline. Doing so helps prevent the unrealistic targets that lack credibility and can kill morale when actual performance falls far short. As I explained in the opioid overdose example above, when an indicator is moving rapidly in the wrong direction, the right target, at least in the near-term, is to slow it down, not turn it around.

Second, avoid setting year-by-year targets. This is especially important when it comes to population indicators like the ones we were working on at the OutcomeStat conference. Most of Baltimore's problems were many years in the making; pretending that even our smartest plans would produce immediate, measurable progress would have been nuts.

We asked the Outcome Leadership Teams to recommend five-year targets, which would give their plans enough time to get traction, and fall beyond the mayor's term in office. You see, ordinary politicians aren't big on targets, because missed targets become campaign fodder. When Mayor O'Malley ran for governor in 2006, his opponent ran television ads criticizing O'Malley for failing to keep his pledge to bring Baltimore's homicides below 175, which he had announced when he took office in 1999. Never mind that violent crime was down some 35 percent during O'Malley's tenure, following a decade in which murders had not once been below three hundred per year.

Maybe O'Malley's target was overly ambitious, but maybe it was the reason for the city's marked crime reduction. In their best-selling book *Built to Last: Successful Habits of Visionary Companies*, Jim Collins and Jerry Porras explain that one of the things that sets visionary companies apart is the use of what they dubbed "Big Hairy Audacious Goals" (BHAGs) to stimulate progress. They compare BHAGs to President Kennedy's proclamation on May 25, 1961, "that this Nation should commit itself to achieving the goal, before this decade is out, of landing a man on the moon and returning him safely to earth." They write, "President Kennedy and his advisors could have gone off into a conference room and drafted something like 'Let's beef up our space program,' or some other such vacuous statement. Given the odds, such a bold commitment was, at the time, outrageous. But that's part of what made it such a powerful mechanism for getting the United States, still groggy from the 1950s and the Eisenhower era, moving vigorously forward."

O'Malley overcame the attack ad and won the election. As governor, he established fifteen "Strategic Policy Goals" for the state, each with a numerical target.

The Outcome Leadership Teams struggled with target setting. Except for the recycling rate, where the state had imposed a target of 35 percent, the teams had to make targets out of whole cloth. The Safer Streets Team knew that absolute targets, like zero shootings, were meaningless, but while they thought a 5 percent reduction in shootings was both ambitious and realistic, they fretted that it signaled acceptance of an unacceptable level of violence.

Some teams wanted to back into their targets by coming up with the Action Plan first and then trying to predict how the strategies in the plan would impact the indicator. The conference facilitators encouraged the teams to instead be aspirational: set targets that represent the way you want things to be in five years, then craft an Action Plan to get there. We had learned through several years of using service performance targets in Outcome Budgeting that target setting is not an exact science, and we told the teams that their targets would be adjusted over time as more data about the baseline and how the strategies were working became available.

The Safer Streets Team never held hands and sang "Kumbaya," but they were able to put their differences aside and agree on an Action Plan with strategies to reduce shootings, cut the property crime rate, and increase the percentage of residents who feel safe in their neighborhoods. Each strategy was assessed for its potential impact on turning the curve and the feasibility of its implementation, based on cost, complexity, political issues, and other factors. The Impact/

Figure 8.5 Impact/Feasibility Matrix

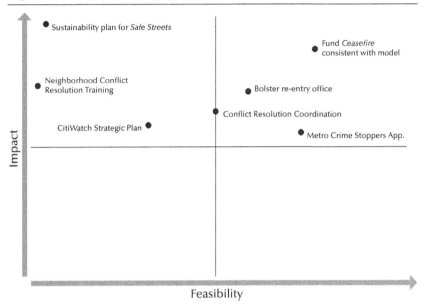

Source: Baltimore Bureau of the Budget and Management Research

Feasibility Matrix for the Number of Shootings indicator is shown in figure 8.5. Several of the team's strategies were to strengthen existing initiatives, through planning and funding. The team also came up with new ideas, such as neighborhood conflict resolution training and a Crime Stoppers mobile app to boost the number of tips and leads that help solve crimes. All of the strategies were judged to be high-impact, with some more feasible than others.

A MARKED MAN

Unfortunately, Mark Grimes did not make it to the OutcomeStat conference. In March of 2015, the *Baltimore Sun* published two investigative articles about Mark. The first article reported that the number of CitiStat meetings had been cut nearly in half from previous years, more than a third of scheduled meetings had been canceled in the past year, and not a single CitiStat report had been posted online in a year and a half. The second article reported that Mark had a contract with the state to represent disabled adults in guardianship cases and that in the first year of the contract, which included his first eight months as CitiStat director, he had billed the state for 1,079 hours of legal work. A *Sun* editorial surmised that Mark was doing his side job on city time while CitiStat "languished."

City Council members, who were not welcome in the CitiStat room and had never shown much interest in performance management, were suddenly concerned enough to hold an oversight hearing, in which they grilled Mark about the *Sun*'s findings. Mark defended himself by explaining that he was in the process of retooling CitiStat, but he was unable to give the councilmembers a timeline and didn't have a good answer for why reports hadn't been posted online.

Initially, Mayor Rawlings-Blake stood by Mark, saying she supported the changes he was making and that what he does on his downtime is his own business; she even urged councilmembers not to hold a hearing on his performance. Five months later, she fired him, telling the press through her spokesman that she "has been frustrated by the pace of change."

Less than a month before the OutcomeStat conference, CitiStat was leaderless.

Where Do We Go from Here?

City government was about to become leaderless, too.

The conference was a success. Ninety-five percent of participants surveyed said they were supportive of OutcomeStat and 88 percent said their team had accomplished its objectives over the two days. The Turn the Curve plans produced at the conference, though still works in progress, would guide the Fiscal 2017 budget build. An OutcomeStat website, to share data and analysis with the public, was just about ready to launch.

The mayor addressed the conference at lunch on Day Two, a Thursday. She told them, "My vision is a city that sets meaningful goals and diligently measures its progress in achieving results for residents, across all of our priority outcomes. You—Baltimore's thinkers and doers—play a crucial role in helping us prioritize our investments and ensure taxpayer dollars have the most meaningful impact . . . I look forward to the thought-provoking conversations, innovative ideas, and successes I know we will have in the coming months. The conference is just the beginning of what I know will be a critical component of achieving our goal of growing Baltimore by 10,000 families."

On Friday, she announced that she would not seek reelection, explaining that she wanted to spend her remaining fifteen months in office focused on the city's future and not her own. I suppose one can't help but be surprised by a forty-five-year-old politician voluntarily giving up her office, but Rawlings-Blake's announcement was not totally unexpected. She had been widely criticized for her response to the Freddie Gray ordeal and was on her heels as an unprecedented surge of violence gripped the city. One veteran political observer put it this way: "She decided she would rather quit than be fired."

Rawlings-Blake wasn't the first Baltimore mayor whose career was cut short by civil unrest. Thomas D'Alesandro III was the son of a popular former mayor and brother of Nancy Pelosi, who would become the first female Speaker of the US House of Representatives. He was younger than Rawlings-Blake when he passed on running for a second term in 1971, having seen his city devastated by a week of rioting after Dr. Martin Luther King Jr.'s assassination in early April of 1968. The 1968 riot was a grim turning point for Baltimore. It accelerated white flight to the suburbs, and hundreds of stores burned and looted in the mayhem never reopened. Many of the vacant and abandoned buildings that formed the backdrop for television coverage of the Freddie Gray unrest were vestiges of the destruction wrought nearly a half century before.

My feelings about Rawlings-Blake's decision were mixed. Part of me was sympathetic, even happy for her. She had been thrust into her job at a difficult moment and made all the right moves to restore dignity to City Hall and lead the city through the Great Recession, but I'm not sure she was ever comfortable in her role. Like me, she is an introvert, and it was pretty obvious that she preferred having her nose in a report on economic development (or her iPhone) to glad-handing with voters. Another part of me was disappointed to lose a leader who had my back on Outcome Budgeting and OutcomeStat, and my disappointment grew as it became apparent that in her long lame-duck period, she would be going through the motions. Her heart just wasn't in it. The "innovation mayor" was gone.

Engaging agency heads and community partners around the Priority Outcomes of an outgoing mayor reminded me of a coaching experience years ago. I was trying to run six-year-olds through soccer drills when an ice cream truck pulled up next to the field. Everyone was distracted and anxious to see the new flavor of the month. That day, practice was almost over, so I just ended it early. I didn't have that option with the city budget and the Turn the Curve plans.

FIVE TAKEAWAYS

1. A complete performance management program includes strategic planning, a budget process that aligns resources with strategies, and ongoing monitoring of plan implementation and actual results. If any of these pieces is missing, you won't be able to reach your performance potential. **Plan-Do-Check-Adjust should be your mantra.**

2. Strategic planning can't be something you do every five years and then lose sight of as you are bombarded by challenges and opportunities you didn't anticipate. **Strategic planning should be a continuous process of goal-setting, data gathering, partnering, and reviewing.** A rolling plan gathers no dust. Mark Friedman's Turn the Curve model takes you through the steps in a logical way.

3. **"Strategic plan" doesn't have to be singular.** Baltimore was building individual plans for each of its most important goals.

4. **Too many organizations update performance data without really knowing where they are headed and why.** Get out of this rut by thinking hard about the factors that have influenced your past performance results (the "Story Behind the Curve") and set specific performance targets for the future. Repeat this exercise regularly.

5. The measure of a performance monitoring or "stat" program is not how many meetings it holds, but whether it leads to better results. Whether it is about health inspections or kindergarten readiness,

the characteristics of an effective performance conversation are **preparation, purpose, and pointedness.** Preparation means having data about the issue at the ready and anticipating the questions the data will raise. Purpose means there is a problem to solve or target for performance improvement; these meetings should never become routine. Pointedness means that the participants are focused on the task and frank with each other about accountability.

FIVE QUESTIONS

1. What are some problems in your city, state, country, or organization that don't seem to be getting better, even though money is being spent to solve them?
2. Spend an hour with your team doing a first run-through of a Turn the Curve plan for a population indicator or service performance measure. To help you, I have reprinted a Population Turn the Curve exercise from *Trying Hard Is Not Good Enough* (see figure 8.6). You can easily adapt it for a service performance measure.
3. Go online and look at what your city is reporting about its budget and performance. What did you find informative? What was missing? What information do you need to evaluate to know if tax dollars are being used effectively to get results?
4. Put yourself in the shoes of Baltimore's Safer Streets Outcome Leadership Team. What could your community do to make you feel safer? Can police build community trust and get tough on crime at the same time?
5. Mayor Rawlings-Blake wanted to make CitiStat more collaborative and less confrontational than it was thought to be under Mayor O'Malley. Do you think she had the right idea? What do you think are the advantages and disadvantages of making performance accountability reviews more collaborative?

FIVE RESOURCES

1. Friedman, Mark. (2005). *Trying Hard Is Not Good Enough: How to Produce Measurable Improvements for Customers and Communities*. FPSI. The Turn the Curve strategic planning

Figure 8.6 Turn the Curve Exercise

Population Turn the Curve Exercise

5 min: Starting Points
- Timekeeper and reporter
- Geographic area

10 min: Baseline
- Choose an indicator
- Create a baseline with history and forecast
- Forecast - OK or not OK?

15 min: Story behind the baseline
- Causes and forces at work   Causes & partners point to action.
- Information & research agenda - causes

20 min: What works? (What would it take?)
- What could work to do better?
- Each partner's contribution
- No-cost/low cost ideas
- Information & research agenda - solutions

10 min: Report Convert notes to one-page report

Population Turn the Curve Report

Result: _____

Indicator
baseline

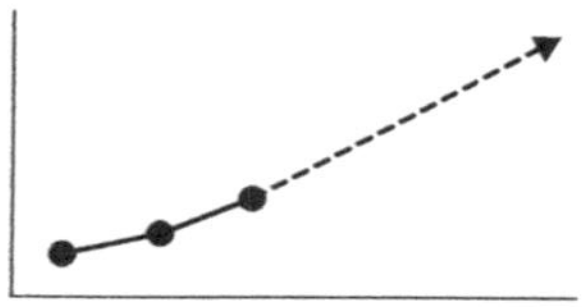

Story behind the baseline
- •
- •
- •
  (list as many as needed)

Partners
- •
- •
- •
  (list as many as needed)

Three best ideas - what works
- •
- •
- •
_____ No-cost/low-cost
_____ Off the wall

Source: *Trying Hard Is Not Good Enough: How to Produce Measurable Improvements for Customers and Communities*, by Mark Friedman

model was the missing link in Baltimore's performance management program. In 2015, Friedman published a companion to "Trying Hard" called "Turning Curves." He also has a website: resultsaccountability.com.

2. Below is a sampling of the evidence and best practices aggregation websites used by Baltimore's Outcome Leadership Teams. Evidence: evidencebasedprograms.org—This site is run by the Coalition for Evidence-Based Policy. It summarizes findings from Randomized Controlled Trials across a range of social issues. clear.dol.gov—This US Department of Labor site focuses on workforce and labor policy. crimesolutions.gov—This site is maintained by the National Institute of Justice. The address is self-explanatory. Best Practices: nycfuture.org/research/innovation-and-the-city—Center for an Urban Future published two reports spotlighting innovative policies from cities around the globe. This first report contains fifteen policies. The second volume has twenty-five more. mrsc.org—The Municipal Research and Services Center is a nonprofit organization in Washington State that compiles research and best practices for a wide variety of city services.

3. Here are two articles about the unrest that erupted in Baltimore following Freddie Gray's death in police custody. The first is from the day after the most intense rioting, the second is from a year later. Dance, Scott, "Riots Erupt across West Baltimore, Downtown," *Baltimore Sun*, April 27, 2015; and Eversley, Melanie, "One Year Later, Baltimore Still Reeling from Freddie Gray Death, Riots," *USA Today*, April 18, 2016.

4. Scharff, Michael, "Rethinking the Role of the Cabinet: Maryland's Center of Government Reforms, 2007—2012," Innovations for Successful Societies, Princeton University, http://www.princeton.edu/successfulsocieties. This article takes an in-depth look at Martin O'Malley's efforts to use the CitiStat model in state government.

5. Collins, Jim, and Porras, Jerry I. (1994). *Built to Last: Successful Habits of Visionary Companies*. New York: HarperBusiness. This book says that visionary companies set "Big Hairy Audacious Goals," something to think about when you are doing strategic

planning. "Government should be run like a business" is a common refrain. The fact is that there are high-performing organizations in every sector that mayors, governors, and other public-sector leaders can learn from. Jim Collins writes about what these organizations have in common in a thirty-five-page monograph called *Good to Great for the Social Sectors*, a companion to his acclaimed book *Good to Great: Why Some Companies Make the Leap and Others Don't.*

9

Pressing Ahead

■ ■ ■

WITHOUT MARK GRIMES and Mayor Rawlings-Blake, I felt more alone than ever, but OutcomeStat had to keep going. My team and I moved ahead on two fronts. The first front was the Fiscal 2017 budget process, where we used the population Turn the Curve plans from the conference for guidance and asked agencies to start developing service Turn the Curve plans for their performance measures. The second front came later, when we raced to take one Priority Outcome, A Growing Economy, through the remaining phases of the OutcomeStat cycle before the end of the mayor's term. We wanted her to get credit for establishing a new model for city management.

BUDGETSTAT

The Turn the Curve plans that came out of the conference were the first drafts of what were intended to be living documents. They all needed more work, particularly on the targets, prioritization of action steps, and implementation details. That said, they were loaded with ideas that agencies could use in their Outcome Budgeting service proposals. A case in point is the plan for the Citizen Perception of Cleanliness indicator, a summary version of which can be found in appendix B.

The most recent survey data showed that less than half of the city's residents rated the cleanliness of their neighborhood as "good" or "excellent." The rating for the city as a whole was below 30 percent. I mentioned in chapter 8 that the Cleaner City Team had found several examples from other cities of litter reduction strategies that were working. These examples all included public outreach and other measures to enlist the help of residents in the cleaning effort. The team's action plan called for Baltimore to do the same.

The Bureau of Solid Waste, which was part of the Cleaner Team, followed through on the Turn the Curve plan right away. The month after the conference, it launched the "Clean Corps," a volunteer initiative to organize block-by-block street and alley cleanups and persuade neighbors to take anti-litter pledges. Around the same time, the bureau proposed a $100,000 budget enhancement for an anti-litter communications campaign, which would serve as "air cover" for the Clean Corps ground attack.

In its proposal, the bureau estimated that it was spending $20 million a year to pick up trash beyond curbside collection and argued, "we cannot collect our way out of the litter problem. What is needed is a long-term, sustainable change in behavior of the littering public." It had brought together a number of nonprofits and other organizations to partner on the campaign and had raised $25,000 from private sources to test anti-littering messages and targeting strategies before the full-scale media blitz. In addition to improving residents' perception of cleanliness, the bureau was banking on the campaign to reduce 311 service request calls about dirty streets, alleys, and lots from seventy thousand to fifty thousand, which would translate into large dollar savings.

In a budget year when few enhancements were funded, the anti-litter campaign was recommended by the Results Team and approved by the mayor. Box 9.1 shows an excerpt from the Fiscal 2017 executive summary budget publication sent to the city council. It illustrates how the Turn the Curve plans were incorporated into the budget presentation. The anti-litter enhancement is highlighted.

Box 9.1 | Citizen Perception of Cleanliness

Figure 9.1 Citizen Perception of Cleanliness

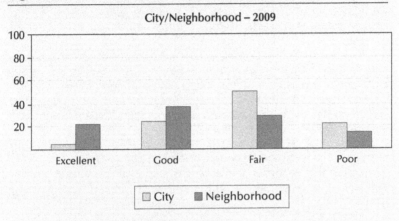

City/Neighborhood – 2009

□ City   ■ Neighborhood

Source: Baltimore Community Survey 2009

Since 2009, the city of Baltimore has administered an annual Community Survey to gauge resident perception of city services and quality of life in Baltimore. One survey question asks respondents to rank the cleanliness of their neighborhood as excellent, good, fair, or poor. Several factors have contributed to the current trend in data, including the following:

Positive Factors	Negative Factors
• Expansion of the mechanical street sweeping program within the city.	• Difficulty in citing illegal dumping violations.
• Community pitch-in and spring/fall cleanup events	• Difficulty in obtaining signage for enforcement of street sweeping parking restrictions.
	• Vacant buildings and lots.

The Fiscal 2017 recommended budget invests in numerous services and programs that will support the Citizen Perception of Cleanliness indicator.

The Municipal Trash Can Program will provide all households with a standard sized, lidded trash can. The trash cans are expected to reduce availability of food sources for rats and provide residents with individual receptacles to encourage disposal into cans and away from streets, alleys, and public right-of-way areas.

Community outreach and education through an Anti-Litter Campaign and Clean Corps, focusing on litter reduction and proper disposal of waste, reinforcing the new Municipal Trash Can Program.

The Environmental Control Board will administer an educational initiative for first-time sanitation violations, with the goal of reducing repeat violators and improving environmental awareness.

Housing Code Enforcement will implement upgrades and replacement to surveillance to better capture illegal dumping activities and improve enforcement.

Cleaning of Business Districts and Street and Alley Cleaning activities will maintain the current level of services.

Household Hazardous Waste Disposal will continue current services and collection at the Northwest Citizen Convenience Center.

Source: Baltimore Bureau of the Budget and Management Research

For the first time, we split the budget proposal process into two phases. The first phase was focused exclusively on service performance measures—updating actual data, documenting data sources, and, most importantly, using Turn the Curve planning. We asked agencies to write the Story Behind the Curve for every measure and a full Turn the Curve plan for two of the measures in each service.

Assisting our agencies was Phil Lee, a disciple of Mark Friedman and president of a local consulting firm that specializes in Results Based Accountability. Phil is from a prominent political family; his forebears include a signer of the Declaration of Independence, governors of Virginia and Maryland, and General Robert E. Lee. Phil talks like a politician himself (meaning, a lot), and he got people excited about Turn the Curve in ways I never could have.

Phil was a corporate lawyer in one of Washington, DC's largest firms when he stumbled across his real passion while doing pro bono work for a violence prevention nonprofit called Voices vs. Violence. He discovered that multiple local government agencies were working with the same troubled families but not talking to each other, which began a quest that soon found its way into a presentation by Friedman.

"I don't want to date myself," Phil laughs, "but back then Mark was still using transparencies to project his Turn the Curve charts up on the screen."

Technology has advanced, of course, and Baltimore's agencies entered their service performance information and Turn the Curve plans into a new software application called Scorecard, which is a product of Phil's firm, Clear Impact. Scorecard has become the central platform for performance measurement and management in Baltimore, fulfilling part of the vision Mark Grimes and I had for OutcomeStat, to marry CitiStat and Outcome Budgeting. As I write these words, Baltimore is well on its way to having a single set of performance measures, all in one place, used at all levels of city government.

Our hope in using Turn the Curve at the service level was that agencies would gain insight about how their services were performing, which in turn would lead to new ideas for performance improvement and more informed budget proposals. We knew not to expect too much from the one month we gave them to do their initial plans, but with Outcome Budgeting and CitiStat now connected like never before, service performance improvement—from outputs to outcomes—was going to become a year-round activity.

A great example of how a Turn the Curve plan has evolved is the Maternal and Child Health Service's measure of the "Percent of Children Receiving Home Visiting Services That Have Completed Social/Emotional Development Screenings at Recommended Intervals."

Rebecca Dineen is Baltimore's assistant commissioner for Maternal and Child Health. She explains that social/emotional screening is critical because, more than physical and speech/language screenings, "it has to do with the whole family." Screenings guide intervention, she says, and early intervention is the key to putting children on a healthy life course.

Rebecca was hired in 2008 to develop an umbrella strategy to improve birth outcomes citywide. The strategy, which came to be known as "B'More for Healthy Babies," has coordinated more than 150 collaborating organizations around evidence-based interventions and a common set of measures. The results in the first decade speak for themselves: infant mortality down by 35 percent, teen births down by 49 percent, 74 percent fewer crib deaths, and a 64 percent reduction in health disparities between black and white babies.

The use of data is in the DNA of the public health-profession, so Turn the Curve came naturally to Rebecca. She welcomed OutcomeStat, because even the Health Department needed a forcing mechanism to make the time for planning. "We are always running from one emergency to the next," she sighs.

Her plan for the social/emotional screening measure has been built over the course of three budget cycles. The latest version, which is shown in box 9.2, represents a team effort to understand why screenings dropped from 2014 to 2015 and come up with ways to get them back toward the 60 percent target. What I like about the plan is that it includes the no-cost/low-cost action step of using the B'More for Healthy Babies website to promote screenings and the "blue sky" idea of offering incentives to mothers for having their children screened. According to Rebecca, the big Turn the Curve breakthrough came from identifying pediatricians and childcare providers as partners and training them to administer the screening.

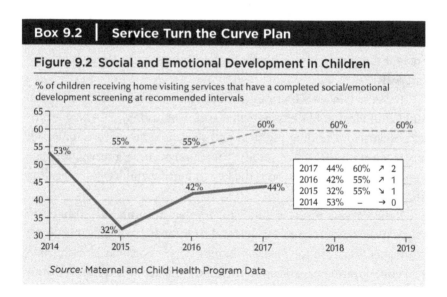

Box 9.2 | Service Turn the Curve Plan

Figure 9.2 Social and Emotional Development in Children

% of children receiving home visiting services that have a completed social/emotional development screening at recommended intervals

2017	44%	60%	↗ 2
2016	42%	55%	↗ 1
2015	32%	55%	↘ 1
2014	53%	–	→ 0

Source: Maternal and Child Health Program Data

Story Behind the Curve

- Social and emotional health and development in young children has been found to predict academic performance in the first grade over and above their cognitive skills and family backgrounds.[1]
- Young children who are on track developmentally get along well with others (parents, teachers, and peers), follow directions, identify and regulate their emotions and behavior, solve problems, persist with tasks, and engage in social conversation and cooperative play.[2] These skills are necessary for succeeding in the classroom, and their development starts in infancy and early childhood.
- One important way in which home visiting programs can have a significant positive impact on children's social and emotional health is by monitoring the social and emotional development of young children at regular intervals using the Ages & Stages Questionnaires: Social-Emotional (ASQ:SE). This screening tool is a set of age-specific behavioral questionnaires that examines a child's strengths and challenges in self-regulation, compliance, communication, adaptive functioning, autonomy, affect, and interpersonal interactions and can identify children with possible social/emotional disabilities.
- Most children with delayed social and emotional development are not identified until pre-K or later, meaning years of valuable intervention time are lost and children enter school lagging significantly behind.
- Because home visiting programs enroll families prenatally and intensively serve infants and young children, they have the ability to identify delays with the ASQ:SE and make referrals to early intervention as early as six months.
- Increasing the percentage of children that received a social/emotional development screening continues to be a priority for the Office of Maternal and Infant Care (M&I). While our screening rate has not yet reached the proposed target of 60 percent, we have seen a steady increase from 32 percent in Fiscal 2015 up to 44 percent in Fiscal 2017.
- The low percentage of children screened with the ASQ:SE at the prescribed intervals is associated with a number of compounding factors.

---

[1]Raver, C., and Knitzer, J. (2002). "Ready to Enter: What Research Tells Policymakers about Strategies to Promote Social and Emotional School Readiness among Three- and Four-Year-Old Children." *National Center for Children in Poverty.*

[2]Smith, B. J. (n.d.). "Recommended Practices: Linking Social Development and Behavior to School Readiness." *Center for Evidence-Based Practice: Young Children with Challenging Behavior.*

- Home visiting programs serve very high-risk women and families in Baltimore who are highly mobile due to housing instability. As a result, home visitors often lose contact with families and are unable to conduct assessments at the recommended frequency.
- The Nurse Family Partnership Program (NFP) requires that these assessments be done at 4, 6, 10, 12, 14, 18, and 24 months of age. Although M&I's client retention rates are fairly high and consistent with national standards, most families become disengaged before their children turn two.
- Close to 100 percent of NFP clients do receive at least one ASQ screening, and all clients are also encouraged to keep well-child visits where the pediatricians may also perform these assessments, but evidence-based model parameters can sometimes counteract a nurse home visitor's ability to do an ASQ. If a family cannot be seen in person, NFP encourages home visitors to place families on "telehealth" while they attempt to reengage them in the program for up to six months after the last contact. It can be challenging for telehealth clients to receive ASQ screenings since they must be done in person.

Partners
Pediatric providers and Baltimore Infants and Toddlers Program (BITP) play an integral role in helping to turn the curve on this measure. Nurse home visitors consider these partners as their main allies in ensuring that children are screened and then referred for any needed social emotional or developmental services.

What Works
Parents benefit from reminders outside of health care settings about the importance of having their children assessed for appropriate development.

Low-Cost/No-Cost Ideas
- Feature an "Ask about the ASQ" campaign on the B'More for Healthy Babies website.
- Advertise the benefits of the ASQ in libraries, day-care settings, churches, and schools. With funding, physical materials could be developed and disseminated in the settings listed above.

Blue Sky
- Offer incentives for clients to successfully keep ASQ appointments.

Action Plan

- Consistently monitor the number of ASQ screenings so that it is always evident when these assessments will be needed.
- When delays are suspected, seamlessly refer children for BITP services.
- Advertise the benefits of ASQ screenings.
- Explore providing incentives for keeping ASQ screening appointments.
- Train pediatric and day-care providers to administer the ASQ screenings.

With the percent of children getting regular screenings up from 32 percent to 44 percent over two years, Rebecca credits OutcomeStat for "ensuring that the conversations are happening about how to do better" and "bringing rigor to our thinking about service performance."

Here's the million-dollar question: How do we connect service performance with citywide outcomes? In Baltimore, we came at the answer from the bottom up and the top down.

Our bottom-up approach was to compile data from all the service performance measures related to each Key Indicator. The example in table 9.1 for Kindergarten Readiness includes Rebecca's social/emotional screening measure, along with several others that collectively tell a story of how well the city is doing on preparing young children for school, with traffic lights for emphasis (Green for meeting the target, Orange for improving, and Red for heading in the wrong direction). Beyond assessing performance, looking at the tables of measures is a great way to find strategic holes that need to be filled.

Our top-down approach is the population Turn the Curve plans, which aren't complete without action steps that spell out specifically what the city and others need to do to get better results, including the role of city services. The second part of this chapter is about our efforts to complete plans for the Growing Economy Priority Outcome.

Table 9.1 Service-Level Performance Measures Supporting Kindergarten Readiness

Type	Key Performance Measure	FY13 Actual	FY14 Actual	FY15 Actual	FY16 Target	FY16 Actual	Trend Indicator	FY17 Target	FY18 Target
Output	# of children receiving Early Head Start/Head Start Services	3,603	3,603	3,603	3,603	3,603	Green	3,603	3,603
	# of Library School Readiness Program participants	53,843	44,425	45,658	47,000	48,578	Green	46,600	49,000
	# of unduplicated families that receive Family League funded home visiting services	418	529	616	520	712	Green	550	1,600
Efficiency	Cost per child - City funded Head Start programs	$9,559	$9,559	$9,559	$9,559	$9,559	Green	$9,559	$9,559
Effectiveness	% of enrollment during contract period (Head Start)	100%	100%	100%	100%	100%	Green	100%	100%
	% of children receiving home visiting services that have completed social/emotional development screening at recommended intervals (Maternal & Child Health)	N/A	53%	32%	55%	42%	Orange	60%	60%
Outcome	% of 3 and 4 year olds "proficient" in each school readiness domain	N/A	N/A	93%	90%	87%	Red	90%	90%
	% of children in Family League home visiting programs who exhibit developmentally on-track social behavior, emotion regulation, and emotional well-being	100%	90%	92%	80%	90%	Orange	90%	90%

A GROWING ECONOMY

In early 2015, Bloomberg Philanthropies (ex-New York City mayor Michael Bloomberg's foundation) announced What Works Cities, which it described as "a national initiative to help 100 mid-sized American cities enhance their use of data and evidence to improve services, inform local decision-making and engage residents." It looked like an opportunity to get much-needed technical assistance for OutcomeStat, so I submitted an application, hoping Baltimore would be part of the first cohort of cities. I figured we were a can't-miss candidate. Michael Bloomberg is a Johns Hopkins alum and had given more than $1 billion to the university, starting with a $5 donation the year after he graduated and continuing with multiple gifts topping $300 million that built a school of public health, a children's hospital, and more. The man has a soft spot for Baltimore, and we were hard up.

Within days after the application deadline, I got a phone call from Zach Markovits, who was coordinating the selection process. He had a few questions for me and seemed upbeat about Baltimore's prospects. He indicated that he would follow up with another call soon, presumably to tell me that Baltimore was in. Then Freddie Gray happened, and the follow-up call never came. A few months later, Bloomberg announced the first eight "What Works Cities," and Baltimore wasn't one of them. The reason was no mystery. Bloomberg wanted to work with cities that had stable leadership, and he correctly predicted that the April unrest would be Mayor Rawlings-Blake's undoing. Fortunately, the story didn't end there.

A few months before the unrest, I had sat next to Beth Blauer on a flight back from a *Governing Magazine* conference in Louisville, Kentucky, where I had spoken on a panel about connecting budgets to results. Beth's story would make for a good movie. On September 10, 2001, she stepped in a pothole and broke her foot, which kept her home from her job in the World Trade Center the next day. After the terrorist attacks, there would be no job to go back to, so Beth and her husband moved to her home state of Maryland to regroup.

An attorney by training, Beth became a probation officer while she figured out what to do with her life. A photography project she ran for girls on probation so impressed the state's director of juvenile services that he hired her as his special assistant. When Martin O'Malley was elected governor soon after, Beth was asked to stay on as her department's chief of staff.

The new governor quickly stood up StateStat, replicating his successful CitiStat model. As in Baltimore, O'Malley ran the early stat sessions himself. From the Department of Juvenile Services (DJS), he wanted a lot of answers, from to how to reduce out-of-state placements of juvenile offenders to why a janitor at a DJS facility was making $200,000 with overtime. As O'Malley tells it, while the DJS director seemed dumbfounded by his questions, he noticed a woman behind him shaking her head and looking exasperated. "I can't bull-shit," Beth admits. Her lousy poker face got her promoted to StateStat director, and she became one of the governor's most trusted aides.

At the time of our flight from Louisville, Beth was at another turning point in her life. She told me that her husband was dying of cancer and that she would soon be starting the Center for Government Excellence (GovEx) at Johns Hopkins with a Bloomberg Philanthropies grant. GovEx would be one of five What Works Cities technical assistance providers. She assured me that Baltimore would be selected as a What Works City, that it wouldn't make sense for Bloomberg to fund GovEx in Baltimore and not help the city. In the aftermath of the unrest, it took strenuous lobbying from Beth and the president of Johns Hopkins to clinch Baltimore's spot.

OutcomeStat was a point in our favor. Amid the mayoral turmoil, it was seen as a good idea that deserved to be brought to scale, led by people who had proven they could get things done.

Baltimore officially became a "What Works City" in June 2016, with an agreement for GovEx to help us take one Priority Outcome—A Growing Economy—through further Turn the Curve planning and into the monitoring phase of OutcomeStat before the mayoral election in November. That gave us four months to take a deeper dive into the Key Indicators, reconvene the Outcome Leadership Team, and hold the first ever public OutcomeStat session, to be led by Mayor Rawlings-Blake.

We had to move fast and were lucky that Beth had tapped her Director of Cities, Sheila Dugan, to be our guide.

John F. Kennedy sarcastically called Washington, DC a city of "Southern efficiency and Northern charm." Sheila proved that Southerners can be both efficient and charming. A native of North Charleston, South Carolina, she was a "typical nerd" growing up. She always had a fresh stack of books from the library and could usually be found reading during recess. "I wasn't the most popular kid in school," she recalls, "but I tried really hard to be likable." It turns out she is extremely likable, even when she is holding you accountable for sticking to the project schedule.

And Sheila is anything but typical. After studying creative writing at the Governor's School for the Arts and Humanities in Greenville and political science at Brown University, she started her career in digital marketing for a company that arranged student trips to the nation's capital. "I learned a lot of what I teach cities about public management in that job," she told me. "We were numbers driven, always measuring everything. We would have these monster performance review meetings to figure out what was working and what needed to change."

As she watched coworkers being laid off during the Great Recession, Sheila decided she was tired of selling people a product they didn't need and would rather be stressed out about helping people. She went back to school for a public policy degree and discovered a passion for expanding broadband access to low-income communities. In her first job out of graduate school, she drove thousands of miles across her home state to bridge the digital divide, from progressive cities like Anderson, which calls itself "The Electric City," to small towns like West Pelzer (population 926), whose City Hall Sheila describes as a "glorified trailer."

Sheila completed her transformation from bookworm to data diva by accepting a one-year Code for America fellowship in Oakland, California, where she was part of a team that improved public-records access for the city. Her role was to rewrite policies and gather user feedback, and she learned a bit of coding, too.

Sheila was one of Beth's first hires at GovEx, and she relished the chance to help her newly adopted city use data to achieve better results for residents. "I saw a ton of potential in Baltimore," she says. "It had a reputation for managing with data, and now it wanted to use data more strategically."

The Growing Economy outcome had three Key Indicators:

1. City Resident Employment Rate
2. Number of Jobs in the City
3. Number of Visitors to the City

The city's core team for the Growing Economy project included the heads of the Mayor's Office of Employment Development (MOED), Baltimore Development Corporation (a nonprofit that functions as the city's economic development arm), and Visit Baltimore (the non-profit tourist bureau funded by the city); Sam Sidh, Beth's former deputy at StateStat who had replaced Mark Grimes as CitiStat director the previous September; and me.

I spent the bulk of my time on the employment rate indicator, and the experience exemplified how asking more questions led us to new insights about what could be done to grow the city's economy.

With Phil Lee as its facilitator, the Growing Economy Outcome Leadership Team had done remarkable work at the OutcomeStat conference the previous September. Its Turn the Curve report was our starting point for this next phase of the OutcomeStat process.

The specific measure of employment rate was the percentage of city residents aged between sixteen to sixty-four years who were employed according to Census Bureau data, regardless of whether they reported being in or out of the labor force. The number had been at around 60 percent from 2012 to 2014, which meant that 40 percent of working-age city residents were not working, either by choice or because they couldn't find a job.

The team had identified nine factors contributing positively to the employment rate and thirteen factors getting in the way of higher employment. Some were obvious, others caught me by surprise. On the positive side, the team listed the growth of the city's anchor institutions, mainly hospitals and universities, a thriving arts community, and increased cargo traffic to the port. It also pointed out that the illegal drug trade finances legal economic activity. On the negative side, the team identified numerous barriers to employment, such as lack of affordable childcare, an underperforming school system, and racial disparities. The team also cited the toll of automation on low-skill jobs, competition for young workers from the underground economy, and the chilling effect of police brutality.

The team's proposed action plan was broad in its scope. It called for employers to relax drug-testing rules and provide on-site childcare, the city to give more contracts to small local firms and demand more jobs in exchange for tax incentives, and workforce development nonprofits to offer more relevant and standardized job training. It even advocated an expanded bike-share network to help residents without cars get to job sites.

In preparation for reconvening the Outcome Leadership Team one year after the conference, Sheila and her GovEx colleagues dove below the surface of the employment rate indicator in hopes of informing more targeted, evidence-based actions. The core team had many questions. Who is unemployed? Who has dropped out of the workforce? How many residents are underemployed? What are other cities doing to help their residents become more employable? Those were just a few of them.

What we learned from the new data opened our eyes to aspects of the employment challenge we hadn't understood before. A few of the facts that had been hidden within the "top line" employment trends sparked intense discussion when we brought the Outcome Leadership Team back together.

Most notably, we discovered a dramatic drop-off in labor force participation among forty-five- to fifty-four-year-olds, people in the prime of their working lives. As shown in the chart in figure 9.3a, this group was doing worse than any other compared to the national average.

Figure 9.3a Baltimore Labor Force Participation by Age (2014)

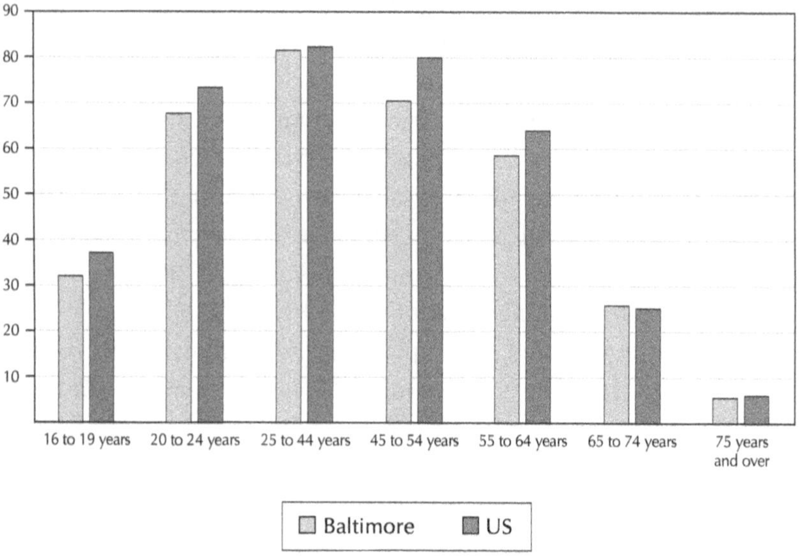

Baltimore ▪ US

Source: US Census Bureau, American Community Survey, 2010–2014

What was behind this group's struggles? We found a few clues. First, older workers were having a hard time getting reemployed in the aftermath of the Great Recession. Respondents to an AARP survey ranked "Employers think I'm too old" as the #3 major barrier to finding a job, just behind "No jobs available" and "I am tied to this area." The same survey found that age discrimination is far more prevalent than race or sex discrimination in hiring decisions. A federal survey of displaced workers put numbers on the problem, finding that workers aged fifty and over are likely to be unemployed six to ten weeks longer than younger workers, and that the odds of being reemployed drop by 2.6 percent for every one-year increase in age.

Beyond age discrimination, older workers suffer from a skills gap in today's economy. In Baltimore, where nearly 20 percent of residents over the age of twenty-five lack a high school credential, this gap can be enormous. According to the American Community Survey, barely more than half of these residents were in the labor force (see figure 9.3b), and a quarter of those who were in the labor force were unemployed.

Figure 9.3b Baltimore Labor Force Participation by Education Level

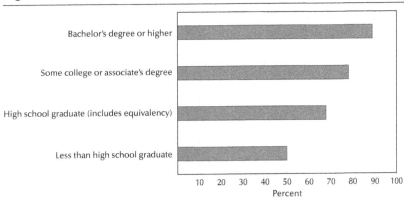

Source: US Census Bureau, American Community Survey, 2010-2014

Another troubling statistic that GovEx put in front of the team tied employment and labor force participation to opioid addiction, which had become an epidemic in Baltimore. The American Time Use Survey reported that of those reporting use of painkillers the day before, more than 60 percent were either unemployed or not in the labor force (see figure 9.3c).

Figure 9.3c Effect of Painkiller Use on Employment Status/ Percentage of People Who Took Painkillers the Day before, by Employment Status.

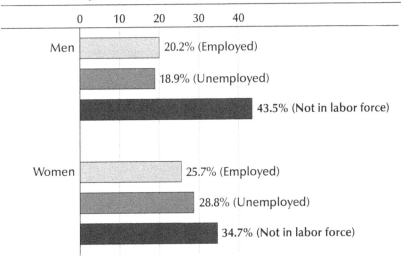

Source: American Time Use Survey via Alan Kreuger

With all this new information, the Outcome Leadership Team zeroed in on adult literacy and General Education Development (GED) attainment as critical not only for improving the employment outcomes of the city's most vulnerable residents but also for saving their lives and giving their children better opportunities.

Jason Perkins-Cohen, director of the MOED, guided the team's conversation around how to improve the availability and quality of adult education, which he said had been neglected for too long. Jason, a large man with a shaved head and a Fu Manchu mustache, looked more like a forklift operator than a government executive, which may explain why he had the team's full attention.

Jason was new to Baltimore city government; he wasn't new to me. The two of us had met more than twenty years earlier, when he was just Jason Cohen. We were Presidential Management Interns being wooed by federal agencies at a job fair. It just so happens that Jason also met his future wife, Alison Perkins, that day, waiting in line at the Department of Housing and Urban Development table.

Jason took a position at the Department of Health and Human Service (HHS), where he worked on President Clinton's welfare reform proposals, specifically initiatives to get welfare recipients into jobs. Welfare reform became a political football, tossed back and forth between the president and the insurgent Republican Congress, led by House Speaker Newt Gingrich. Jason's bosses at HHS, Peter Edelman and Wendell Primus, resigned in protest after Clinton signed a compromise welfare reform bill that they believed would tear up the social safety net.

Jason wasn't far behind, leaving HHS to help the District of Columbia implement the welfare-to-work provisions of the new law. The District had already contracted with several small nonprofits to deliver job training, including one run by a dentist. When Jason visited the training sites, he found most of them empty. If welfare reform was going to have a chance, something had to change. Jason reworked every contract so that the vendors were paid for their performance on four basic metrics: how many clients they saw, how many graduated from the training, how many got a job, and how many kept the job for at least six months. At vendor meetings, he put their scores up on the wall for all to see, which was another dose of motivation for better performance.

When he came to MOED, Jason brought a few firmly held convictions with him. One is that, as he puts it, "a job is the solution to every social ill." Another is that measurement drives performance. He found an agency more concerned about compliance with the requirements of state and federal grants than helping as many people as possible find jobs and increase their earnings. For Jason, meeting federal job placement standards is not enough, and his focus on results accountability, technical assistance, and vendor oversight doubled job placements from 2,300 to 4,600 in two years. He credits OutcomeStat with being a "great conversation starter" about performance and helping him get "under the hood" of services that are falling short of his expectations.

The Outcome Leadership Team came up with ideas for grassroots outreach to the target population for adult education, with an emphasis on helping them overcome the shame they felt about their educational status. There was much talk about improving Baltimore City Community College, which was fighting to maintain its accreditation. Representatives from the city's largest foundations offered solutions that they were funding in other cities, including an "adult high school" in Indianapolis. A dean from Morgan State University said that the school had the capacity to launch online programs for adult training.

The promise of OutcomeStat was palpable that September day. Sheila had worked with many other cities, and rarely had she seen such a diverse and deeply invested group of stakeholders engaged on an issue. That we were in the last months of the mayor's term made it all the more extraordinary.

OutcomeStat's promise has not yet been fulfilled in Baltimore. Exactly one month after it reconvened, the Growing Economy Team reported to the mayor on the Turn the Curve plans for its three indicators, a session that was recorded and posted on the city's new OutcomeStat website, the first "stat" session ever shared with the public. Our vision was for regular meetings of all seven Outcome Leadership Teams, to continuously gather new data, prioritize strategies, strengthen partnerships, inform budgets, implement the Turn the Curve plans, and monitor progress.

Catherine Pugh took office as Baltimore's fiftieth mayor in December of 2016, having narrowly turned back Sheila Dixon's comeback bid in the Democratic primary. Pugh had yearned to be mayor her entire adult life, and it took her almost that long to realize her dream. At sixty-six, she had served almost twenty years in the Baltimore City Council and Maryland General Assembly; otherwise, her résumé was eclectic. She had been a print journalist, talk show host, college dean, and small business owner, started a charter school, founded the Baltimore Marathon, and has even written children's books.

Although Pugh had vowed to continue several of Rawlings-Blake's strategic initiatives, the city's ongoing violent crime wave became her almost singular focus.

OutcomeStat lives on in Mayor Pugh's violence reduction plan, which is data driven and takes a comprehensive approach to the problem, from law enforcement to public health to housing, and also in Baltimore's efforts to consolidate Outcome Budgeting and CitiStat service performance measures, which have been described earlier in this chapter.

I am hopeful that other cities will be inspired by Baltimore's idea and use OutcomeStat to its fullest potential. Sheila, whose perspective on city performance management is as broad as anyone's, found much in OutcomeStat for other cities to emulate. "GovEx exists because many cities struggle with the most basic use of data to manage," she explains. "OutcomeStat shifts the focus from counting widgets to measuring outcomes and engages the community in a structured way around the mayor's priorities."

What really sets OutcomeStat apart, though, is how it connects performance and budgeting. "Baltimore was unique," Sheila says. "Few cities bring performance management and budgeting together, except in a superficial way, like publishing performance measures in the budget book."

We've come a long way in this book. The next chapter takes a step back to reflect on Value, Lessons Learned, and the Future of Outcome Budgeting.

FIVE TAKEAWAYS

1. **Connecting service performance measures to citywide outcomes is important.** These measures are part of the resources-to-results logic model. If outcomes aren't moving in the right direction, service performance may be one of the culprits.
2. Agencies spend a lot of time "putting out fires." They may not like being forced to **take a time out to think about how to improve performance,** but they will thank you later.
3. **City government cannot achieve big outcomes on its own,** but it can convene partners to develop and implement a collective action plan that turns the curve.
4. **Key Indicators, like the employment rate, can tell you only so much.** Drilling down into the data often reveals opportunities for action.
5. **When you are brainstorming ways to improve service performance, be sure to come up with both low-cost/no-cost ideas and "blue sky" ideas.** Your plan should include steps you can take right now and dreams for the future to work toward.

FIVE QUESTIONS

1. Read the Turn the Curve plan for Citizen Perception of Cleanliness in appendix B. Can you think of more action steps to turn the curve? Where would your ideas fall on the Impact/Feasibility Matrix?
2. After looking at the data on Baltimore's employment rate, do you agree that the city should focus on adult literacy and GED attainment? What other areas of focus might be more impactful on the employment rate?
3. What additional data related to employment should Baltimore be looking at? Gather employment data for your locality and see what issues it points to.

4. This chapter discusses a few examples of making performance information public to motivate improvement. What are some ways your organization could use this strategy?
5. Achieving great outcomes is a team effort. Choose an outcome that's important in your community and come up with a list of all the partners that would need to work together to turn the curve on that outcome.

FIVE RESOURCES

1. The What Works Cities website (whatworkscities.bloomberg.org) is full of features about what cities are doing to use data and evidence to improve results for residents.
2. The Center for Government Excellence website (govex.jhu.edu) has even more of these kinds of stories.
3. The B'More for Healthy Babies website (healthybabiesbaltimore. com) has information on the wide range of initiatives that have dramatically improved maternal and child health in Baltimore.
4. You can get more information about Clear Impact, Phil Lee's consulting firm, and its Scorecard performance management software at clearimpact.com.
5. A video of the Growing Economy OutcomeStat meeting is at www. cityontheline.com.

10

The Bottom Line

■ ■ ■

BEFORE I WRAP things up, I want to bring us back to Value, which I have called government's bottom line, and leave you with my thoughts about Lessons Learned and the Future of Outcome Budgeting.

VALUE

As a reminder, in chapter 1 I defined Value as Results per Dollar Spent. Here's the equation:

$$Value = \frac{Results}{Dollars\ Spent}$$

I explained that in Outcome Budgeting, we are looking for service proposals that increase Value in one of three ways, as shown in box 10.1.

Box 10.1 | Value

More results for the same money
OR
The same results for less money
OR, BEST OF ALL
More results for less money

Both the numerator and denominator of the Value equation—Results and Dollars Spent—are elusive concepts. My goal is to pin them down for you (though I can't guarantee that they won't still be trying to wriggle away).

Let's start with Dollars Spent. Most government budgets don't tell you how much services really cost. That's because most governments don't go to the trouble of (1) figuring out the full cost of services and (2) assigning those costs to service budgets.

It is easier to budget centrally for many costs that services consume. When we started Outcome Budgeting in Baltimore, service budgets did not include the costs of employee pensions, workers' compensation, space usage, computer hardware, fleet maintenance and fuel, capital repairs, debt service, and more. We changed that, because without knowing the full cost, a service that looks like a bargain might actually be bloated. Baltimore's Department of Transportation pegged the cost for its in-house crews to repave a lane mile of neighborhood street at $85,000; upon further inspection, the full cost turned out to be $135,000, and the mayor's office started asking about putting the work out for bid.

My office produced a cost analysis handbook that includes a case study of Baltimore's mixed refuse collection service. The study found that the service's indirect costs (including overhead like finance, legal support, and capital assets) were nearly as large as its direct costs (salaries, vehicles, equipment). It also determined that the mix of collection, transport, and disposal costs varied greatly across the city's four quadrants and recommended redrawing collection routes and exploring the feasibility of a second waste transfer station. You can find the report at the website: www.cityontheline.com.

Accounting for Dollars Spent gets more complicated at the community level, where multiple organizations are investing in a Result.

Even so, measuring Dollars Spent is usually easier than measuring Results. What is a "Result"? The dictionary says it's "a consequence, effect, or outcome of something." That's not very helpful. Let's think about some examples. In government, the Results we care about fall along a continuum, similar to the Logic Model described in chapter 5.

At one end are simple outputs, like the number of hypodermic needles distributed to drug users. At the other end are complex outcomes, like the number of heroin overdose deaths per thousand residents. In between are many measures of the effectiveness of government services, such as the number of residents trained to administer Naloxone (the opioid overdose reversal drug) and the success rate of drug treatment programs, as well as intermediate outcomes, such as reported mental health status and nonfatal overdoses (see figure 10.1).

We lean heavily on performance measures to put numbers on Results. Performance measures are useful as indicators of where Results are heading, and for simple Results, they may be all we need. The closer we get to outcomes, the more important it is to pair performance measures with evidence. By evidence, I mean rigorous evaluations of the impact a service is having on its intended Result.

Outcome Budgeting asks services for performance measures and evidence. A good example is Baltimore's Safe Streets program, which deploys "violence interrupters" in targeted neighborhoods (what it calls "sites") to mediate disputes that could escalate into deadly conflict. Safe Streets reports the number of shootings in its sites, but when that number goes down, how can we be sure it is because of the program versus any number of other causes, such as increased police presence, lower unemployment, or a disruption in the illegal drug supply chain? That's where evidence comes in. A team of researchers at Johns Hopkins University has studied Safe Streets, sorting through the various causes of shootings and zeroing in on the impact of the violence interrupters.

The researchers found that when implemented properly, Safe Streets causes reduced shootings. This finding gives credibility to the program's performance measures and makes it a candidate for favorable budget treatment. In theory, it also allows us to compare the

Figure 10.1 Results Continuum

Value of Safe Streets against other interventions that can demonstrate an impact on shootings, in Baltimore or other cities.

Unfortunately, evidence is hard to come by. In the book *Moneyball for Government*, Jim Nussle and Peter Orszag write that "less than one dollar out of every hundred dollars the federal government spends is backed by even the most basic evidence." The ratio might be even worse in state and local government. A nonprofit advocacy group called Results for America is trying to change that, and as one of its "Moneyball Fellows," I got the ball rolling on evaluations of the city's recycling, permanent supportive housing, and youth homelessness programs. These evaluations will inform future budget decisions.

Value is more than a metric. It is the mind-set of Outcome Budgeting. As long as people expect more from government than they are willing to pay for, government has no choice but to deliver bigger, better Results for every Dollar Spent.

LESSONS LEARNED

In one way or another, I have shared with you many, many lessons learned in these pages. Here I distill the ten that I most want you to remember, plus one to grow on.

1. **Leadership support isn't the Be-All and End-All.** Yes, it's important, but the leaders aren't in the trenches with you. They can't dive on every grenade, which is why you need a good team and as many friends as you can recruit. Make sure leadership sets the tone for change and reinforces the change message at every opportunity and be prepared to fight some battles without them.

2. **You can't do Outcome Budgeting halfway.** The purpose of Outcome Budgeting is to take stock of all your resources and align them as best you can with your goals. In Baltimore, we went all in because we had limited resources and unlimited challenges; we needed to put everything on the table. I'm not a fan of piloting Outcome Budgeting, but if that's the only way to get it started in your organization, run your pilot around one or two outcomes, not agencies.

3. **Results Teams can get siloed, too.** Don't let Results Teams get lost in the minutiae of service proposals and lose sight of their Priority Outcomes. If that means asking them for strategic guidance on

service funding levels, rather than specific dollar amounts, so be it. You want them to think beyond the proposals in front of them, because those proposals may not be enough to turn the curves of Key Indicators.

4. **If you need a friend, get an agency head.** Agency heads can feel threatened by Outcome Budgeting because they are used to having more say about how their services are funded. Some will see the opportunity to win resources that wouldn't have otherwise been available. Others will go through the motions and count on leadership to back down from cutting "essential" services. If I had to do it over again, I would meet even more with agency heads, individually and collectively, and give them a larger role in guiding Outcome Budgeting. It would have softened resistance and promoted collaboration.

5. **Listen.** Don't take everything you hear at face value. Most people are too polite to criticize you to your face. Find ways to get the straight scoop, like the focus groups we arranged after the first three cycles of Outcome Budgeting. Most of all, be willing to ask questions even when you know you won't like the answer.

6. **Don't stop at Outcome Budgeting.** Outcome Budgeting is limited only by the imagination and ingenuity of the people writing service proposals. Thankfully, there are plenty of ways to replenish these commodities, like Lean, an Innovation Fund, data analytics, program evaluation, a book club, and more.

7. **Community members are key.** They ask the "dumb" questions that need asking, and they're not afraid to question authority. In addition, they tend to think that government is not the solution to every problem and that communities can and should take more responsibility for their own well-being.

8. **Outcome Budgeting can be scary.** I was lucky to implement Outcome Budgeting in the city that invented CitiStat, which meant that people were accustomed to being held accountable for performance. That didn't mean they liked it, though, and some had suffered beatdowns over performance failures. Measuring outcomes, which are outside our span of control, dialed up the fear factor. When I would talk to agency heads and program managers about setting ambitious performance targets, I would appeal to their sense of identity as public servants. "If we're not here to make residents' lives better, why are we here?"

9. **You don't have to be loud, just persistent.** Management guru Jim Collins found that the most successful corporate CEOs do not fit the stereotype of brash, outgoing leaders. Instead, they are quietly persistent, with "personal humility and professional will." That

was my way. I believed in what we were doing, and when I ran into resistance, I talked it out, thought it through, or maneuvered around it.

10. **You can't communicate too much.** I would sometimes feel frustrated that people weren't "getting" Outcome Budgeting. We trained, coached, even sent out newsletters, but the message didn't always stick. Doing more of all of this—and doing it year-round instead of just during the budget process—would have helped. But before you flood people with communication, be sure it is effective. Make it simple, use concrete examples, tell stories, and appeal to emotions when you can. If you're not sure what I mean, read Chip and Dan Heath's book *Made to Stick*.

11. **Outcome Budgeting Is a Long-Term Investment.** Baltimore is one of America's most challenging cities, with social and economic problems that sometimes seem intractable. Outcome Budgeting did not solve those problems. It is not a magic bullet. What it did was change the way people think about those problems and how the city, through its spending, services, and stewardship, can more strategically address them. Outcome Budgeting was a seed, and from it grew efforts to deliver services more efficiently, use data and evidence to make decisions, engage the community, become financially sustainable, innovate, and, through OutcomeStat, bring partners together to plan for a better future.

THE FUTURE OF OUTCOME BUDGETING

In 2012, Baltimore hosted a conference we called "BFO 2.0," BFO standing for "Budgeting for Outcomes." It was a gathering of cities and counties that were early adopters of this new way of budgeting to talk about what the next version of what we were all doing would look like. Participants included Fort Collins, Colorado; Redmond, Washington; Mesa County, Colorado; New Orleans, Louisiana; Roanoke, Virginia; and Lakeland, Florida. We met in Camden Station, a beautifully restored Baltimore and Ohio Railroad terminal, where Abraham Lincoln awaited his train on the way to Gettysburg.

Mayor Rawlings-Blake's speech to the group was no Gettysburg Address, but she encouraged us to draw on our success stories and develop a "playbook" for improving Outcome Budgeting.

Photo 10.1 Camden Station *Source:* Andrew Home

Mike Mucha, the Director of Research and Consulting for the Government Finance Officers Association, recapped the playbook in an article for *Government Finance Review* ("Budgeting for Outcomes: Improving on a Best Practice," December 2012). In rereading Mike's article, I was struck by how much the plays we formulated back then are still forward-looking today.

Merge Outcome Budgeting with Overall Performance Management Efforts

Outcome Budgeting cannot work in isolation. It should be part of an organization's larger performance management program, which also includes strategic planning, performance measurement, process improvement, and program evaluation.

I'm not aware of any city that started a comprehensive performance management program from scratch. Performance management initiatives are started at different times, by different leaders, and reside in different parts of the organization, and budget is often an outlier. That was certainly the case for the BFO 2.0 conferees, and for dozens of other jurisdictions I have gotten to know.

Unless you are starting a new city (wouldn't that be fun?), you will have to step back and figure out how to get things organized and what's missing. OutcomeStat, which I described in chapters 8 and 9, was Baltimore's attempt to fit its performance management pieces together. I hope it serves as a model for other organizations.

Develop Effective Leadership to Support Outcome Budgeting

Commitment from the mayor, governor, or CEO is essential, but they come and go. The future of Outcome Budgeting depends on lasting leadership. In our first year of Outcome Budgeting, Mayor Dixon convened an Outcome Budgeting Advisory Team, made up of leaders from labor, business, philanthropy, academia, churches, civic groups, the city council, and city agencies. In her invitation letter, she explained that the purpose of the team was to

- help me guide the overall process for implementing Outcome Budgeting in Baltimore;
- assure the integrity and credibility of the Outcome Budgeting process;
- provide feedback to me on the quality of the process and the degree to which the process meets expectations for creativity, innovation, and maximum results for each dollar the city spends; and
- provide the view of citizens and to play a role in educating other Baltimore citizens about Outcome Budgeting.

The Advisory Team was short-lived because of Mayor Dixon's scandal and resignation. Looking back, I wish I had kept it together under Mayor Rawlings-Blake. Keeping influential people plugged into Outcome Budgeting can go a long way to ensuring its survival across political transitions and building support for the tough budget trade-offs that are required to achieve citywide outcomes.

Reduce the Administrative Burden of Budgeting for Outcomes

I have explained that Outcome Budgeting is more work than traditional budgeting. To sustain Outcome Budgeting, it must be simplified. In Baltimore, we ran the full process annually, because our homegrown budgeting system didn't allow for multiyear planning.

It took a toll on everyone involved and was the #1 complaint from agency heads. I strongly recommend biennial budgeting, or even triennial budgeting, like they do in Oakland County, Michigan. The off years can be devoted to the kind of strategic and analytical work that never gets the attention it deserves when budget cycles seem endless.

If it makes sense to reduce the frequency of budgeting, the same goes for the length of budget proposals. The old saw is true: the more you say, the less they hear. After the conference, we ratcheted down the word count for proposals, and the proposals got better. Agencies complained at first, because it takes some work to organize your words and focus on what's most important. What the agencies didn't realize is that the Results Teams were able to give their shorter proposals more thoughtful review, and if there were any gaps in the information transfer, they could be filled via follow-up questions or face-to-face conferences.

Looking ahead, the search for the essence of Outcome Budgeting should continue. My longtime deputy, Bob Cenname, always thought that in an ideal world, there would be one perfect performance measure for each service. He may be at the extreme, but he's thinking in the right direction (and by the way, it helps to have someone on your team whose job is to keep things simple). The human mind is easily distracted by unnecessary data, which is why the valuable stuff gets lost. Maybe my next book will be about Lean Budgeting.

Find Technologies to Support the Process

Mike wrote, "[Outcome Budgeting] remains a process that is managed outside of the main financial system." That statement is still true. I have yet to find a software that integrates all phases of Outcome Budgeting with the "nuts and bolts" tasks of entering line-item data, estimating personnel costs, projecting revenue and expenses, and so on. In Baltimore, we created a web tool for agencies to enter budget proposals and performance measures. Later, we adapted Scorecard software, which was built for "Turn the Curve" planning (see chapter 8), to replace the web tool, but we still didn't have a unified budget system.

State-of-the-art Outcome Budgeting software would feature the following:

- A single point of entry for budget and personnel data
- Flexible text fields for budget proposals
- Performance management tools like Turn the Curve planning that can be a common platform for strategic planning, budgeting, and stat
- The full Results Team workflow, including proposal review, scoring and ranking, as well as communication with agencies and presentation to decision makers
- Easy reporting of budget and performance data by Priority Outcome and Key Indicator

Implement a True Outcome Budgeting Approach

What this means to me is that Outcome Budgeting should include as many funding sources and bidders as possible, and it should intentionally shift dollars to achieve Priority Outcomes.

Funding Sources

In Baltimore, every service under the mayor is required to complete an Outcome Budgeting proposal, but only General Fund dollars are allocated to Results Teams, because those are the dollars with which the mayor has the most discretion. Grant, utility, and other dedicated funds have less flexibility for repurposing, but they should still be part of the conversation.

Two opportunities for cities to expand the scope of Outcome Budgeting are capital funds and Community Development Block Grant (CDBG) funding.

Capital investments are critical to achieving Priority Outcomes. For example, modernizing schools may be a strategy for improving test scores, and an expanded crime camera network can contribute to reducing shootings. Capital budget proposals should be reviewed and ranked alongside operating budget proposals by Results Teams.

Federal CDBG funds are available for a wide range of anti-poverty, affordable housing, and infrastructure initiatives. Baltimore, like many cities, subgrants a large portion of CDBG dollars to politically connected nonprofit agencies with limited accountability for results. Decisions about how to allocate CDBG funds should be made through the Outcome Budgeting process, based on alignment with Priority Outcomes, performance, and evidence of impact.

Bidders

I've made the point in this book that government services can become like classic monopolies: inefficient, expensive, and indifferent to customers. Outcome Budgeting works best when agencies are entrepreneurial and innovative, thinking urgently about how to improve and help meet Priority Outcomes, at the lowest cost possible. Sadly, some agencies are accustomed to getting their way and aren't motivated to change. Police departments are notoriously entitled.

Shaking agencies out of their complacency is a leadership challenge. Outcome Budgeting can help by bringing new players into the budget game. Opening up the budget proposal call to outside bidders is part of a True Outcome Budgeting Approach. What if a university offered to share the cost of a private security force, reducing the need for sworn officers? Or a nonprofit proposed to take over homeless services and deliver better results? Or a private company showed that it could maintain the city's fleet at lower cost and greater reliability? If outcomes for residents is what we really care about most, these are the kinds of proposals we want to see.

A wide-open bidding process could be a chaotic, unmanageable free-for-all and would give lawyers, procurement managers, and union leaders fits. A smart first step is to choose one or two Key Indicators, such as reducing childhood asthma, and accept proposals from all comers related to just those results. Work with the administrators and lawmakers to carve out limited exceptions to existing rules that stifle creativity. For inspiration, read about Iowa's experiment with Charter Agencies, which freed agencies from bureaucratic restrictions in exchange for measurable results, at www.cityontheline.com. Cities outsource all sorts of operations, from trash collection to mowing to case management. Why can't they outsource outcomes?

Shifting Dollars

In chapter 2, I told you about the Monopoly money game, which revealed that the way the city was actually spending money was far different than the mayor and senior team's ideal allocation by Priority Outcome. Safer Streets, mainly the police and fire departments, was eating up half of discretionary General Fund dollars, and not enough was going to health, neighborhoods, economic development, and other needs.

In a True Outcome Budgeting Approach, leaders reallocate funding at the front end of the budget planning process, then consider the trade-offs that arise when the Results Teams report back. In one scenario, shifting 10 percent of Safer Streets funding to other Priority Outcomes might cause an unacceptable increase in emergency response times. In another, it could turn out that closing two fire companies would not compromise response times and the savings could be used to make a big dent in opioid overdose deaths. The latter scenario might never come to light without re-slicing the budget pie. The Safer Streets team would not have had to push the fire department to examine company closures, and the Healthier City team would not have had room to pay for the opioid overdose program.

I had a hard time convincing Baltimore's leaders to re-slice the pie; the allocations were somehow abstract to them. I knew they had real consequences, and I managed to shift funding gradually toward a more balanced spending strategy.

Consider Service Levels

With all the talk of services being ranked "above the line" and "below the line," it's easy to get the impression that Outcome Budgeting is an all-or-nothing exercise. As I explained in chapter 4, we encouraged Results Teams to explore alternative service funding levels to reach what they considered an optimal "investment portfolio." A future goal is for agencies to be able to produce robust "scaling" options. What I mean by that is options for increasing or decreasing funding that accurately estimate how the funding changes would impact performance. In our experience, agencies had difficulty with scaling; success will require training, coaching, and perhaps technology solutions.

A play I would add to Mike's list is **Be Transparent.** In my dreams, Baltimore shared service proposals online and let residents review and weigh in on them. We also posted Results Team evaluations and rankings. It was a totally open process, which motivated both agencies and Results Teams to do their best work, generated new ideas, and lent credibility to the budget that came out at the end. Some governments, like Fort Collins, are close to this ideal.

The reality in Baltimore was that the mayor and senior team didn't want to have political fights over predecisional recommendations. That's a reasonable fear, because hard but smart choices could be killed in the crib. At the same time, it's really a fear of the unknown, and it assumes the worst from people. I hope if this book convinces you to try Outcome Budgeting, you will have the courage to let the sunshine in.

If you are convinced to try Outcome Budgeting, the next chapter will help you get ready.

11

Are You Ready?

■ ■ ■

I HOPE THIS BOOK has gotten you interested in trying Outcome Budgeting in your organization. If it has, here are ten questions to check your readiness.

DO YOU KNOW YOUR OUTCOMES?

Outcomes are the starting point for Outcome Budgeting. Many organizations have a list of initiatives, strategies, and investments that they want to carry out, but they haven't articulated how they want their community to be different five or ten years from now.

Start with big-picture outcomes, like Safer Streets, and then come up with three or four specific measures (Key Indicators) that will help you focus your resources and track your progress.

The power of outcomes is that they don't specify solutions. Outcomes invite inquiry, analysis, and new thinking about how to get from here to there.

WILL YOUR LEADERSHIP OWN OUTCOME BUDGETING?

You will want more than just the "go ahead" to implement Outcome Budgeting. Your leadership needs to be fully informed and aware of what Outcome Budgeting means, including its pitfalls, and be committed to the change.

How do you sell leadership on Outcome Budgeting? With data and emotion. The data might show that the organization is not on track to achieve its goals, current strategies aren't working, budgets are constrained year after year, and budget changes have been incremental. In other words, we keep doing the same thing and we're not getting the results we want. The emotion is in stories about what the organization's success looks like for real people and an appeal to the leadership's identity as innovators.

Before you close the deal, remind leadership that Outcome Budgeting is a disruptive change and has the potential to roil parts of the organization, especially those that can't get unstuck from business as usual—which leads to the next question.

DO YOU HAVE A PLAN TO MANAGE THE CHANGE?

Selling leadership on Outcome Budgeting is not enough. You need to bring as many people on board as you can, from the top to the bottom of your organization. You will have holdouts, but if you have a critical mass of champions in the right places, your chances of success are good.

Meet with people one-on-one and in groups. You can make the same case you made to leadership, but you also need to find out where people are and what they're ready for. They may not see the problems the way you do and be confused or scared about what you're proposing. Change is coming, but unless you're in a crisis, be willing to slow down if necessary to keep the organization together.

Just as you want to be flexible on the pace of change, give others a voice in its shape. Savannah, Georgia, formed a Value Team of agency heads to guide its Outcome Budgeting process. You can do something similar.

Also, prepare yourself for change. The book *Leadership on the Line*, which I referenced in chapter 5, is a great resource for brave souls who take on the status quo.

DO YOU HAVE A LONG-TERM FINANCIAL PLAN?

Outcome Budgeting is first and foremost about using your existing resources more strategically. It can be part of the solution to an organization's financial problems, but your organization might need to do more to become financially sustainable.

If your financial foundation is unstable, Outcome Budgeting will look like fiddling while Rome burns. Make Outcome Budgeting one of the strategies in a larger plan to address the structural issues.

DO YOU HAVE A COMMUNICATION STRATEGY?

Outcome Budgeting asks people to think differently. If they don't, and just go through the motions, it will become a frustrating paperwork exercise. To prevent this from happening, you need to communicate effectively. By communicate, I mean deliver information and inspiration to everyone who has a role in Outcome Budgeting, including the public. It includes training, coaching, testimonials, manuals, newsletters, tweets, YouTube videos, newspaper articles, guest speakers, posters, and practically any other media you can come up with.

To avoid the Curse of Knowledge that I wrote about in chapter 6, test your messages on a "focus group" of people who are on the front lines of service proposal writing, including agency heads and program managers. They are probably your most critical audience, because their work is the raw material for getting better results.

I also suggest forming discussion circles around each Outcome, including staff from all relevant agencies. The circles should start meeting as soon as the Requests for Results are ready and continue meeting through the budget process, and possibly year-round. The purpose of the circles is to answer questions about Outcome Budgeting, incubate ideas about how to achieve the Outcomes, and foster cross-agency collaborations without Results Teams as the middleman. If you decide to implement OutcomeStat, they could mature into the Outcome Leadership Teams described in chapters 8 and 9.

DO YOU HAVE THE TECHNOLOGY?

I wish I could recommend an out-of-the-box software solution that practically does Outcome Budgeting for you, but it doesn't exist (yet).

In chapter 10, I listed some features I'd like to see in an Outcome Budgeting software application. The most important for getting started is a tool for agencies to write their service proposals and for those proposals to be published for review by Results Teams. Baltimore built its own proposal tool, then adapted Scorecard software for the purpose, software that has the added benefit of supporting the "Turn the Curve" planning that is core to OutcomeStat.

ARE YOUR SERVICES WELL DEFINED?

Services are the units of analysis for Outcome Budgeting, as I explained in chapter 2. There are three steps to defining a service: Scope It, Cost It, and Measure It.

Scope It means that a service should be a set of activities with a common purpose, customers who care about it, and someone in charge of it.

Cost It means you should know the full costs of delivering the service, both direct and indirect.

Measure It means that each service should have a set of no more than five performance measures that tell the story of the Results it's delivering for the Dollars Spent.

DO YOU HAVE THE TALENT?

Talent is not technical skill and experience; it is attitude, analytical thinking, and emotional intelligence. I'm guessing you have plenty of talent in your organization, but you might have to look around to find all of it, because it's not labeled.

Outcome Budgeting is an opportunity to identify, develop, and promote talented people. Do everything you can to get talented people on your Outcome Budgeting implementation team, including finding people outside of your organization who are willing to help.

DO YOU HAVE A PERFORMANCE
MANAGEMENT PROGRAM?

Chapters 8 and 9 describe how Baltimore implemented Outcome Budgeting without the benefit of a strategic plan and struggled to integrate Outcome Budgeting and CitiStat.

Try to avoid the same mistakes. Make sure Outcome Budgeting is part of a complete performance management cycle, which at a minimum includes strategic planning, budgeting, and performance accountability, and should also include Lean, data analytics, program evaluation, and innovation.

As I've said, I hope to see some cities realize the full potential of the OutcomeStat model, a trifecta of performance management best practices—Results Based Accountability, Outcome Budgeting, and CitiStat—working in harmony.

DO YOU NEED OUTSIDE HELP?

Baltimore hired consultants to help us get Outcome Budgeting started. They gave us training, coaching, tools, and templates, helped us troubleshoot problems, and taught us the language of Outcome Budgeting. They also gave Outcome Budgeting credibility, because they had implemented it successfully in other cities. Most importantly, they prepared us to be self-sufficient after Year One.

For us, outside help was well worth the investment. If cost is an issue, you may be able to find a partner to foot the bill. Outcome Budgeting is attractive to the business community because it shows that government is trying to make the best possible use of tax dollars. In Dallas, the local chamber of commerce paid for the city's Outcome Budgeting consultants.

I like to think this book makes DIY Outcome Budgeting much easier than when I began my journey ten years ago, but even when you have a map, it's nice to have a trusted companion by your side.

Writing this book was a joy. I am privileged to be able to share with the world the stories of the many people who brought Outcome

Budgeting to life in Baltimore, and of the city itself, which, for all its flaws and frustrations, found a way to capture my heart.

As you've read, Baltimore's Outcome Budgeting experience has been one of trial and error. I hope the lessons we learned will light the way for the next generation of cities, counties, states, and other organizations that decide traditional budgeting isn't getting them the results they need.

Acknowledgments

■ ■ ■

WHAT I ENJOYED most about writing this book was interviewing the people whose stories you have read. They are all people I had worked with, but there was so much about them I didn't know. Each one of them opened up to me about their childhood, dreams, triumphs, and disappointments, for which I am forever grateful. I learned amazing things in every conversation, and I hope I have done their stories justice.

I have many other people to thank for making Outcome Budgeting successful in Baltimore. I will start with Mayor Sheila Dixon, who saw the potential of Outcome Budgeting and hired me to implement it, and Mayor Stephanie Rawlings-Blake, who stuck with it through thick and thin. The finance directors I worked under—Ed Gallagher, Harry Black, and Henry Raymond—were unfailingly supportive of me, even as I was disrupting the normal order and making mistakes along the way.

My special thanks to the people who worked with me in the Bureau of the Budget and Management Research (BBMR). As I wrote in this book, I had the most talented, dynamic team in all of city government. I can't name them all, but I will name a few who were instrumental in getting Outcome Budgeting going and keeping it going. My deputies, Thomas Kim and Bob Cenname, did the dirty work of adjusting our budget systems to the new process and always gave me wise counsel about implementation issues (some of which I foolishly ignored). Kristin Dawson, Laura Larsen, Emma Tessier, and Mira Green each did the enormously challenging job of coordinating the budget process, and each made it better in her own way. Emma simultaneously played a huge role in the OutcomeStat initiative. Jessica Clarke took the baton from Emma and ran with it, bringing Outcome Budgeting and CitiStat closer together than ever before. Jessica also assisted me in retrieving some old computer files for my research.

Thanks also to Amy Costanzo and Kirsten Silveira, who were my point people for the Innovation Fund, Lean Government, and community engagement, all of which I discuss in the book, and to my assistant Jeanine Murphy-Baumgardner, whom I hired as a temp and has become like family.

Several people gave me feedback during the writing of the book. Steve Goldsmith, Liz Farmer, Mark Funkhouser, Jim Chrisinger, Nelsie Birch, Jay Newman, Jeff Page, Roy Meyers, Maia Jachimowicz, Shayne Kavanagh, Phil Lee, Adam Leucking, and David Osborne read a draft of the first few chapters and rooted me on.

David Gottesman, Michael Jacobson, and Oliver Wise brought practitioners' perspectives to their reading of the full manuscript and made many suggestions to clarify information and keep me out of trouble. J. B. Wogan gave me invaluable advice about pitching the book to a publisher, and his in-depth review of the final draft made it better in many ways.

I was thrilled when Peter Hutchinson, one of my public administration heroes, agreed to write the foreword for the book. Big thanks to him.

From my publisher Rowman & Littlefield, I couldn't have asked for a better editor than Traci Crowell, who was enthusiastic about the book and patient with a first-time author. Her assistant Mary Malley expertly managed the details of book publication.

Three organizations provided financial support for the publishing and promotion of the book, for which I am very grateful. Results for America, Clear Impact, and Operational Performance Solutions are all leaders in making government work better.

Most of all, I want to thank my family.

My father, Bob Kleine, showed me how to be steady and disciplined, while also being funny. All of those qualities went into writing this book. My mother, Gail Kleine, taught me to speak up for myself and always corrected my grammar. My love of the written word comes from her.

My wife Kelly doesn't share my interest in public budgeting, but she shares most of my other interests and has been my rock of love, support, and encouragement for half of my life. My daughter Sara Gail was my library buddy for many of my writing sessions. My son Schroeder didn't help with the book, but watching him play sports was a wonderful diversion.

Andrew Kleine
Silver Spring, Maryland

Appendix A

Request for Results: Make Baltimore a Cleaner, Greener, and More Sustainable City

■ ■ ■

SECTION 1: MAYORAL OBJECTIVE

Make Baltimore a Cleaner, Greener, and More Sustainable City
Sustainability is defined as "meeting the current environmental, social, and economic needs of our community without compromising the ability of future generations to meet these needs." The objective is to create a better world for future generations.

SECTION 2: PRIORITY INDICATORS

The following five indicators will be used to monitor the overall of progress on this Mayoral Objective. Proposals that "move the needle" on these indicators will receive priority consideration for funding. At the same time, we recognize that many other indicators are important toward achieving the objective of a Cleaner, Greener, and more Sustainable city.

1. Percentage of Household Waste Recycled
The percentage of household waste recycled is equal to tons of recycled household waste divided by total tons of all household waste (see figure A.1). The two ways to improve the metric are (1) increase

the amount of recycling and (2) decrease the overall amount of household waste. In Baltimore, we are concerned about both.

Figure A.1 Percentage of Household Waste Recycled

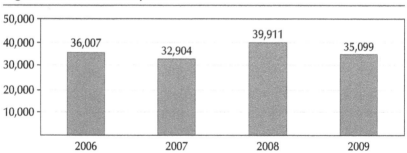

Source: Baltimore City Department of Public Works, Bureau of Solid Waste

2. Number of Rat Complaints

The control and eradication of Baltimore's rat population helps the city by reducing the spread of disease and destruction of property and removing a particularly visible and offensive sign of trash and blight. This indicator consists of two measures: rat complaints and resident satisfaction with rat removal services (see figures A.2 and A.3).

Figure A.2 311 Rat Complaints

Source: Baltimore City 311 Data, Mayor's Office of Information Technology

Figure A.3 Satisfaction with Rat Removal Services

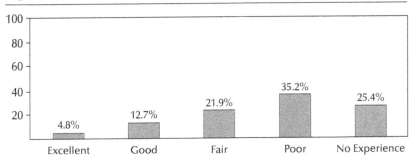

Source: Baltimore Community Survey 2009

3. Percentage of Tree Canopy Cover

The tree canopy is slowly recovering from a particularly challenging period. A healthy tree canopy directly benefits Baltimore in several ways including improved air quality and a reduction in summer air temperature and energy use resulting from increased shade.

The tree canopy is measured (from space) only once every five to ten years. The increase in the percentage of tree canopy cover can be tracked on a yearly basis with the following measures:

a. Ratio of trees planted to trees removed by Division of Forestry crews. This ratio in 2009 was 1 to 1.6.
b. Percentage of new street trees alive after two years. In 2009, 75 percent of new street trees are projected to be alive after two years.
c. Number of trees planted (see figure A.4).

Figure A.4 Trees Planted (2009)

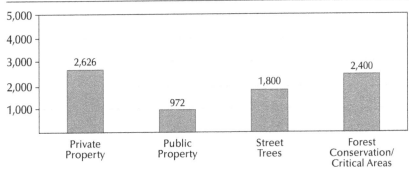

Source: TreeBaltimore, Department of Recreation and Parks

4. Green House Gas Emissions

Baltimore's Greenhouse Gas Inventory uses the Clean Air/Cool Planet software, the most recent, nationally accepted protocol, to measure Baltimore City's emissions of carbon dioxide annually. Table A.1 shows Baltimore's emissions by category and sector for the year 2007, our baseline data.

Table A.1 Greenhouse Gas Emissions

Sector	Tons of carbon dioxide equivalent, CO_2e	Percentage
Industrial	2,382,109	27%
Transportation	2,254,410	24%
Commercial	2,157,649	23%
Residential	2,166,818	23%
Waste	265,088	3%
Total	9,226,074	100%

Baltimore Office of Sustainability

5. Citizen Perception of Cleanliness in the City

Resident satisfaction with the city's cleanliness should reflect progress on the broad array of issues covered by this city goal. The Baltimore Citizen Survey 2009 asked residents about how they rate cleanliness of the city and their neighborhood (see figure A.5).

Figure A.5 Neighborhood Cleanliness Chart

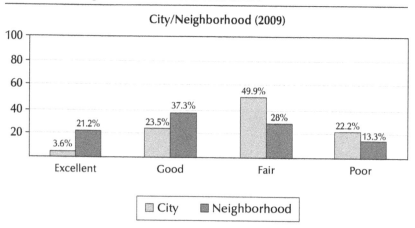

Source: Baltimore Community Survey 2009

SECTION 3: CAUSE-AND-EFFECT MAP

The Cause-and-Effect Map is shown in figure A.6.

Figure A.6 Cause-and-Effect Map

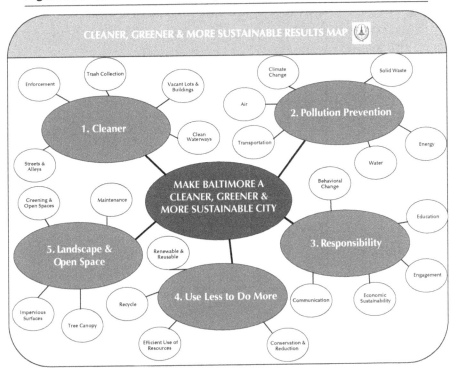

Source: Baltimore Bureau of the Budget and Management Research

SECTION 4: STRATEGIES

Five primary factors can lead to a Cleaner, Greener, and More Sustainable Baltimore. (See the Cause-and-Effect Map in figure A.6). These factors in priority order are the following:

1. Make Baltimore Cleaner
2. Prevent Pollution
3. Responsibility
4. Use Less to Do More
5. Landscape and Open Space

Strategy 1: Make Baltimore Cleaner

A key component to a cleaner city is effective waste management. This includes collection, operations, education, legislation, and enforcement. All of these items must work together to be effective and include all waste-related pollution, including chemicals, trash, yard waste, household materials, and so forth.

We are seeking proposals that (in priority order)

1. provide a solid waste collection program that supports proper disposal for all types of solid waste;
2. increase compliance with laws and regulations designed to make the city cleaner.

Agencies should think beyond traditional enforcement strategies and consider alternative means of promoting compliance, such as education, partnering, incentives, etc.

Strategy 2: Prevent Pollution

The impact of pollution and waste on our health and quality of life is becoming more and more evident. Every day, Baltimoreans breathe air ranked as the 9th, 10th, and 22nd most polluted nationally for ozone, short-term particle pollution, and year-round particle pollution, respectively. Pollution in our streams, rivers, and the bay impedes our use of these resources as centers of recreation and natural beauty, as well as their ability to sustain crucial wildlife habitats. Brownfield sites in Baltimore can be difficult to redevelop because of the presence of hazardous substances.

We are seeking budget proposals that (in priority order)

1. **Optimize transportation choices within the city.** Our current transportation system is economically, environmentally, and socially unsustainable. We are seeking proposals that reduce congestion and support increased use of public transit, walking, and bicycling.
2. **Improve stream and bay water quality.** Baltimore is striving to restore healthy water quality levels by 2020 in accordance with the federal Clean Water Act. Pollutants enter the water through leakage from sewer pipes, drainage from stormwater pipes, and private land that include sediment, chemicals, and trash. We are

seeking proposals that reduce the levels of trash, chemicals, and bacteria in our water bodies through strategic deployment of resources, engineering solutions, and citizen education.

Strategy 3: Promote Personal Responsibility

Individual residents, community groups, institutions, and businesses must recognize how their decisions impact the sustainability of their community. Government can promote personal responsibility through education, awareness, and enforcement of rules.

We are seeking budget proposals that encourage personal and organizational responsibility for the environment through education, communication, behavioral change, and engagement.

Strategy 4: Use Less to Do More

The "Three R's" of Sustainability are Reduce consumption; Reuse materials and products over and over or draw from naturally renewable sources; and Recycle waste materials into new products.

We are seeking budget proposals that (in priority order)

1. **Conserve energy and resources (Reduce).** The cheapest energy and resources are the ones we do not use. This strategy has been more aggressively implemented than the others because it has produced near-term economic benefits in addition to long-term environmental benefits. Proposals should support conservation of resources such as electricity, water, and fuel.

2. **Encourage the development and use of renewable and reusable resources and products. (Reuse).** Baltimore is finding itself short of energy and fuel, while increasing fuel costs are driving away industry and development. The only option for the future will be renewable resources such as wind, solar, and biomass/waste and new, alternative fuels. Re-Use of materials such as containers, refurbished electronics, and building materials is also imperative for success. Proposals should support an increase in the use of resources and products that can be reused over and over.

3. **Increase recycling (Recycling).** The City of Baltimore has increased its recycling of solid waste material but has only scratched the surface of its potential. Baltimore recycles approximately 16 percent

of the residential solid waste, whereas cities with more aggressive programs are approaching 50 percent recycling. Proposals should support recycling of all materials from all potential markets.

Strategy 5: Provide More Landscaping and Open Space

A green city enjoys significant health, infrastructure, and economic advantages. Baltimore should strive to leverage its natural resources to provide more habitat, shade, water and air purification, food, and recreational opportunities.

We are seeking budget proposals that (in priority order)

1. **Increase the coverage of the tree canopy.** The Tree Baltimore initiative aims to double Baltimore's tree canopy from 20 to 40 percent by 2037. We are seeking proposals that support research of the existing urban forest, protect existing forests, increase the number of trees planted on both public and private property, and enhance tree survival through design, construction, and maintenance of public spaces.

2. **Provide cost-effective maintenance programs for Baltimore's landscape.** Properly maintained lots, parks, and open spaces increase surrounding property values, reduce crime, and increase the strength of our communities. We are seeking proposals that support maintenance and management of our open spaces and that support effective plans and strategies for open space management.

3. **Reduce the percentage of impervious surfaces.** Impervious surfaces increase the volume of rain water and pollutants that enter stream systems during storms, causing stream bank erosion and sediment and pollutant discharge into the harbor and bay. Examples of ways to increase pervious surfaces include green medians in streets, green roofs, and "green" alleys made of porous asphalt.

4. **Optimize the greening and use of available open spaces (i.e., vacant lots, parking lots, roofs).** There are nearly thirty thousand abandoned properties in Baltimore City, and many of them are vacant lots. Vacant lots often become targets of illegal dumping and crime. Lots can be transformed into useful, green spaces where

appropriate through community adoption, greening, and farming. Also, as redevelopment takes place, parking lots and side yards can be landscaped and solar or green roofs installed as part of these projects. Proposals should support greening, maintenance, and the removal of barriers to greening of our vacant lots and underutilized open spaces.

SECTION 5: CRITERIA

Value. Proposals that demonstrate good value tell us what we can expect to be delivered per dollar spent. Value is a measure of both efficiency and the effectiveness of a service.

Strength of alignment with the Mayoral Objective, Priority Indicators, and strategies.

Innovation. Innovative proposals demonstrate new solutions or the degree to which the service improves or reengineers the way a service is currently delivered. Even high-value services as they currently are delivered have areas for improvement.

Multiple Mayoral Objectives. We seek proposals that demonstrate the ability to address multiple Mayoral Objectives concurrently.

Leverage. We seek proposals that demonstrate the ability to leverage other funds or resources for service delivery and/or collaborate with other internal or external entities. Partnerships can also be with neighborhood groups or other non–service providers.

Evidence-based. We seek proposals that deliver a service that is proven effective through empirical data or professional best practices. This can be an agency's data gathered through CitiStat or some other performance measurement effort, or reliable data gathered by another organization.

Part of a Strategic Plan. We seek proposals that advance an existing or emerging strategic plan. Strategic plans outline clear goals and objectives with specific action items, funding sources, individual roles, and time lines. Examples include the Sustainability Plan, Comprehensive Master Plan, Ten-Year Plan to End Homelessness, Birth Outcomes Plan, and so forth.

Customer Service Focus. We seek proposals that focus on providing excellent customer service. Think of customers broadly and to include internal customers, such as other city agencies or city staff members, and external customers, including residents and users of city services.

Life Cycle Cost Analysis.* We seek proposals that encourage decision-making based on holistic and full life cycle cost considerations. Life Cycle Cost is the total discounted dollar cost of owning, operating, maintaining, and disposing of a building, product, or system over a period of time.

*Unique to the Cleaner, Greener, More Sustainable Request for Results

Appendix B

Excerpt from A CLEANER CITY Preliminary Turn the Curve Plan

■ ■ ■

INDICATOR 1: CITIZEN PERCEPTION OF CLEANLINESS

Indicator Baseline

Figure B.1 shows the percentage of residents who rated the cleanliness of their neighborhood as "Good" or "Excellent" on the community survey.

Figure B.1 Citizen Perception of Cleanliness

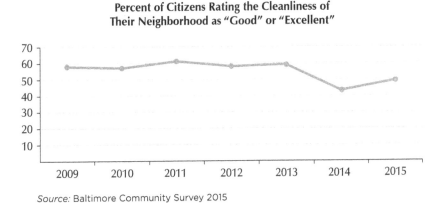

Source: Baltimore Community Survey 2015

About the Indicator

Each year, the City of Baltimore administers the annual Community Survey to gauge resident perception of city services and quality of life in Baltimore. One survey question asks respondents to rank the cleanliness of their neighborhood as Excellent, Good, Fair, Poor, Don't Know, or Refuse to Answer. This indicator measures responses of "Good" or "Excellent." Since 2009, the percentage of participants rating neighborhood cleanliness as "Good" or "Excellent" has remained relatively the same, with a steep drop to 43 percent in 2014.

One possible explanation for the drop is that 2014 was the first year the survey included cell phones as well as landlines. Thus, the survey reached a portion of the city's population that had previously not been reached. It appears that this group of residents is not as satisfied about the city's cleanliness as those who had previously been reached.

Story Behind the Curve

Positive factors contributing to the baseline are listed below:

1. **Municipal Trash Can Pilot Program:** In June 2014, the Department of Public Works (DPW) launched a pilot program that provided 64-gallon trash containers to nine thousand households in the Belair-Edison and Greater Mondawmin communities. The wheeled receptacles had attached, tight-fitting lids and were delivered equipped with a tracking device to prevent theft. The 2014 pilot yielded desired results. Most notably, the number of calls for rat extermination dropped by 26 percent and fewer workers experienced injuries related to lifting trash cans. Recently, Mayor Rawlings-Blake announced that $10 million will be dedicated to providing the same trash cans in the pilot program to all city households, with the goal of continuing progress in reducing the city's rat problems, worker injuries with lifting trash cans, and promoting cleaner streets.

2. **Baltimore City recycling cans:** The City of Baltimore, partnering with the Baltimore Community Foundation and local partners, has made recycling bins available for purchase at eleven locations. Twenty-five-gallon bins are $12.00 and 18-gallon bins are $5.00. Lids can be purchased for $3.00. In addition, recycle bins are being brought to community meetings and other gatherings to bring them closer to residents who don't have transportation to purchase

bins on-site at DPW locations. Though residents can recycle without using the designated bins, residents seem to prefer using them. The city picks up recycling weekly, and since 2009 there has been a gradual increase in the percentage of residents who recycle, increasing from 6 percent in 2009 to 20 percent in 2014. However, the message is continually reiterated that residents can recycle in any container other than plastic bags.

3. **Big Belly trash compactors:** The solar-powered "Big Belly Compactors" were installed throughout the Inner Harbor promenade in fall 2011. When full, the cordless 42-gallon bins automatically compact trash to one-eighth its original volume. The self-contained units reduce the need for bigger and/or more cans and reduce odors and overflow from trash in high-traffic areas.

4. **Single stream and 1+1:** The city has curbside, single stream recycling every week. This practice started in 2009. The amount of recyclables that may be set out is unlimited. Residents are required to put recyclables at the same location where trash is left for collection. There are also eight city-operated drop-offs that accept single stream recycling.

5. **Mechanical street sweeping:** In April 2014, the mechanical sweeping operation was serving more than 1,500 miles of streets weekly. Additionally, in 2014 a mechanical alley sweeping program was piloted in fourteen neighborhoods. In July 2014, citywide street sweeping began operating in four quadrants that previously saw no service or scattered, inefficient service. Instead of sweeping only the central areas of the city and some of our main commuter routes, all neighborhoods are now being reached using a fleet of thirty-six vehicles. An additional eleven sweepers have been purchased, and these will be used to replace older vehicles and ensure continuous sweeping operations. The amount removed per mile has decreased from 0.14 tons per mile in April 2015 to 0.10 tons by July 2015. In 2011, 74,048 miles were swept and 7,161 tons of debris were collected. Totals for 2014, which include nine months of expanded street sweeping, were 101,476 miles swept and 11,106 tons of debris collected.

6. **Mayor's spring and fall cleanups:** This spring was the sixteenth annual cleanup. These events involve neighborhood associations with sweeping, raking, planting, and painting. Taking part in these cleanups can make residents eligible for storm water fee reduction credits.

7. **Community pitch-in:** DPW supports more than a thousand community cleanup events annually.

Negative Factors Contributing to the Baseline

1. **Lack of signage about parking restrictions during sweeping times:** To avoid neighborhood clutter, signs were not posted for the street sweeping program telling citizens when to move their cars. Instead, postcards were mailed and temporary signs were provided to communities to remind citizens of their sweeping day. Street sweeping days were also listed on the DPW calendar. Sweeping is done on an odd-even alternating basis on Wednesdays. Residents must move their cars from the sides of streets being swept in order to expedite the work. On the first Wednesday of the month, the odd sides of streets in northwest (NW) and southeast (SE) Baltimore are swept; on the second Wednesday, the even sides of NW and SE; on the third Wednesday, the odd sides of NE and SW; and on the fourth Wednesday, the even sides of NE and SW.

2. **Lack of responsiveness from city agencies or miscommunication/ communication challenges:** Residents routinely complain that 311 calls regarding trash, rats, and other issues of cleanliness are not being properly addressed. Complaints include not being able to get through to 311, being directed to various operators or departments over and over again, or calls not being responded to in a timely fashion or at all. This is an issue, as resdients are routinely encouraged to call 311. Additionally, residents may resist having to purchase proper containers to deal with their trash and recycling, as cans being stolen is a common occurrence.

3. **Lack of personal responsibility and accountability:** Similar to the culture of litter, a lack of personal accountability and responsibility for the cleanliness of one's neighborhood leads to spaces that are unkempt and untidy. Many residents do not know what their

responsibilities are, for example, alley cleaning, sidewalk cleaning, and so forth. Residents expect the city to maintain areas for which they are responsible.

4. **Vacant buildings and vacant lots:** There are an estimated sixteen thousand vacant houses and fourteen thousand vacant lots in Baltimore. Although vacant properties are being demolished, rehabilitated, or redeveloped, the problem remains and contributes to the negative perception of cleanliness in neighborhoods.

5. **Difficulty of giving citations for illegal dumping:** There are issues with the 311 system that contribute to this. For example, 311 operators say they cannot enter a ticket as illegal dumping if the person calling in the complaint did not actually witness the dumping. Also, across the various 311 platforms (e.g., online, phone call) there are different ways to report the same basic issue. These seem to be system design issues that should easily be able to be remedied.

6. **Correlation of trash and rats:** Rats will survive if there is a ready supply of fresh food or trash available. Residents who have placed trash in bags or in uncovered trash cans contribute to the rat population by providing a constant source of food. Though rats can survive on extremely small amounts of food, a constant supply of trash can be assumed to contribute to the rat problem, and to people's perception of a dirty city.

7. **Block Captain program:** The city used to have a program that was a partnership between DPW and the Baltimore Community Foundation. There had been at one time roughly a thousand block captains in the city. These block captains were charged with helping to make sure that their areas of the city were kept clean. The group asserted that this program had success. But it was discontinued around 2000 and has not been replaced by anything comparable.

What Works

1. **Enforce strict prohibition on illegal dumping with fines:** The City of Chicago saw a decrease in illegal dumping by instituting a strict policy that fined and/or punished illegal dumpers, compensated citizens who helped with neighborhood surveillance,

and set up a task force that patrolled neighborhoods. This effort reduced cleanup costs from $14 million to $8 million a year. This also included significant public outreach, with flyers, brochures, postcards, PSAs, events, and a website launched to educate the public about the illegal dumping issue. From January 1997 to July 1999, the Department of the Environment (DOE) in Chicago cited 179 dumpers, collected $998,118 in fines and settlements, and filed $7 million in liens. DOE also required offenders to clean up 710,892 cubic yards of debris. For comparison, prior to the pilot program in 1995, Chicago had only cited 45 dumpers from 1992 to 1994. After the pilot was implemented, 135 dumpers were cited in 1995–1996, thereby prompting the city to keep moving forward in expanding its enforcement program against illegal dumping.

2. **Use funding to help neighborhoods help themselves:** Keep Indianapolis Beautiful partnered with the city to create the Project 180°/IPL Revive a Neighborhood program, in which neighborhoods can apply for funding to do a project—from something as simple as a neighborhood cleanup day to planting trees or building a new neighborhood vegetable garden.

3. **Use "carrot and stick" approach—free dumpsters and citations combo:** Keep Houston Beautiful targeted specific neighborhoods and wards, coming up with slogans to create buy-in and owner-ship: "Keep Five Alive" for their Fifth Ward, for example. They also found corporate partners (Conoco in Houston) to fund improvement projects. The neighborhoods held several commu-nity meetings and workshops to identify key issues and create action plans. Additionally, press conferences, community out-reach efforts, and incorporating the message into school curricu-lums were included. The city used a "carrot and stick" approach to reducing illegal dumping. The "carrot" approach employed the provision of 60-cubic-yard public dumpsters in several well-known dumping sites. The community liaisons monitored the dumpsters and notified the Department of Solid Waste when they were full. The "stick" approach included issuing warnings and citations for illegal dumping and other trash-related nuisances using a network

of enforcement groups—the community teams, Public Works, Solid Waste, and Houston Police worked together.

4. **Municipal Trash Can Program:** The Municipal Trash Can Pilot began in the Belair-Edison and Mondawmin neighborhoods in 2014. Expanding this program to the entire city, which the mayor's office has announced it will be doing, could help reduce the amount of litter in alleys and therefore improve people's perceptions of cleanliness.

Action Plan

1. Municipal Trash Can Program

   a. Connect with community leaders
   b. Use social media to spread message
   c. Use can program start-up to get Cleaner City message out to residents

2. Develop a long-standing, sustainable, citywide Cleaner City communications campaign (low to medium cost) by working with

   a. Office of Sustainability
   b. DPW
   c. NGOs
   d. Department of Housing and Community Development
   e. Professional marketing agency
   f. Social media

3. Enforce strict prohibition on illegal dumping and other sanitary violations with fines

   a. Fully staff housing code enforcement
   b. Reprioritize their enforcement priorities
   c. Create a dedicated team for sanitary violations

4. Help neighborhoods help themselves (low cost)

   a. Peer-to-peer networking
   b. Increased resources for community pitch-in program (medium cost)
   c. Adopt a lot

Figure B.2 shows how the team rated the impact and feasibility of recommended actions.

Figure B.2 Impact/Feasibility Matrix

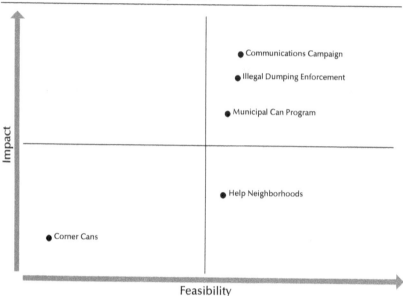

Source: Baltimore Bureau of the Budget and Management Research

An action that was discussed but was put as a lower priority involved corner trash cans.

5. Corner cans (high cost—each can costs $750, but other supports are necessary)
   a. Domed lids for corner cans
   b. Can captains
   c. Gateways and bus routes

Target

The group seemed to think that in the absence of any major new initiatives, citizen perception of cleanliness would likely stay about the same or improve slightly. The target is for the percentage of residents who rate the cleanliness of the city as either "Good" or "Excellent" to increase from 49 percent to 59 percent in five years.

Appendix C

Excerpt from Citizen's Guide to the Fiscal 2013 Budget

■ ■ ■

Figure C.1 Listening to Citizens

Listening To Citizens

What You Said
What the Budget Does

In the Fiscal 2013 budget planning process residents were invited to participate in citizen budget workshops where they were able to develop a budget that reflects their priorities (the exercise was also available online). During the workshops citizens were asked to make budget decisions to close the city's $48 million budget deficit. This could be done by making spending cuts, increasing revenue, or enhancing funding for high priority services.

These charts show how the recommended budget aligns with citizen input. All bars in light gray are reflected in the Fiscal 2013 budget plan. Recommendations not reflected in the Fiscal 2013 budget have been targeted for further review for Fiscal 2014.

Chart 1:
Top Citizen Recommended Spending Cuts

Category	Percent
Turn off city cable channel	66%
Reduce 311 Call Center hours	59%
Continue furlough plan	58%
Cut city admin budgets	55%
Reduce funding for elections	54%
Eliminate police Marine Unit	53%
Eliminate business district cleaning	51%
Freeze pay	49%

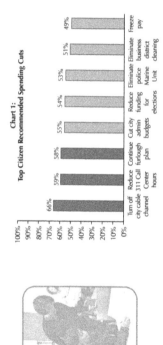

- The City cable channel will continue to be funded in Fiscal 2013; however, this service has seen its budget reduced 24% since Fiscal 2010.
- The 311 night shift was eliminated in fiscal 2011. For Fiscal 2013, the 311 Call Center will be merged with the 911 Call Center to increase effectiveness.
- The recommended budget ends furloughs and generates new savings through health benefit reforms.
- City administrative budgets were reduced by $1.3 million from the current level of service following 10% reductions in Fiscal 2011 and 2012.
- Funding for city elections was reduced by 5%. Recent State action will align the City's election cycle with federal elections. This shift will reduce the number of elections, generating future cost savings for the City.
- The Police Marine Unit will be funded for an on-call basis for a savings of $650,000.
- Business District Cleaning will utilize mechanical sidewalk sweepers that will improve overall effectiveness while reducing the cost of the service.
- City employees will not receive a cost of living increase, though ending furloughs is an effective 1-2% increase in take home pay.

**Chart 2:
Spending Cuts OPPOSED By Citizens**

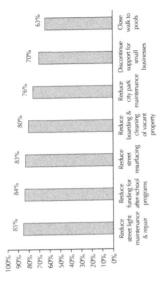

	85%	84%	83%	80%	76%	70%	63%
	Reduce street light maintenance & repair	Reduce funding for after-school programs	Reduce street resurfacing	Reduce boarding & cleaning of vacant property	Reduce city park maintenance	Discontinue support for small businesses	Close walk to pools

- The City will continue the conversion of street lights to LED technology. This transition will ultimately lead to nearly $2 million in savings in lighting and maintenance costs.
- Funding for after-school programs has been protected throughout the economic downturn. In Fiscal 2013, the Family League will engage 8,000 students, a 50% increase.
- The current level of service has been maintained for street resurfacing and street light maintenance. This translates into 200 lane miles resurfaced.
- The City will continue to clean & board 42,000 vacant properties in Fiscal 2013.
- Recommended funding for Park Maintenance will allow the service to partner with other city agencies to maintain park services.
- Services for small and emerging businesses will be maintained.
- The proposed pool season for the summer of 2012 is consistent with the 2011 season and keeps walk-to neighborhood pools open.

Citizen Input & Revenue

- 84% of participants opposed raising the property tax. In Fiscal 2013 homeowners will see the first phase of a new homeowner's property tax credit. Ultimately the credit will reduce the property tax by 20 cents by 2020 for owner occupied residential properties.
- 61% of respondents support selling sponsorships and advertising on public building and parks. Current efforts are underway to determine how this project can be carried out.
- This budget does not include any new taxes or tax increases to City residents.

Did You Know?

The Mayor hosts budget workshops in the fall and winter to allow citizens the opportunity to balance the budget and share recommendations. This exercise is also available online. Be sure to check out the City's budget website for more details: www.baltimorecity.gov/budget.

Source: Baltimore Bureau of the Budget and Management Research

Glossary

Base Budget—The way your organization currently spends money. In traditional budgeting, the base budget changes only incrementally from year to year, and the changes are usually made across the board. Outcome Budgeting reexamines the base budget and helps repurpose dollars to achieve measurable results.

Baseline (Budget)—A projection of future revenues versus the cost of maintaining current levels of service (CLS, see below). If your baseline shows costs growing faster than revenue, Outcome Budgeting can help you spend less money while making more impact.

Baseline (Performance)—A projection of future performance if nothing changes. For example, you might project that the infant mortality rate in your city will rise from 10 per 1,000 births to 12 per 1,000 births over the next five years in the absence of an intervention. Performance targets should be set against a baseline, not the current performance level. This concept is discussed in chapter 8.

Below the Line—In Outcome Budgeting, Results Teams rank service proposals for funding based on their alignment with Priority Outcomes and their performance. The teams have budgets, which are typically insufficient to fund all of the services. Services that rank too low for funding are considered to be "below the line." See chapter 4 for more on this concept.

Board of Estimates (BOE)—Baltimore's fiscal policy body. The BOE is made up of the mayor, city council president, comptroller, and two mayoral appointees. The BOE reviews the mayor's budget proposal and can make changes before submitting it to the city council for final approval.

Cause-and-Effect Map—A tool used by Results Teams to develop their Requests for Results (RFRs, see below). The map is used to identify the primary and secondary factors that lead to a Priority Outcome. Cause-and-Effect Mapping is described in detail in chapter 4.

CitiStat—A performance accountability program pioneered by Baltimore. The traditional CitiStat model is to meet biweekly to review agency operational metrics and solve performance problems. Outcome Budgeting and OutcomeStat shifted CitiStat's focus more toward longer-term results.

Current Level of Service (CLS)—An estimate of the cost to maintain the same service delivery level from one year to the next. CLS is the base budget plus or minus adjustments for pay raises, inflation, one-time costs, and so on.

Drilling Platform—A visual to represent the Results Team's ranking of services, illustrating that with limited resources, some services will fall below the water line and not be recommended for funding. Chapter 4 includes a Drilling Platform graphic.

Effectiveness—A type of performance measure Baltimore uses to track the quality, timeliness, and accuracy of service delivery. An example is the percentage of potholes filled within forty-eight hours of a service request. A primer on performance measurement is in chapter 3.

Efficiency—A type of performance measure Baltimore used to track the cost per unit of output or outcome delivered by a service. An example is the cost per street mile paved.

Intermediate Outcome—A measure that is part of the Logic Model for achieving an outcome and can indicate progress (or lack of progress) toward the outcome. An example would be that nonfatal shootings is an intermediate outcome for the outcome of fatal shootings. Another is that crib deaths is an intermediate outcome for the outcome of infant mortality.

Key Indicator—A measure used to track progress on the city's Priority Outcomes. Each Priority Outcome has three to four Key Indicators. For example, under the Cleaner City Priority Outcome, one of the Key Indicators is the Recycling Rate. Baltimore's OutcomeStat initiative developed "Turn the Curve" plans for each Key Indicator. Baltimore also published tables in its budget book showing the service performance measures related to each Key Indicator.

Lean—A set of tools for reviewing business processes and making them more customer-friendly and efficient. As an offshoot of Outcome Budgeting, Baltimore trained more than a thousand employees in Lean thinking. One of Baltimore's many Lean success stories can be found in chapter 7.

Logic Model—A model for visualizing how inputs are turned into outcomes. The logic model shown in chapter 5 starts with an outcome in the far left column, and from left to right shows the intermediate outcomes, outputs, activities, and inputs that are needed to support the outcome. For planning purposes, start with the outcome and ask, "How?" several times until you have formed a complete logic chain.

Outcome—A condition you want to improve in your community or organization. Outcomes can also be thought of as the end results you are trying to achieve, whether for a state, city, neighborhood, service, or household. Baltimore's service-level outcomes ranged from street smoothness to fleet availability to viral loads in HIV patients.

Outcome Quotient—The percentage of budget decisions that are based on priority, performance, and rational analysis, versus political considerations.

Output—A type of performance measure Baltimore used to track the direct results or production of service activities. Examples are the number of rat burrows baited or students treated in school health clinics.

Priority Outcome—Baltimore's citywide outcomes. They included Better Schools, Safer Streets, and Stronger Neighborhoods. Each was measured by three to four Key Indicators, (see above).

Request for Results (RFR)—Document issued by Results Teams to agency bidders that spells out what the team is looking for in service proposals. The RFR is like a mini strategic plan for achieving the Priority Outcome. A sample RFR is in appendix A.

Result—A broad term for whatever you are trying to accomplish through your efforts.

Results Based Accountability (RBA)—A data-driven process for taking action to solve problems and improve communities. Baltimore used RBA's "Turn the Curve" planning model for its OutcomeStat initiative, which is described in chapters 8 and 9.

Results Team—A team of employees and residents that issues a Request for Results for its Priority Outcome, reviews and ranks service proposals, and recommends an investment portfolio to leadership. Results Teams are described in chapter 4.

Scaling—Writing alternative service proposals at different funding levels to show the relationship between dollars and performance.

Service—A set of activities and actions to provide a benefit to city residents. Defining services is one of the first steps in Outcome Budgeting. Services should have a discrete purpose, clear lines of accountability, performance measures, and a budget. Baltimore's full definition of a service can be found in chapter 2.

Service Proposal—A request for funding in Baltimore's Outcome Budgeting process. It includes performance measures, explanation of performance and how it will be improved, description of how the service aligns with Priority Outcomes and Key Indicators, and evidence of service impact. Chapter 3 is all about writing great Service Proposals.

Story Behind the Curve—Part of "Turn the Curve" planning, it is an analysis of the factors influencing the trend of a Key Indicator or performance measure. More details can be found in chapter 8.

Structural Budget Deficit—A fiscal situation in which costs to provide desired services exceed revenue, even in normal economic conditions.

Tollgate—Milestone meetings in Baltimore's Outcome Budgeting process, which included approval of RFRs, Results Team recommendations to the mayor, and final budget approval by the mayor.

"Turn the Curve" Plan—The planning method used in Results Based Accountability to improve performance. It is described in detail in chapter 8.

Value—Results per Dollar Spent, which is described in this book as government's bottom line. Value is discussed in chapter 1 and chapter 10.

Index

About the Author

■ ■ ■

ANDREW KLEINE served as budget director for the City of Baltimore, Maryland, from 2008 to 2018. He received the 2016 National Public Service Award from the American Society for Public Administration and the National Academy of Public Administration. He lives in Silver Spring, Maryland.

John Robinette